Stan Frankenthaler and Sally Sampson

Photographs by Webb Chappell

Simon & Schuster New York London Toronto Sydney Singapore

the occidental tourist

More Than 130 Asian-Inspired Recipes

 SIMON & SCHUSTER
Rockefeller Center
1230 Avenue of the Americas
New York, New York 10020

SIMON & SCHUSTER and colophon are registered trademarks
of Simon & Schuster Inc.

For information about special discounts for bulk purchases,
please contact Simon & Schuster Special Sales:
1-800-456-6798 or business@simonandschuster.com

Designed by Bonni Leon-Berman
Interior illustrations by Alexis Seabrook

Manufactured in the United States of America
10   9   8   7   6   5   4   3   2   1

Library of Congress Cataloging-in-Publication Data

Frankenthaler, Stan.
    The occidental tourist : more than 130 Asian-inspired recipes /
  Stan Frankenthaler and Sally Sampson; photographs by Webb Chappell.
      p. cm.
    1. Cookery, Asian.   I. Sampson, Sally.   II. Title.

TX724.5.A1 F724   2001
641.595—dc21   2001049322

ISBN: 0-684-87307-9

This book is dedicated to four women who have shared so much with me: my mother, Ginny Boyd Frankenthaler; and my grandmothers, Carrie Boyd and Jeanette Frankenthaler, who encouraged me and taught me to cook, who had fun in the kitchen, who told their stories through food, who loved to bring family and friends together to share a meal at the table, and who have excited my imagination and my wonder for all things gastronomic my entire life . . .

And to the woman of so much significance to me — Laura Marie.
—S.F.

For Lauren and Ben, my little travelers who literally transport me.
—S.S.

acknowledgments

Creating *The Occidental Tourist* was a tremendous undertaking and a wonderful adventure. It was an adventure in learning about writing and about my own cooking style, and also in learning about how people cook at home. I wanted to bring to you a book of mouth-watering recipes that opened your palate and your pantry doors to a whole new set of flavors; a book that provided real knowledge and that encouraged a sense of culinary adventure.

There are so many people to thank. First I must acknowledge the help of my two working partners—Jim Smith, my business partner and friend, for all his encouragement and support, for his belief in the project since the beginning, and for carrying the weight of the restaurant any time the book has pulled me away. And to my writing partner, Sally, my friend of almost fifteen years—thanks for your patience, prodding, and all the hard work you invested in our book.

Thanks to my executive sous chef, Michael McEwen, who helped me test and retest recipe after recipe. He and I spent more hours in grocery stores than either of us ever dreamed. Michael was instrumental in organizing our photo shoots and farm visits. Our chef de cuisine, Andrea Jorgensen, helped in developing the book; and our first cook, Michelle McEwen, was always there for me to test recipes and prep for photo shoots. Thanks to Kyu Kim for working with me on many of the pastry recipes, and to the entire staff of Salamander present and past. And special thanks to our current management team: Rego, Moriya, Jan, Dan, Kerry, chef Dave, Billie Jo, and chef Tim.

Webb Chappell, our photographer, was amazing. He produced beautiful images, and together we hit on a fresh, uncomplicated, yet texturally rich composition that reflects a style of food photography unlike what appears in other books. Thanks to Patsy Chappell, Webb's mom, who was a huge support to us. She and Michel Berthier gave us the opportunity to work in their home kitchen and to use many of her beautiful things. To Keri Fisher, once of Salamander, who did great research for the book, thanks also.

Thank you to Carla Glasser and Jenny Alperen at the Betsy Nolan Literary Agency. And especially to Sydny Miner, our editor at Simon and Schuster, who believed in the project before it ever really began. Thanks to Chris Tracy and Ann Jenkins and everyone at Calphalon. To Chris and KitchenAid for their support. To all my chef friends—Peter Hoffman, Rick Bayless, Greg Higgins, Ming, Chris, Ann, Joann, Jesse, Lora, Jasper White, and more who encouraged the process and me. To Eero Ruuttila and Pat Woodbury, two of the greatest growers I know! To my family, my dad, and all my friends who put up with me during the last two years.

contents

introduction   13

essentials   17
   the essential pantry   18
   essential equipment   22
spice rubs and pastes   25

stocks   33

serving accompaniments   43
   flavored oils   44
   dipping sauces   48
   relishes and chutneys   53
   pickles   61

starters   71

shellfish   101

fish   121

poultry   151

meats   175

vegetarian entrees   193

salads   207

vegetable side dishes   229

rice and noodles   239

sweets and treats   255

desserts   273

index   297

the occidental tourist

introduction

I grew up in a family that celebrated every special occasion and every single holiday, not in a church or in a shopping mall, but around the dinner table. My childhood food memories are rich ones: riding in the milk truck with the local dairyman, gardening with my grandmothers, and ringing the dinner bell. I remember the first time I got to bring the huge, steaming platter of roast beef and Yorkshire pudding into the dining room—it was Christmas and I was about six or seven years old. We were a household of cooks, and I can vividly recall the feeling that I was now a part of a revered club within my family.

From that moment on, whenever there was a need, whether it was to shell beans or peel carrots, my name was called. My great-grandmother, Alva Tuchler, made the richest, smoothest Bavarian creams and I just about swooned each time she invited me, whom she called "angel," to slice and sugar the berries. My mother often recounted the story of one evening when Carrie, her mother, who was a stern, Bible-thumping Southern Baptist, brought a platter of fried chicken to the table. She and I had cut up the two chickens earlier that day, and when my mother realized there were only three chicken legs on the platter, she began to investigate. Her mother calmly replied, without missing a beat, that one of the chickens was one-legged. The truth—that she and I had eaten the hot, crispy leg that very afternoon—was not divulged. This was not my strict grandmother's style: she who forbade my grandfather to smoke inside and my father to keep beer in her refrigerator, who never allowed us to eat unless we were sitting at the table. I knew then, during that uncharacteristic moment of conspiracy, that I had truly arrived.

Once I had established myself as a co-cook, gone were the Legos, the trucks, the matchbox cars and G.I. Joes of childhood. I starting getting the tools of the trade as gifts: omelet pans, kitchen gadgets, cast-iron skillets, even Grandma's old Dutch oven. In elementary school, I walked home every day to have lunch with my mother; we shared grilled cheese, fried bologna (my favorite), or tuna fish sandwiches with crushed potato chips while we watched *The Galloping Gourmet* and, sometimes, *Jeopardy*.

As a preteen, I took up Boy Scouts and backpacking. Cooking had always been in the company of women—a kitchen filled with grandmothers and aunts—and now, finally, it was a cool, rugged guy thing. As Scouts we foraged for wild ingredients; we camped and hiked for days; and, sometimes longer. Weeks in advance, we planned what food to bring on backpacking trips. We grilled steaks on a wood fire and stewed stews, and all the while I lugged around my grandmother's Dutch oven. I baked cobblers with coals banked all around the oven and on the top.

My family moved around a lot, from the South to the Midwest to New Jersey. When I was fourteen we returned to Savannah, where my parents bought a campground on the Ogeechee River. They worked long hours, and dinner became my happy responsibility. When we were young, my paternal grandparents took my sister and me out to very nice restaurants, where they allowed us to order whatever we wanted, including escargots, Delmonico steaks, and veal piccata. We became friendly with the family who ran the local Chinese restaurant. While I cooked frogs legs (with frogs we had caught), grilled anything (my dad was a big meat eater), and made Southern specialties like biscuits with sorghum syrup, mustard greens with bacon and vinegar, and Savannah red rice (stewed tomatoes with white rice) for my family, I daydreamed of becoming a chef in a Chinese restaurant. I loved the food, and I also loved that dining in a Chinese restaurant was like sitting around a family dinner table, the dishes all arriving family-style. I loved that the other people dining around us were often of three different generations. It was just like home.

I finished college in 1982 with a degree in English literature, and forsaking the original plans for law school, I moved on to the Culinary Institute of America. Back then, the CIA was very focused on classic French cooking. My time there left me wondering what we weren't learning about other cultures. I had become fascinated with Asia—huge in size and diverse in history, geography, and most important to me, cuisine and ingredients. I studied Chinese history and Asian philosophy, and I had a voracious appetite for all types of Asian food, whenever and wherever I could find it. I shopped in ethnic markets, buying exotic ingredients, and experimented at home and made lots of mistakes. I cooked constantly for my family and friends, shaping what would later become the Salamander cuisine.

My appetite naturally extended to Asian cookbooks: Ken Hom's *Chinese Technique,* books on Indian cuisine, and cookbooks by Barbara Tropp, Sri Owen, and Copeland Marks, among others. I had a bad case of wanderlust: I hung out in Boston's Chinatown, eating, shopping, and looking for adventure, I traveled to other cities and eventually to Asia, but professionally I wasn't quite where I wanted to be. At work I was cooking French nouvelle, regional American, and French bistro dishes. However, when I was allowed to run my own specials—Soft-shell Crabs with Cold Chinese Noodles and Sesame Sauce, or Scallops Stir-Fried with Tiny Haricots, Coriander, and Lime—I was transported. The positive feedback whet my appetite.

When I opened Salamander in 1994, I wanted to integrate my personal history and my experience, my loves and my passions, into my professional life: the Southern hospitality and nurturing that I got from my grandmothers, my home-cooking experiments, and my explorations into Asian cultures and the cuisines. Finally I had a place where I could continue my evolution as a chef.

The cuisine at Salamander is an adventurous exploration of Asian flavors and cooking techniques. Using a palette of ingredients drawn from Vietnam, Thailand, Japan, and the diverse regions of China, we have developed a unique style. The flavors and aromas that punctuate these cuisines are seductive and sensual: lime leaves, lemongrass, ginger and cilantro, mint and coriander, star anise and coconut. I want our diners to be transported on an adventure through the foods and flavors of exotic lands. Our goal is to harmonize flavors, to balance and layer spices and textures, all the while using the highest-quality locally grown ingredients and presenting them in a warm, memorable, and sophisticated way.

15

I often deviate from traditional recipes: If the original recipe calls for stewing an old capon for five hours, I might braise a young chicken or a squab instead. There are those in the food community and media who describe this as "fusion," but in truth, this merging of elements has been going on forever. For centuries, regional dishes, techniques, and ingredients have traveled from family to family, country to country. And what, after all, is most "traditional" American food but fusion cuisine from the ultimate melting pot?

What inspires me about Asian cooking is that I am able to continuously learn, to hone and develop my skills by using exotic techniques, interesting taste combinations, unusual ingredients, and varied cooking methods. It is always an exploration, a curiosity satisfied, a flavor as an emotional reaction. I love the vibrancy of Asian cooking, which defines the flavors individually and yet presents them with harmony and balance. Each dish complements and contrasts, providing the four main elements of salt, sweet, sour, and bitter all at once, with both soft and crisp textures.

Now that you know why a German Jewish/Lutheran/Southern Baptist guy is cooking Asian food, go check out my rules of the road and get cooking!

essentials

For all kinds of cooking, a little advance preparation makes things so much easier. I encourage you to do a bit of planning: A few containers of frozen stock, or a spice rub in the fridge, can be a big help when you decide to make a soup or a stew or to roast some flavorful chicken breasts. When you're reading these recipes, don't be put off by unfamiliar ingredients or cooking methods. I describe these techniques and identify the ingredients—soon lemongrass and lime leaves will be as familiar to you as nutmeg and parsley!

And although there are lots of pieces of kitchen equipment that are nice to have, you really need only five things: a good knife, a large cutting board, a few really good pans, some mixing bowls, and good storage containers. Good food is based on quality ingredients, a loving hand, and a bit of patience at the stove—that's all!

staples

These are the items I always have on hand. With a fully stocked pantry, you can make most everything in this book. When I have a preference regarding a particular brand, I indicate it here. You can find Asian ingredients in a well-stocked supermarket, gourmet store, or Asian market. You can also use the Resource List (see page 21) for mail-order and Web sources.

Asian noodles, assorted, including soba, somen, rice sticks, udon, rice vermicelli
baking (unsweetened) chocolate (Callebaut or El Rey)
baking powder

baking soda
brown sugar: dark and light
chickpeas, canned and dry
chili garlic paste (Lee Um Eke or Red Rooster)

Shopping for the pantry

cocoa powder, unsweetened (Droste or
  Callebaut)

coconut milk (Chaokoh or Thai Kitchen)

cornmeal, stone-ground yellow

curry paste: yellow (Maser), green (Prick
  King Green or Maser), and red (Maser)

fish sauce

flour: all-purpose white, cake, and tempura

hoisin sauce (Lee Um Eke)

honey

lentils, dried: red and green

mirin

mustard: Dijon grainy and smooth

nuts: almonds, cashews, peanuts, walnuts

oil: light and dark Asian toasted sesame
  (Eden), soy, chili, olive

peanut butter, organic

rice: jasmine, sushi, and basmati

rice paper wrappers

salt, kosher

sesame tahini, canned

soy sauce (Kikkoman)

spring roll wrappers

sugar, white

tamari (Eden)

tamarind

tomato paste (Muir Glen)

tomatoes: canned whole and canned
  crushed (Muir Glen) and canned diced

tropical juice: mango or pineapple

vinegar: balsamic, cider, and rice (Orlando)

wine: red and white

wonton skins

spices and extracts

Spices are best purchased whole rather than preground. Ground spices quickly lose their aroma and flavor, so it's wise to buy them in small quantities. Whole spices can be ground as needed—we toast and then grind ours in a coffee grinder. If you cook a lot, you'll find that it's worth having one grinder specifically designated for spices. Store spices in airtight containers in a cool, dark place for no more than six months.

allspice berries

anise seeds

bay leaves

black pepper

cardamom pods

cayenne pepper

cinnamon: ground and sticks

cloves

coriander seeds

cumin seeds

curry powder (Madras)

fennel seeds

five-spice powder

Korean hot chili powder

lime leaves

mustard seeds: brown and yellow

nutmeg: whole or ground

peppercorns: Szechuan and black

Red onion

Star anise pods and coriander seeds

Salts

red chili flakes, crushed

saffron threads

sesame seeds: black and white

star anise

turmeric, ground

vanilla beans

vanilla extract, pure

fresh fruits and vegetables

carrots

celery

galangal

garlic

ginger

lemongrass

lemons

limes

onions: Spanish and red

scallions

shallots

tomatoes: beefsteak or plum

refrigerator and freezer

bacon, slab

butter, unsalted

eggs

milk

resource list

At the time of this printing, the following web sites were all still in business . . . but . . .

www.chefscatalog.com; www.tabletools.com (good places to purchase kitchen equipment)

www.kingarthurflour.com; www.cooksnook.com (product information and specialty products)

www.asiafoods.com; www.ethnicgrocer.com; www.gongshee.com; www.orientalpantry.com (Asian products)

www.globalchefs.com (book reviews, career information, organic-food sources, chef biographies, wines); www.starchefs.com

www.epicurious.com (information and recipes)

www.ecofish.com (seafood delivery)

www.calphalon.com (cookware)

essential equipment

Having good equipment won't make you a good cook, but it will make cooking easier and often more enjoyable. Here's a list of what I consider essential.

blender

box grater, four-sided

coffee grinder, electric (for grinding spices)

colander

cutting board (a big, heavy wooden one that won't move around)

food processor

Japanese mandoline—a slicing device in which the food moves over a knife blade, achieving a consistent thickness. There are French, German, and Swiss mandolines, but we use the hardworking, inexpensive, readily available Japanese version.

ladles: 2-, 4-, and 6-ounce

measuring cups

measuring spoons

mixing bowls, stainless-steel

potato masher

sieve, ricer, or food mill

slotted spoons

spatulas

stand mixer

tongs

vegetable peeler

whisks

wooden spoons

zester

pots and pans

wok

8-quart stockpot

8-inch cast-iron skillet

10-inch skillet

14-inch skillet

12-inch sauté pan

Large roasting pan

3-quart saucepan

knives

8-inch chef's

9- or 10-inch slicing

boning

cleaver

paring

serrated bread

charcoal, hardwood
grill: charcoal or (preferably) wood-burning
metal flue (chimney)—a cylinder made of
  sheet metal that you fill with newspaper
and then top with charcoal. It heats the
charcoal faster than placing the charcoal
directly in the pit, and it makes lighting
the grill much easier.

Cooking methods: Here's a quick description of some of the most common cooking methods.

Baking: To cook food in an oven, surrounded by dry heat.

Braising: A two-part cooking process: First the food is seared, or browned in fat, on top of the stove. Then the food is placed in a braising pan, covered with liquid, tightly sealed, and cooked in the oven or on top of the stove. This process breaks down tough cuts of meat, rendering them tender and flavorful.

Broiling: To cook food directly under or over a heat source. Often, when an appliance cooks food from above it is called a salamander, and when it cooks food from below it is called a grill.

Frying: To cook food in fat over high heat. If the food is completely submerged in the fat, it is called deep-frying. If there is a very small amount of fat, it is called sautéing.

Grilling: To cook food directly over a heat source.

Poaching: To cook food in liquid just below the simmering point, usually 185°F. This gentle cooking process is ideal for tender or fragile foods.

Sautéing: To cook food in a small amount of fat over high heat, stirring often. The term comes from the French *sauter,* which means "to jump."

Stir-frying: To cook food (typically cut in small, uniform pieces) in a small amount of fat over intense heat in a wok.

spice rubs and pastes

Spice rubs are a type of dry, intensely flavored marinade that should be used sparingly. As opposed to a liquidy oil-based marinade, spice rubs and pastes are massaged directly onto the surface of meats, chicken, or fish. These powerful rubs can pack a lot of flavor, as you will see with the Korean and East Indian blends, resulting in a dish that is deliciously aromatic and flavorful.

This spice rub has an interesting subtlety in spite of being composed of complex flavors; it won't knock you over the head. The spices are those typically found in curry powder, with the addition of yellow mustard seeds, brown mustard seeds, and cardamom. It is particularly good with chicken, eggplant, cod, halibut, and salmon. Simply rub the spices in, cover, and refrigerate for at least 10 minutes, or, better still, for up to 24 hours. Then cook as you choose: sauté, roast, or grill.

1 tablespoon fennel seeds
1 tablespoon coriander seeds
2 tablespoons cumin seeds
1 tablespoon anise seeds
1 teaspoon crushed red chili flakes
1 teaspoon amchoor
2 tablespoons minced fresh ginger
1 tablespoon yellow mustard seeds
1 tablespoon brown mustard seeds, or 1 additional tablespoon yellow
12 cardamom pods
¼ cup soy oil

Place the fennel, coriander, cumin, and anise seeds in a skillet and cook over medium heat, stirring often, until dark and very fragrant, 2 to 3 minutes. Set aside to cool.

Place the cooled seeds in a spice grinder and pulse until coarsely cracked. Transfer to a bowl, add all the remaining ingredients, and mix to combine. Cover and refrigerate for up to 1 month.

2/3 to 3/4 cup

Soy oil: When I need a neutral oil, I like to use soy because it is relatively flavorless and it is healthful. It also has a high smoking point; in other words, it has the ability to hold a high temperature without smoking or imparting unpleasant flavors when sautéing.

Amchoor: Amchoor, also known as mango powder, is an East Indian seasoning made of ground sun-dried unripe mango. The powder has a tart, acidic, fruity flavor that adds depth to many curry dishes. As a paste, it is also used to tenderize poultry, meat, and fish. Amchoor is readily available at Indian markets.

Ginger: More than almost any other flavor, ginger defines Asian cooking. While it is often mistakenly called a root, ginger is in fact a tropical rhizome (underground stem) native to Southeast Asia. Long relied upon for its medicinal value (it is said to aid digestion, stimulate the appetite, and cure upset stomachs), ginger is used in a myriad of forms throughout Asia and, more recently, in the United States. The flavor is clean and spicy, with a hint of sweetness, and marries well with garlic. Fresh ginger will keep well at

Fresh ginger

room temperature for at least 1 week. To store it longer, wrap the ginger loosely in a paper towel (to absorb moisture), place it in a plastic bag, and keep it in the refrigerator.

korean chili spice blend

Similar to a spice mix I tasted in Japanese noodle shops, this is one of my favorite condiments; keep it next to the salt and pepper on your dinner table. Salty, crunchy, and spicy, it is great sprinkled on soups, cold chicken, fried squid, tempura, even cottage cheese. Without exception, everyone I have given it to has pleaded for more. I've seen cooks in our kitchen put this blend on their sandwiches at lunch!

Do not substitute American chili powder for Korean: Korean is coarsely ground, whereas American is finely ground. My favorite brand is Wang; it can be found at any Asian market.

½ cup white sesame seeds
¼ cup black sesame seeds
2 tablespoons coriander seeds
½ cup Korean (coarsely ground) chili powder
1 sheet nori, finely diced

Place the white and black sesame seeds and the coriander seeds in a skillet and cook over medium heat, stirring often, until dark and very fragrant, 2 to 3 minutes. Set aside to cool.

Add the chili powder and nori to the cooled seeds, and mix to combine. Transfer to a glass jar, cover, and keep at room temperature for up to 2 months.

About 1¼ cups

Nori: Most commonly seen in the United States wrapped around rice and raw fish, nori is paper-thin sheets of dried seaweed. The color ranges from green to almost black, and the flavor is fairly sweet and reminiscent of the ocean. While they are most often used as a wrapping, the sheets may be chopped or sliced and added to any number of Asian preparations, or sprinkled as a garnish. Nori is rich in protein, iron, and vitamins.

Sesame seeds: Dating back to 3000 B.C., sesame seeds are one of the first recorded seasonings. Grown widely in India and the Orient, the seeds were originally brought to North America by African slaves. Grown in shades of brown, red, black, and white, sesame seeds have a nutty, slightly sweet flavor. White sesame seeds are hulled and are often toasted for more flavor.

southeast asian green curry paste

When I was in Thailand I loved to watch the vendors at the market work their woks, creating curry dishes that are very different from those of India and its neighbors. Southeast Asian curry dishes start with a paste of fresh ingredients—lemongrass, fresh herbs, ginger, galangal, garlic—combined with dried spices and chilies. The paste is stir-fried with coconut milk, an assortment of vegetables, and a protein such as meat or tofu. The curry is usually thinner than Indian curries and has a much broader spectrum of flavors.

2½ inches fresh ginger, cut into thick slices
8 garlic cloves
1 inch galangal, or 1 additional inch fresh ginger
¼ to 1 cup packed fresh cilantro leaves
5 kaffir lime leaves (see page 32)
1 stalk lemongrass, outer husk discarded, inner heart sliced
2 jalapeño peppers, seeded and sliced
About ½ cup packed fresh mint leaves
About ½ cup packed fresh Thai basil leaves
4 shallots, sliced
2 tablespoons coriander seeds, toasted and cracked
1 tablespoon star anise pods, toasted and ground
½ cup light sesame oil

Place all the ingredients in a food processor and process until it forms a paste. Transfer to a glass container, cover, and refrigerate for up to 2 months.

1⅔ to 1¾ cups

Galangal: A rhizome (underground stem) with a ginger-pepper flavor, galangal grows throughout Southeast Asia and is especially popular in Thai cooking. This creamy-fleshed tuber can be used as a substitute for ginger. Galangal has a stronger attack, or first flavor, on your palate than ginger, and a lingering taste that is mildly astringent and aromatic. The sharp flavors of galangal marry well with the flavors of the regions in which it grows: Cambodia, Thailand, Vietnam, and Indonesia.

How to use curry pastes: To make a great and quick curry dish, simply sauté onions, ginger, and garlic, and carrots and celery if desired. When the vegetables have softened, add some curry paste, starting with 1 tablespoon and adding more as desired. Add chicken stock, coconut milk, and diced tomatoes. When the mixture has heated through, add cut-up cooked chicken, pork, or fish. When that has poached, add some Asian noodles and—*ta-da!*—dinner is on the table!

Why use paste instead of curry powder? The resulting flavors are more complicated, and more interesting, because the paste has a wider range of ingredients.

Star anise: Similar in flavor to anise (both get their flavor from an oil called anethol), yet slightly more bitter and from a different plant family, star anise is a star-shaped, dark brown pod that contains a single large seed in each of its eight segments. Native to China, star anise comes from a small evergreen tree that is related to the magnolia. To toast star anise, place a small pan over medium heat and add the star anise. Cook, stirring often, until fragrant and darkened, 3 to 5 minutes. Transfer it to a plate and set aside to cool.

Star anise

yellow curry paste

Yellow curries contain a higher percentage of dried spices, most notably turmeric, than either green or red curries. This gives the paste a bright yellow color and a dusty, earthy flavor. Peanuts are traditionally included in this curry and lend a distinctive flavor and richness to the finished dish. Be careful, though: Be sure to inquire if any of your guests is allergic to nuts. This assertive, nutty, moderately hot curry lends itself to pork, duck, and noodle stir-fries as well as to soups.

Turmeric: Easily recognized by its bright yellow-orange color and pungent aroma when ground, turmeric has been used in cooking for more than 2,000 years. Ground from the root of a plant similar to ginger, turmeric is popular in East Indian cooking and in curry preparations in cuisines stretching across the Indian Ocean. It is also what gives American mustard its telltale bright yellow color.

2½ inches fresh ginger, cut into thick slices
8 garlic cloves
1 inch galangal (see page 30), or 1 additional inch
  fresh ginger
¼ to 1 cup packed fresh cilantro leaves
1 stalk lemongrass, outer husk discarded, inner
  heart sliced
½ cup packed fresh mint leaves
½ cup packed fresh Thai basil leaves
4 shallots, sliced
2 jalapeño peppers, seeded and sliced
1 tablespoon ground turmeric
½ cup light sesame oil
1 cup unsalted peanuts (optional), toasted

Place all the ingredients in a food processor and process until it forms a paste. Transfer to a glass container, cover, and refrigerate for up to 1 month.

About 2½ cups

The color of a curry generally identifies the predominant flavor or combination of ingredients and the heat level. Green curry is mostly fresh herbs, yellow predominantly dried spices. Red curry paste gets its flavor from Thai bird chilies, the third-hottest variety of chili to be found any-where. The flavors of this paste marry well with beef, lamb, and assertive seafood like clams, mussels, or bluefish.

2½ inches fresh ginger, cut into thick slices
8 garlic cloves
1 inch galangal (see page 30), or
  1 additional inch fresh ginger
⅓ cup fresh cilantro leaves
1 stalk lemongrass, outer husk discarded,
  inner heart sliced
4 shallots, sliced
5 fresh or frozen kaffir lime leaves
½ to ¼ cup red Thai bird chilies, stems
  trimmed
2 tablespoons coriander seeds, toasted and
  cracked
1 tablespoon star anise pods, toasted and
  ground
½ cup light sesame oil

   Place all the ingredients in a food processor and process until it forms a red-speckled paste. Transfer to a glass container, cover, and refrigerate for up to 2 months.

About 2 cups

Lime leaves: Kaffir lime leaves are an essential ingredient in Southeast Asian cuisines and can be found fresh or frozen in most Asian markets. If you find them fresh, buy more than you need and freeze the extra for future use. I'm not a big fan of dried lime leaves because they lose their fragrance in the drying and storage process.

Using pastes as marinades: I like to turn these curry pastes into quick marinades when I'm short on time and want a big flavor burst. Simply add 2 to 3 tablespoons curry paste to ½ cup light sesame oil, stir, and toss with chicken breasts, pork chops, flank steak, scallops, or shrimp. Let sit at least 2 hours or up to overnight. Cook as desired: broil, sauté, or grill.

Thai bird chilies: The thin-fleshed Thai chili, small (only 1 or 2 inches long) but powerful, ranges in color from green to red. It's a popular addition in many Southeast Asian dishes due to its strong flavor and staying power. Unlike many chilies, Thai chilies do not lose their flavor when cooked.

stocks

Stocks and broths are easy to make, and they freeze well for up to 6 months.

A stock can be made from veal bones, chicken bones, shrimp shells, even lobster bodies. Each type of stock simmers for a different length of time to fully extract the flavors of all the ingredients—3 to 4 hours for shellfish; overnight for veal stock.

Stocks are prepared with bones or shells, aromatic vegetables, herbs and spices, water, and sometimes wine. A broth is the liquid that results from poaching or braising poultry or meat.

Most of the time butchers will sell or give you necks and backs to make chicken stock, but I prefer to use chicken rib cages—they are cleaner, have bits of meat still attached, and have softer bones, all of which results in a finished stock with better body and clarity. Rib cages are not always put in the display case, but you can ask your butcher for some; the cages come from producing boneless chicken breasts, so you can be sure there will be no shortage!

5 pounds chicken rib cages
4 carrots, coarsely chopped
2 large or 4 small Spanish onions, coarsely chopped
4 celery stalks, coarsely chopped
1 head garlic, halved horizontally to expose the cloves
1 leek, green top only, coarsely chopped
1 bottle (750 ml) high-acid, not overly fruity white wine, such as
  Sauvignon Blanc or Orvieto
6 quarts cold water

Stock tips: Two important rules apply to making stocks: Always start with cold water, and always simmer rather than boil your stock. When making stocks, it sometimes helps to think about consommés and how they work. A consommé is a clarified stock. The stock is clarified by the addition of egg whites. We toss the whites with julienned vegetables and, as the cold stock heats, the egg white—coated vegetables clump together, with the protein in the eggs acting as a net to catch any impurities. All of this material forms a "raft" that floats to the top of the stock, taking all of the little unwanted bits with it. Making a good stock works much the same way. If you start with cold water, the protein from the bits of meat and bones will gather the little bits from the water and ensure a good clear stock. This too is why you never want to boil your stock or consommé; the agitation will cause the "net" to rupture, releasing the impurities back into the stock.

Preheat the oven to 400°F.

Place the rib cages in a large roasting pan, place it in the oven, and roast until they are light golden and fragrant, 15 to 20 minutes. Add the carrots, onions, celery, garlic, and leek greens, and toss to combine. Return the pan to the oven and roast until the vegetables are caramelized and the bones are a deep golden color, about 30 minutes. Stir, and cook for an additional 15 minutes.

Transfer all the roasted ingredients to a large stockpot, being careful to scrape up the brown bits from the roasting pan.

Place the roasting pan over medium heat and add the wine. Bring to a boil, scraping up any bits still in the pan. When the bottom of the pan is clean, pour the contents into the stockpot. Add the water and bring to a boil over high heat. Reduce the heat to low and simmer, uncovered, for 3½ to 4 hours, skimming the foam off as necessary.

Strain the stock and discard the solids. Transfer the stock to one large or several small containers, cover, and refrigerate for up to 5 days or freeze for up to 6 months.

3 quarts

The aroma of simmering veal stock has to be about as homey as the sight of a fire burning in the fireplace or the scent of cookies baking in the oven. Making your own stock is easy, affordable, and essential. Having containers of homemade stock in your refrigerator or freezer will enable you to produce wonderful soups and rich sauces, and many recipes in this book, with ease. You won't believe the difference it will make to your cooking!

5 pounds veal shin or shoulder bones
4 carrots, coarsely chopped
2 large or 4 small Spanish onions, coarsely chopped
4 celery stalks, coarsely chopped
1 head garlic, halved horizontally to expose the cloves
1 leek, green top only, coarsely chopped
1 6-ounce can tomato paste
1 bottle (750 ml) high-acid, not overly fruity red wine, such as Merlot or Cabernet
  Sauvignon
6 quarts cold water

Preheat the oven to 400°F.

Place the bones in a large roasting pan, place it in the oven, and roast until they are very light golden and fragrant, 15 to 20 minutes. Add the carrots, onions, celery, garlic, and leek greens, and toss to combine. Return the pan to the oven and roast until the vegetables are caramelized and the bones are a deep golden color, about 45 minutes. Add the tomato paste, stir, and cook an additional 15 minutes.

Drain off as much fat as possible from the roasting pan. Transfer the bones and vegetables to a large stockpot, being careful to scrape up the brown bits stuck to the bottom of the pan.

Place the roasting pan over medium heat and add the wine. Bring to a boil, scraping up any bits still in the pan. When the bottom of the pan is clean, pour the contents into the stockpot. Add the water and bring to a boil over high heat. Reduce the heat to low and cook, uncovered, for 8 to 12 hours, skimming the foam off as necessary.

Strain the stock and discard the solids. Transfer the stock to one large or several small containers, cover, and refrigerate for up to 5 days or freeze for up to 6 months.

3 quarts

vegetable stock

It is very important to start your soups, sauces, and braises with a flavorful liquid. Unlike most vegetable stocks, which are often no more than onion water, this broth is rich, flavorful, and nutritious. If you have a large, shallow sauté pan, use that rather than a stockpot; the wider cooking surface will allow the vegetables to caramelize more effectively, enriching the stock.

You can use this vegetable stock as a replacement for water or for any meat-, chicken-, or fish-based stock.

1 tablespoon soy oil
2 large or 4 small Spanish onions, coarsely
    chopped
1 leek, green top only, coarsely chopped
1 head garlic, halved horizontally to expose
    the cloves
3 carrots, coarsely chopped
1 fennel bulb, coarsely chopped
10 ounces (3 to 4 cups) fresh whole button
    mushrooms
4 celery stalks, coarsely chopped
4 quarts cold water

Seed packets

Place a large sauté pan or stockpot over medium heat. When it is hot, add the oil. Then add the onions, leek greens, garlic, carrots, fennel, mushrooms, and celery. Cook, uncovered, until the vegetables are tender and are just starting to fall apart, about 30 minutes.

Add the water and bring to a boil over high heat. Reduce the heat to low and cook, uncovered, until the vegetables are falling apart, about 30 minutes to 1 hour.

Strain the stock and discard the solids. Transfer the stock to one large or several small containers, cover, and refrigerate for up to 7 days or freeze for up to 6 months.

3 quarts

At Salamander, we all drink dashi; it's fortifying and soothing in the way that consommé is. In fact, we believe that it's what keeps us so healthy.

Essentially, we make an Asian-flavored vegetable broth and enrich it with konbu, dried kelp (seaweed) widely used in Japanese cooking. Bonito flakes (bonito fish is similar to mackerel) are a traditional ingredient in dashi broth, but we have chosen to keep this version vegetarian. Use the dashi as a soup broth or sauce base.

When you use the dashi, never bring it to a boil or you'll lose the nutritional value and delicate nuances of flavor.

1 tablespoon light sesame oil
2 small onions, coarsely chopped
1 leek, white part plus 1 inch of green, coarsely chopped
4 carrots, coarsely chopped
1 fennel bulb, coarsely chopped
1 head garlic, halved horizontally to expose the cloves
2 inches fresh ginger, sliced
2 teaspoons kosher salt
1 teaspoon Szechuan peppercorns
1 tablespoon coriander seeds
2 star anise pods
4 quarts cold water
4 ounces konbu
¼ cup tamari
1 teaspoon dark sesame oil
½ teaspoon chili oil

Konbu: Also known as *kombu* or kelp, konbu is sun-dried seaweed; it comes in sheets. It is used as a flavor enhancer and is most often encountered in dashi, the Japanese soup stock. When you add konbu to a recipe, you should allow it to infuse, like tea; do not let it boil. Once the package is opened, it can be stored in a cool, dark place for up to 6 months. Konbu is available in Asian specialty stores.

Place a large (6-quart) saucepan or stockpot over medium heat. When it is hot, add the light sesame oil. Then add the onions, leek, carrots, fennel, garlic, ginger, salt, peppercorns, coriander seeds, and star anise. Cook, stirring occasionally, until the vegetables begin to caramelize, 8 to 10 minutes.

Add the water and bring to a boil over high heat. Reduce the heat to low and simmer for about 30 minutes.

Meanwhile, using a damp cloth, wipe the strips of konbu to remove any salty dust that may remain from the drying process. With the tip of a sharp knife, gently score the konbu throughout the length and on both sides.

Remove the pan from the heat, and add the konbu, tamari, dark sesame oil, and chili oil. Set aside to cool to room temperature, 1 to 1½ hours.

Strain the stock and discard the solids. Transfer the stock to one large or several small containers, cover, and refrigerate for up to 2 weeks or freeze for up to 6 months.

4 quarts

A *fumet* is a light fish stock made with wine. I use only flatfish bones (sole, flounder, and halibut), and I cook the stock very briefly—a fumet should be more of an infusion than an extraction. When a fish stock or sauce has been overcooked or overly reduced, the aroma and taste completely overwhelm the dish and your palate. With fish fumet, it is better to err on the side of too light rather than too fishy.

Do not substitute other vegetables; be sure to use only white (pale-colored) vegetables.

1 tablespoon soy oil
2 large or 4 small onions, halved and thinly sliced
2 large leeks, white part plus 1 inch of green, thinly sliced
2 celery stalks, thinly sliced
1 head garlic, halved horizontally to expose the cloves
2 cups dry white wine
5 pounds flatfish bones, cleaned of head, tail, and entrails, well rinsed under cold water
4 quarts very cold water

Place a large (8-quart) stockpot over medium heat and add the oil. When the oil is hot, add the onions, leeks, celery, and garlic. Cook until the vegetables wilt (do not let them color), 1 to 2 minutes. Add the wine and cook until reduced by half, 5 to 8 minutes. Add the fish bones and the water, and bring to a full rolling boil. Reduce the heat to low and simmer for just 3 to 5 minutes, skimming off the foam as necessary. Set the pot aside to cool for 20 minutes.

Strain the fumet and discard the solids. Transfer the fumet to one large or several small containers, cover, and refrigerate for up to 5 days or freeze for up to 6 months.

4 quarts

shellfish stock

I always keep shellfish stock on hand. To produce a truly nice one, take the time to get a good sear on the crab and lobster bodies: You want the shells deeply browned and the aroma deep and intense. Ask your fishmonger to quarter the crabs and to split the lobster bodies. This will make your job easier.

2 tablespoons soy oil
5 pounds shellfish bodies (lobster, crab, and/or shrimp; uncooked shells are best)
2 large or 4 small Spanish onions, coarsely chopped
2 carrots, coarsely chopped
4 celery stalks, coarsely chopped
1 head garlic, halved horizontally to expose the cloves
1 leek, white part plus 1 inch of green, coarsely chopped
1 6-ounce can tomato paste
1 bottle (750 ml) dry white wine
6 quarts cold water
½ cup brandy (optional)
1 orange, halved
2 stalks lemongrass, sliced

Place a large sauté pan or stockpot over medium-high heat. When it is hot, add the oil. Add the shellfish bodies and cook until well seared and caramelized, 6 to 8 minutes. Be careful to keep the heat high enough so that the bodies do not steam or stew.

Reduce the heat to medium, and add the onions, carrots, celery, garlic, and leeks. Cook until the vegetables brown, 5 to 8 minutes. Add the tomato paste and stir to combine. Add the white wine and the water, and brandy if desired, and bring to a boil. Reduce the heat and simmer, uncovered, for 3 hours, skimming off the foam as necessary.

Remove the pan from the heat; add the orange and lemongrass; steep for 1 hour. Then strain the stock and discard the solids. Transfer the stock to one large or several small containers, cover, and refrigerate for up to 5 days or freeze for up to 6 months.

4 quarts

serving accompaniments

Condiments are a cook's secret weapon. My refrigerator holds jars and jars of things I've made (and bought) that really help me cook at home with ease. The recipes that follow are meant to add flavor and balance to the dishes in the rest of the book. Pickles, relishes, and chutneys perfectly accent roasted and grilled foods, and when you can just spoon some out of a container you will add a huge punch to a meal. Flavored oils can be used for marinades and to enhance the flavors of soups and curries. Dipping sauces are the perfect companion to savory appetizers such as spring rolls, sushi, wontons, and scallion pancakes. The sauce should complement and balance the flavors of the dishes being served with it. A luxuriously rich peanut sauce is a perfect pairing to grilled satay. A spicy dish may require a sweet, fruity, or lime-flavored dipping sauce. Prepare your dipping sauces in advance if you have time, to allow the flavors to meld—and keep some on hand for last-minute impulses. Dipping sauces also pair well with grilled meats and seafood.

flavored oils
fragrant chili and spice oil

This lip-smacking oil is especially good over cold roasted meats—chicken, beef, or pork—or drizzled over soups or noodles just prior to serving. Flavored oils are made differently depending on whether you are using dried ingredients like spices, or fresh ingredients like herbs. For this oil, I simply steep toasted spices and other ingredients in a small amount of warmed oil to create a strong infusion. When it has cooled, I add more oil to balance the flavors. As a rule, use about 2 tablespoons of spices or chilies to flavor 1 cup of oil.

Arbol chilies: Similar in flavor but less hot than cayenne chilies, these have a tannic, grassy, slightly smoky flavor. They are red and pointed and usually 2 to 3 inches long.

4 arbol chilies
1 3-inch cinnamon stick
5 cardamom pods
3 star anise pods
1 tablespoon coriander seeds
1 cup light sesame oil
1 tablespoon dark sesame oil
1 teaspoon kosher salt
¼ teaspoon black pepper

Place the chilies, cinnamon stick, cardamom pods, star anise, and coriander in a large skillet and cook over medium heat, stirring often, until dark and fragrant, 2 to 3 minutes. Add ½ cup of the light sesame oil and cook until heated through, about 2 minutes. Remove from the heat and let steep for 10 minutes.

Transfer the mixture to a glass container, and add the remaining ½ cup light sesame oil, the dark sesame oil, salt, and pepper. Cover and refrigerate for up to 2 months.

1¼ cups

serving accompaniments

scallion oil

The rich green, mellow oniony flavor makes this oil perfect to use on steamed vegetables, cold noodles, or a simple Asian salad. To make an herb-flavored oil, or an oil flavored with fresh ingredients like garlic, roasted peppers, or citrus zest, simply puree the main ingredients and then add enough oil to produce a flavorful mixture. The oil will be flavorful enough to use right away. The purpose of blanching the scallions is to intensify their color and to remove some of the raw flavor.

2 cups water
2 bunches (about 16) scallions, green tops only
  (save the whites for another use)
1 tablespoon finely minced fresh ginger
1 cup soy oil
¼ cup dark sesame oil
1 teaspoon kosher salt
¼ teaspoon black pepper

Prepare an ice bath.

Place the water in a saucepan and bring to a boil over high heat. Add the scallion greens and blanch for 30 seconds. Drain the scallions and transfer them to the ice bath. When they are cool, drain and wring them out or press them dry between paper towels.

Place the scallions, ginger, soy and sesame oils, salt, and pepper in a food processor and process until smooth.

Transfer the mixture to a glass container, cover, and refrigerate for up to 2 months.

About 1¼ cups

Ice bath: An ice bath is used to quickly bring down the temperature of food. This is done for one of two reasons: to stop the cooking process or to get the food out of the "temperature danger zone," where bacteria is most likely to grow (40° to 140°F). To make an ice bath, fill a large container with ice and very cold water. Place the food you wish to cool in the ice bath, either in the original cooking vessel or in another container. Be sure that the food container is taller than the ice bath so water does not get into your food. Alternatively, for foods like blanched vegetables, the food itself can be placed directly into the ice water, with or without a wire basket, then removed, drained, and stored.

I love to add cilantro flavor by drizzling this deep green oil on soups and noodles, but I also like to use it for purely decorative purposes, using a squeeze bottle to make lines and zigzags on the plates I send out to the dining room. You can do this too! This oil can also be used as a marinade for chicken, shrimp, or just about anything to which you want to give a quick burst of flavor. At Salamander we use bushels of fresh cilantro, along with a variety of mints and Asian basils. The taste and fragrance of these herbs are essential to my cooking; the flavor they add to sauces, rice, noodles, and soups is immeasurable.

Light versus dark sesame oil: When describing sesame oil, I often compare the uses and flavors of the dark and light to the same variations in olive oil. The darker, heavier, and more flavorful the oil, the more appropriate it is for seasoning, drizzling over noodles or vegetables, or for vinaigrettes. The lighter oils are best used for sautéing and marinades.

¾ to 1 cup packed fresh cilantro leaves
2 garlic cloves
1 tablespoon minced fresh ginger
1 teaspoon kosher salt
¼ teaspoon black pepper
1 cup light sesame oil
1 tablespoon dark sesame oil

Place the cilantro, garlic, ginger, salt, and pepper in a food processor and process until smooth, about 2 minutes. Add the oil and process until smooth. Transfer to a glass container, cover, and refrigerate for up to 2 weeks.

About 1¼ cups

serving accompaniments

curry oil

My friend Matt Murphy worked at Salamander for more than a year when we first opened. Matty had come to Salamander to build solid cooking skills before opening his own place (he now runs Matt Murphy's Pub in Brookline Village). At Salamander he did prep and prepared hot and cold appetizers. Every Saturday this curry oil was on Matty's prep list, and every Saturday half of this recipe was on his apron! Try this flavor-packed oil on your apron, or better yet, on grilled marinated vegetables or on the Indian-Spiced Leg of Lamb with Creamy Yogurt Sauce (page 176).

Chopping ginger: When I need to mince fresh ginger, I never grate it. Instead, I slice it with the grain and then cut it into tiny dice. Instead of the stringy, dry ginger you get from grating, this method renders it moist, fragrant, and easy to use.

1 tablespoon cumin seeds
1 tablespoon coriander seeds
1 tablespoon fennel seeds
1 tablespoon curry powder
1 tablespoon ground turmeric
1 cup plus 1 tablespoon light sesame oil
1 tablespoon minced fresh ginger
4 garlic cloves, minced
1 cup pineapple or mango juice
1 teaspoon kosher salt
¼ teaspoon black pepper

Place the cumin, coriander, and fennel in a spice grinder and grind to a coarse powder. Add the curry powder and turmeric and pulse to combine.

Place a small pan over medium heat. When it is hot, add the 1 tablespoon sesame oil. Then add the ginger and garlic and cook until lightly browned. Add the ground spices and cook until they are toasted and very fragrant, about 2 minutes. Add the pineapple juice and cook until reduced to ¼ cup, 5 to 8 minutes.

Transfer the mixture to a food processor, add the remaining 1 cup sesame oil, salt, and pepper, and process until smooth.

Transfer the curry oil to a glass container, cover, and refrigerate for up to 2 weeks.

About 1¼ cups

dipping sauces
hoisin and spice
dipping sauce

I was such a freak for Chinese food as a kid; I yearned to be a cook in a Chinese restaurant! This dipping sauce has universal appeal and a broad variety of uses. It's great with Vietnamese Summer Rolls (page 74), Spring Rolls (page 72), cold and hot meats, like Twice-Cooked Philippines-style Chicken (page 167), dumplings, Asian wraps, scallion pancakes, and fried snacks. It is best when made one day ahead.

2 tablespoons minced fresh ginger
2 garlic cloves, minced
1 cup hoisin sauce
½ cup orange juice
2 tablespoons soy sauce
¼ cup rice vinegar
1 tablespoon dark sesame oil
1 teaspoon kosher salt
¼ teaspoon black pepper
¼ cup chopped unsalted peanuts, toasted (optional)

Place all the ingredients in a bowl or food processor and mix to combine. Transfer to a container, cover, and refrigerate for up to 1 week.

2 cups

Hoisin: An indispensable part of Chinese cooking, hoisin is a thick, reddish brown, sweet and spicy sauce made with soybeans. It is readily found in Asian markets and many large supermarkets. Once opened, it should be transferred to a non-metal container, covered, and refrigerated.

serving accompaniments

spicy peanut sauce

I could eat this classic peanut sauce straight out of the jar (and have been caught doing so on many occasions). However, it's best as an accompaniment to fresh rolls and dumplings, tossed with Chinese egg noodles, dolloped over Malaysian Sweet Spice–Rubbed Chicken (page 160), served with pork or beef, and of course, classically paired with chicken or beef satay.

For a change, try substituting cashew or almond butter for the peanut butter.

Mirin: Mirin is a low-alcohol sweet wine made from glutinous rice. Also known as rice wine, mirin is used primarily as a sweetener in Japanese cooking. It's available in Asian markets and in good supermarkets.

1 tablespoon light sesame oil
¼ cup minced fresh ginger
8 garlic cloves, minced
¼ cup tomato paste
½ cup natural unsweetened peanut butter
1 tablespoon chili garlic paste (see page 82)
½ cup hot water
¼ cup soy sauce
¼ cup mirin
¼ cup rice vinegar
1 teaspoon kosher salt
¼ teaspoon black pepper

Place a skillet over medium-high heat. When it is hot, add the oil. Then add the ginger and garlic and cook until lightly browned, about 2 minutes. Add the tomato paste, peanut butter, and chili garlic paste. Lower the heat to medium and cook, stirring constantly to prevent scorching, until the tomato paste has lost its sweet raw flavor and the mixture is a dark reddish brown and very fragrant, 2 to 3 minutes.

Transfer the mixture to a mixer fitted with a whisk attachment or to a blender. With the machine running on medium-high speed, slowly drizzle in the water, followed by the soy sauce, mirin, and rice vinegar. Mix until just combined. Add the salt and pepper. Transfer to a container, cover, and refrigerate for up to 2 weeks.

About 2 cups

This mild citrusy tamari sauce is a simple and easy variation inspired by a Japanese sauce called *ponzu,* which I remember enjoying tremendously with giant oysters in Tokyo. I especially like this sauce with lighter meats or seafoods, maki or other sushi, grilled or broiled fish and shellfish, Lobster Tempura (page 111), as well as crispy tofu.

For the best results, make this 24 hours in advance.

1 cup Versatile Dashi (page 38)
⅓ cup fresh orange juice (about 1 large orange)
⅓ cup fresh lemon juice (about 2 lemons)
¼ cup tamari

Place all the ingredients in a bowl, and mix to combine. Transfer the sauce to a container, cover, and refrigerate for up to 2 weeks.

About 2 cups

Sweet and Hot Pepper Relish, Cool Lime Dip, and Golden Shallot Relish

cool lime dip

I guarantee that you will become hooked on this intoxicating spicy lime dipping sauce! If you taste it as you make it, you will find flavors swirling about your palate in complementary layers of fragrance, spice, heat, and lime, creating images of faraway lands. You can just imagine what it does for whatever you dunk into it! Try this with crispy whole fish, steamed or grilled shrimp and scallops, satay, and spring rolls.

Fish sauce: A clear, salty, protein-rich sauce produced from the salting and fermenting of small fish, such as anchovies. In Southeast Asia, it is used in much the same ways the Chinese use soy sauce or the Americans use salt. Fish sauce is found in jars in specialty markets.

1 tablespoon coriander seeds
1 teaspoon Szechuan peppercorns
2 star anise pods
¼ cup sugar
2 arbol chilies
¼ cup water
½ cup rice vinegar
½ cup fresh lime juice (3 or 4 limes)
4 fresh or frozen kaffir lime leaves (see page 32)
1 inch fresh ginger, sliced
1 tablespoon dark sesame oil
¼ cup fish sauce

Place the coriander, peppercorns, and star anise in a 1-quart saucepan and toast over medium heat, stirring often, until dark and very fragrant, 2 to 3 minutes. Add the sugar and chilies, and cook until melted and lightly caramelized, about 2 minutes. Carefully and gradually add the water, and bring to a boil over high heat. Stir until the caramel has dissolved. Remove from the heat.

Place the rice vinegar, lime juice, lime leaves, ginger, sesame oil, and fish sauce in a bowl and mix to combine. Pour the sugar syrup into the bowl, stir to combine, and cover. Leave at room temperature for at least 12 and up to 24 hours. Then strain, and discard the solids. Transfer the sauce to a container, cover, and refrigerate for up to 2 weeks.

About 1½ cups

Almost twenty years ago, I first created this sauce to serve with soft-shell crabs. Every year during soft-shell season, I make sure to enjoy this combination of two of my favorite flavors at least once. The sauce is also great with hot or cold noodles, cold boiled shrimp, and crab cakes, as a dip for crudités, and as a sauce for panko-coated strips of fried chicken and shrimp.

1 tablespoon light sesame oil
1 tablespoon minced fresh ginger
2 garlic cloves, minced
½ cup sesame tahini
2 tablespoons hot water
2 tablespoons soy sauce
¼ cup mirin
¼ cup rice vinegar
1 tablespoon black or white sesame seeds, toasted
1 tablespoon chili garlic paste
1 teaspoon kosher salt
¼ teaspoon black pepper

How to toast seeds:
Place a small pan over medium heat and add the spices. Cook, stirring often, until fragrant and darkened, 3 to 5 minutes. Transfer to a plate and set aside to cool.

Place a skillet over medium-high heat. When it is hot, add the oil. Then add the ginger and garlic, and cook until lightly browned, about 2 minutes. Transfer the mixture to a blender, add the tahini and hot water, and blend until smooth. With the machine running, gradually drizzle in the soy sauce, mirin, and rice vinegar; blend until smooth. Stir in the sesame seeds, salt, and pepper. Transfer to a container, cover, and refrigerate for up to 2 weeks.

About 1½ cups

serving accompaniments

relishes and chutneys
tamarind fruits

This sweet-and-spicy tropical fruit chutney is an absolute hit as an accompaniment to grilled lamb and beef and richly flavored fish like tuna, bass, mackerel, and bluefish. All of these are particularly good if rubbed first with the Malaysian Spice Rub (page 160) before grilling. I think I fell in love with that tamarind undertone in steak sauces before I ever knew what it was. Now I seek it out, in everything from soda to Thai candies.

1 tablespoon light sesame oil
2 shallots, sliced
2 tablespoons minced fresh ginger
6 garlic cloves, minced
2 red bell peppers, cut into small dice
1 cup Tamarind Juice (recipe follows)
2 cups pineapple or mango juice
½ cup cider vinegar
¼ cup lime juice
2 firm pears, cut into small dice
2 papayas, cut into small dice
1 small golden pineapple, cut into small dice
1 cup raisins
2 teaspoons coriander seeds, toasted and ground
1 3-inch cinnamon stick, toasted and ground
2 star anise pods, toasted and ground
1 teaspoon kosher salt
¼ teaspoon black pepper

Tamarind: Tamarind is a naturally sour tropical fruit whose flavor is most recognizable in A.1. and Worcestershire sauces. It is used to accentuate a sweet-and-sour blend of flavors. In tropical climates you will find tamarind sodas and juices—in fact you can also find them here in any good Caribbean grocery store.

How to toast cinnamon sticks: Break up the cinnamon sticks a bit with your hands. Place a small pan over medium heat and add the cinnamon. Cook, stirring often, until fragrant and darkened, 3 to 5 minutes. Transfer to a plate and set aside to cool.

Place a large (4-quart) heavy-bottomed saucepan over medium heat. When it is hot, add the oil. Add the shallots, ginger, and garlic and cook until lightly browned, 2 to

3 minutes. Add the bell peppers and cook until lightly browned, 3 to 5 minutes. Add the tamarind juice, pineapple juice, vinegar, and lime juice, and bring to a boil. Reduce the heat to low, and add the pears, papayas, pineapple, raisins, coriander, cinnamon, star anise, salt, and pepper. Simmer until the mixture is reduced to a thick, rich, chutney-like consistency, 25 to 30 minutes. Transfer to a container, cover, and refrigerate for up to 2 weeks.

About 6 cups

tamarind juice

1 4-ounce package tamarind
paste
2 cups mango or pineapple juice
1 cup water
2 tablespoons sugar

Tamarind Fruits

Place all the ingredients in a saucepan and bring to a boil over medium heat. Remove from the heat, stir, and let steep for 5 minutes. Then strain the mixture well, pressing as much pulp through the sieve as possible. Return the liquid to the saucepan and bring to a boil over medium heat. Cook until reduced to 1 cup, about 15 minutes. Transfer to a container, cover, and refrigerate for up to 1 month.

1 cup

sweet and hot pepper relish

I grew up on sweet relishes and pickles. This one is zippier than most and is yummy on samosas, or on grilled pork, salmon, or portobello mushrooms. I also like to use this relish on ham and cheddar or smoked turkey and cucumber sandwiches.

1 tablespoon soy oil
6 garlic cloves, minced
2 large or 4 small Spanish onions, finely diced
1 teaspoon yellow mustard seeds
1 teaspoon brown mustard seeds
1 teaspoon anise seeds
2 bay leaves
4 red bell peppers, finely diced (at least 1 cup diced)
¼ cup palm sugar or white sugar
¼ cup cider vinegar
4 Thai bird chilies
1 inch fresh ginger, sliced
1 teaspoon kosher salt
½ teaspoon black pepper

Palm sugar: Palm sugar, also known as jaggery, is an unrefined, dark sugar made from boiling the sap of several different kinds of palm trees, among them sugar palm, coconut palm, and the palmyra palm. It's easy to use, has an interesting sweet, winelike fragrance and flavor, and gives a nice body to the syrup. You can find it in any Asian and East Indian markets. Any time a recipe calls for making a caramel or infused syrup, I substitute palm sugar for the white sugar.

Place a stainless steel–lined pan over medium heat, and when it is hot, add the oil. Add the garlic and onions, and cook until lightly browned, 3 to 4 minutes. Add the mustard seeds, anise seeds, and bay leaves, and toast for 1 minute. Then add the bell peppers and cook for 2 to 3 minutes, until slightly softened.

Add the palm sugar, cider vinegar, chilies, and ginger. Raise the heat to high and bring to a boil. Reduce the heat to low and cook until syrupy, 8 to 10 minutes. Add the salt and pepper, and set aside to cool.

Transfer the cooled relish to a container, cover, and refrigerate for up to 2 weeks.

About 2 cups

Saffron brings a certain allure to a dish. In this recipe shallots are braised until they are tender and are completely infused with lusty saffron in a sweet-and-sour mixture of wine and cider vinegar. The colors are lovely in this relish. It is perfect with roasted meats and birds soaked in Ginger Citrus Brine (page 107).

1½ teaspoons soy oil
12 shallots
2 garlic cloves
1 cup dry white wine
⅓ cup sugar
¼ cup cider vinegar
1 teaspoon kosher salt
12 saffron threads
¼ cup black raisins
¼ cup golden raisins
1 red bell pepper, roasted, peeled, and diced
1 teaspoon minced garlic
¼ cup lemon juice
½ teaspoon yellow mustard seeds
½ teaspoon brown mustard seeds
1 teaspoon kosher salt
½ teaspoon black pepper

Place a 1-quart saucepan over medium heat, and when it is hot, add the oil. Then add the shallots and cook until browned on all sides, 4 to 5 minutes. Add the garlic and cook for 2 minutes.

Add the wine, sugar, vinegar, salt, and saffron, and bring to a boil. Reduce the heat to low, cover, and cook, stirring often, until the liquid has evaporated and the shallots are tender and a saffron-gold color, 12 to 15 minutes. Set aside to cool.

Chop the shallots and transfer them to a large mixing bowl. Add the raisins, roasted pepper, garlic, lemon juice, mustard seeds, salt, and pepper, and mix to combine. Transfer to a container, cover, and refrigerate for up to 2 weeks.

About 2 cups

Saffron: It takes over 14,000 stigmas from a variety of small purple crocus to produce 1 ounce of saffron. These stigmas must be handpicked and then dried, an extremely labor-intensive process that makes saffron the world's most expensive spice. Used to both color and flavor food, a little bit of this aromatic spice goes a long way.

How to roast peppers: Roasting peppers makes them tender, sweet, and incredibly versatile. You can add roasted peppers to salads, pastas, and relishes; you can even puree them for a simple sauce or dip. There are many methods for roasting peppers. If you have a gas cooktop or an outdoor grill, the best way is to place the peppers directly over the flame. Place the pepper on the heating element, or spear it on a long-handled fork, and watch it carefully while you turn it so that the entire pepper develops a black, papery coating. Alternatively, you can place the peppers under an oven broiler until the same result is achieved. Remove the peppers from the heat, place them in a container, and cover tightly with plastic wrap. Let the peppers steam for about 15 minutes; this will make it easy to remove the skin. When the peppers are cool enough to handle, peel off the burnt skin, revealing the soft, lush flesh. Do not rinse the peppers; that would remove some of the flavor.

sweet curried mango chutney

Our executive sous-chef, Michael McEwen, and I often joke about which one of us loves this sweet-and-spicy mango relish more. But I have no doubt—it's me! Delicious with roast lamb, duck, or beef, and with curries and rice, it should be a frequent offering on your table. Be sure the mango is ripe; there is no substitute for its intense flavor and luscious texture.

1 cup distilled vinegar
½ cup sugar
1 teaspoon chili garlic paste (see page 82)
½ teaspoon curry powder
1 inch fresh ginger, thinly sliced
2 perfectly ripe mangoes, sliced ¼ inch thick
2 tablespoons lime juice

Prepare an ice bath.

Place the vinegar, sugar, chili garlic paste, curry powder, and ginger in a 1- or 2-quart stainless steel–lined saucepan and bring to a boil over medium-high heat. Cook until reduced by half, 10 to 12 minutes.

Add the mango slices and lime juice, stir to combine, and return to a boil. Then remove the pan from the heat and place it in the ice bath so that it cools quickly. Transfer the cooled chutney to a container, cover, and refrigerate for up to 1 week.

About 2 cups

Curry powder: From the southern Indian word *kari,* meaning "sauce," "curry" is used to refer to any number of hot, spicy, gravy-based dishes of East Indian origin. Curry powder bears no relation to curry leaves, which smell of tangerine and are rarely found outside of India. Curry powder is a British invention, designed to imitate the flavor of Indian foods. It is a mixture of spices that may contain any or all of the following: cumin, coriander, black pepper, chilies, fenugreek, ginger, salt, cinnamon, cloves, and cardamom.

spicy eggplant chutney

I find that a lot of people (particularly men) say they don't like eggplant, but this wonderfully balanced spicy-sweet tropical chutney wins them over every time. It's great with grilled and roasted vegetables, heartily spiced fish dishes, and lamb.

Coriander seed: Coriander is the seed of *Coriandrum sativum,* a plant in the parsley family. Grown primarily in Morocco and Romania, coriander seed is used in Indian, South American, Mediterranean, African, and Asian cuisines. Although it is from the same plant as cilantro, the leaf and the seed are very different in flavor and cannot be used interchangeably. Coriander seed has a warm, nutty aroma and is an essential ingredient in curry powder. It was probably one of the first spices used by mankind, having been known as early as 5000 B.C. Sanskrit writings dating from about 1500 B.C. also mention it. In the Old Testament, "manna" is described as "white like Coriander Seed" (Exodus 16:31). The Romans spread it throughout Europe, and it was one of the first spices to arrive in America.

Be sure to add the herbs after the chutney has completely cooled so they don't wilt. I always recommend Japanese eggplant, but you can substitute the more common Mediterranean variety; just remember that they are much larger and seedier, so be sure to cut away some of the seeds when you are dicing them.

1 tablespoon soy oil
2 teaspoons minced fresh ginger
2 garlic cloves, minced
1 large or 2 small Spanish onions, minced
2 large Japanese eggplants, cut into medium dice
*   (about 2 cups)*
½ teaspoon yellow mustard seeds
½ teaspoon brown mustard seeds
2 teaspoons coriander seeds
1 cup canned diced tomatoes, drained
½ cup mango or pineapple juice
2 tablespoons cider vinegar
2 tablespoons soy sauce
1 teaspoon chili garlic paste (see page 82)
2 teaspoons kosher salt
½ teaspoon black pepper
2 scallions, white and green parts, sliced
1 tablespoon chopped fresh cilantro leaves
1 tablespoon chopped fresh mint leaves

Place a saucepan over medium heat, and when it is hot, add the oil. Then add the ginger and garlic, and cook until lightly browned, 2 to 3 minutes. Add the onions and cook until lightly browned, 2 to 3 minutes. Add the eggplant, reduce the heat to low, and cook until the eggplant is lightly browned and starting to soften, 4 to 5 minutes.

Add the mustard seeds and coriander seeds, and cook for 1 minute. Then add the tomatoes, mango juice, vinegar, soy sauce, chili garlic paste, salt, and pepper. Cook, stirring occasionally, until the mixture is nearly dry, 10 to 12 minutes. Set the mixture aside and allow it to cool thoroughly.

When the mixture is cool, stir in the scallions, cilantro, and mint. Transfer the chutney to a container, cover, and refrigerate for up to 2 weeks.

About 4 cups

I am a huge fan of pickling. From green beans and red onions to green tomatoes, melon rinds, and pineapple, I will pickle just about anything and everything. The right pickle can make a savory dish even greater. How sweet, how tart, and how spicy the pickle is can all be determined by you. This fruit pickle is atypical in that the pickling liquid, which usually consists only of vinegar and water, has tropical fruit juice in it, making these pickles doubly tropical. These are perfect with Honey and Five-Spice Barbecued Pork Ribs (page 191) and with Black Tea–Brined Chicken (page 153).

2 cups pineapple or mango juice
¼ cup sugar
2 cups cider vinegar
1 teaspoon kosher salt
2 3-inch cinnamon sticks
6 star anise pods
4 arbol chilies
1 tablespoon coriander seeds
1 teaspoon Szechuan peppercorns
1 ripe mango, cut into large dice (about 1 cup)
1 pineapple, cut into large dice (about 2 cups)
1 papaya, cut into large dice (about 1 cup)

Prepare an ice bath.

Place the pineapple juice, sugar, vinegar, and salt in a 2- or 3-quart stainless-steel saucepan and bring to a boil over high heat. Boil for 5 minutes.

Meanwhile, place a skillet over medium heat and add the cinnamon sticks, star anise, chilies, coriander, and peppercorns. Cook, stirring often, until the spices are dark and very fragrant, 2 to 3 minutes. Set them aside to cool.

Wrap the toasted spices in a cheesecloth bag and add it to the juice mixture. Bring the liquid back to a boil, and add the mango, pineapple, and papaya. Stir once and let return to a boil.

Place the saucepan in the ice bath. When the pickles have cooled, transfer the mixture to a container, cover, and refrigerate for up to 4 weeks.

About 1½ quarts

In the summer of 2000, I went on a culinary adventure to Japan and saw the most beautiful daikons all over the marketplaces. Daikon is a large white radish commonly used in many Asian cuisines, especially Japanese, Chinese, and Korean. Served raw, pickled, or combined with chilies and vinegar as a fresh condiment, daikon has a nice crisp, cool, wet texture, which can be retained only by very brief cooking. I serve these pickles to accompany Grilled Soy-Soaked Flank Steak (page 180) and Scallion Noodle Cakes (page 244), as well as Scallion and Oyster Popovers (page 97) and Spring Rolls (page 72).

1½ pounds daikon, julienned (3 to 4 cups)
3 teaspoons kosher salt
1 cup orange juice
¼ cup sugar
2 cups cider vinegar
1 cup rice vinegar
1 teaspoon ground turmeric
2 teaspoons chili garlic paste (see page 82)
Grated zest of 1 well-washed orange

Prepare an ice bath.

Set a colander over a bowl, and put the daikon in the colander. Sprinkle 2 teaspoons of the salt over the daikon. Cover with plastic wrap, and let sit for at least 4 hours or up to 24 hours; the daikon should be wilted and should have released some liquid. It will also be very pungent. Rinse the daikon well under cold water.

Place the orange juice, sugar, both vinegars, turmeric, chili garlic paste, orange zest, and the remaining 1 teaspoon salt in a stainless steel–lined saucepan and bring to a boil over high heat. Let boil for 15 minutes. Then add the rinsed daikon, and when the mixture returns to a boil, remove it from the heat. Transfer the pot to the ice bath and allow the daikon to cool completely.

Transfer the daikon to a container, cover, and refrigerate for up to 4 weeks.

1 to 1½ quarts

serving accompaniments

napa cabbage chi

Our chef du cuisine, Andrea Jorgensen, makes the best *chi* (the Korean term for any pickled and naturally fermented vegetable). AJ is marrying into a Korean family and has learned to make *chi* out of anything: baby turnips, young garlic, and spring onions are some of my favorites. Cabbage *chi (kim chi)* is perhaps the most common, served throughout the year. *Kim chi* is used to accompany soups, dumplings, and barbecued meats.

This may seem like a large quantity, but it takes some time for the cabbage to pickle, and if you love *kim chi* it will go fast.

*1 large or 2 small heads
  napa cabbage (about
  2 pounds), quartered
  lengthwise*
1 tablespoon kosher salt
12 garlic cloves, crushed
*1 inch fresh ginger, thinly
  sliced*
*4 bunches scallions (30 to
  35), white and green
  parts, cut into 1-inch
  lengths*
*4 small onions, halved and
  julienned*
*2 cups julienned daikon
  (about 1 pound)*
1½ cups fish sauce
1 cup Korean chili flakes
1 cup hot water

Fish sauce

Place the cabbage quarters in a colander, set the colander over a bowl, and sprinkle the salt over the cabbage. Cover with plastic wrap, and let sit overnight.

Rinse the cabbage and squeeze out any excess water. Transfer the cabbage to a large mixing bowl, and add the garlic, ginger, scallions, half of the onions, daikon, fish sauce, chili flakes, and hot water. Mix well, making sure the liquid reaches all the crevices and layers in the cabbage.

Spread the remaining onions in the bottom of a heavy plastic or ceramic container, and cover with the cabbage mixture. Place a double layer of plastic wrap directly on top of the cabbage, and top it with two plates or bowls to weight it down. Let the cabbage marinate at room temperature for 2 to 3 days. Then cover and refrigerate for at least 2 or 3 days before serving. The *kim chi* will keep in the refrigerator for up to 2 months.

About 4 quarts

Korean chili flakes: Large, coarse, and spiky, Korean chili flakes create a mild, sweet burn followed by a slow heat. They are available in Asian markets.

Kim chi

sweet cucumber pickles

My grandmother, Mama Boyd, made the best bread-and-butter pickles—perfectly crisp and sweet but not cloying. This recipe is hers, except that she wouldn't have used ginger, whereas I can hardly make a thing without it. Also, she would have used brown, not palm, sugar. Preserving, canning, and pickling always remind me of the hot summers I spent with her in the Deep South, weeding her garden and drinking Dr Pepper and coffee ice cream floats.

We should all make an effort to preserve more fresh fruits and vegetables, either from our own gardens or from local farm stands. It's a way of enjoying the seasons after they have gone by, you get better flavor all year long, you support local farmers . . . oh, don't get me started. But the truth is, you can't make good fresh tomato sauce in January with tomatoes from the supermarket, and I would rather eat raspberry jam in the winter from raspberries I picked in the summer!

4 cucumbers, decoratively scored and cut into ¼-inch-thick rounds
3 teaspoons kosher salt
½ cup palm sugar or light brown sugar (packed)
3 cups cider vinegar
1 inch fresh ginger, sliced
2 shallots, sliced
2 teaspoons white sesame seeds, toasted
½ teaspoon celery seeds

Place the cucumbers in a colander, and set the colander over a bowl. Sprinkle 2 teaspoons of the salt over the cucumbers, cover with plastic wrap, and let sit for at least 4 hours or up to 24 hours. Rinse well under cold water.

Prepare an ice bath.

Place the sugar, vinegar, ginger, shallots, sesame seeds, celery seeds, and remaining 1 teaspoon salt in a 2- or 3-quart stainless steel–lined saucepan. Bring to a boil over high heat, and boil for 5 minutes.

Add the cucumbers and return to a boil. Then transfer the pan to the ice bath and allow to cool.

When the pickles are cool, place them in a container, pour the brine over them, cover, and refrigerate for up to 2 months.

1½ quarts

miso vegetable pickles

These lightly acidic, unusually mellow pickles are the perfect accompaniment to Miso Soup (page 99) and to cold noodle dishes such as Chilled Soba Noodles with a Tamari Wasabi Vinaigrette (page 249). Spend some time thinking about how you cut the vegetables: I like to roll-cut the carrots and to score the eggplants and cut them on the diagonal. The more decorative the cuts are, the prettier the pickles will be. Also try playing around with the combination of ingredients; try substituting or adding shiitake mushrooms, baby turnips, or asparagus.

1½ cups rice vinegar
1½ cups distilled vinegar
½ cup sugar
½ inch fresh ginger, sliced
2 garlic cloves, sliced
2 teaspoons kosher salt
2 carrots, roll-cut or cut into medium dice
1 cup cauliflower florets (1 small head)
½ cup pearl onions (about ¼ pound)
1 Japanese eggplant, scored, halved, and cut into ¼-inch-thick diagonal slices
1 red bell pepper, cut into large dice
1 small fennel bulb, outer root removed, bulb halved and cut into thin wedges with the
*   inner root intact*
1 tablespoon blond miso

Prepare an ice bath.

Place the vinegars, sugar, ginger, garlic, and salt in a 3-quart stainless steel–lined saucepan and bring to a boil over high heat. Boil for 5 minutes.

Add the carrots, cauliflower, onions, eggplant, bell pepper, and fennel. Return to a boil, and boil until the carrots and cauliflower are slightly tender, 3 to 5 minutes.

Transfer the pan to the ice bath and when the mixture has cooled slightly, stir in the miso. When the mixture is thoroughly cool, place it in a container, cover, and refrigerate for up to 3 months.

About 1½ quarts

Roll-cutting: The roll cut is a traditional cut used typically in rustic preparations of long, slender vegetables such as parsnips and carrots. Starting from the bottom, approximately 1 inch is cut off at a 45-degree angle. The vegetable is then rotated a quarter-turn and sliced again at a 45-degree angle. This process is repeated up the length of the vegetable.

Miso: Essentially a bean paste made by fermenting soybeans, sometimes with one other ingredient to add flavor, miso is an integral part of the Japanese diet. A morning bowl of miso soup is a daily ritual. There are many different types of miso, named for the extra ingredient added during fermentation. White, or blond, miso gets its color and flavor from rice. Try experimenting with different types of miso; the additional ingredients can add a depth of flavor. Just make sure you never boil miso; the high temperature will reduce its flavor and nutritional value.

You may never have had a watermelon pickle, but I can remember the first time I did: It was at a birthday party in Savannah, Georgia, and my immediate response was that they were not unlike a sweet cucumber pickle. They have a poached fruit–like consistency, are tender, sweet, almost candied but not cloying, and have a soothing texture.

A bowl of these pickles is a great complement to any summer picnic table. I love to pair them with most sandwiches, from lobster salad to ripe tomato with mayonnaise. They're great with Vietnamese-Style Shrimp Fritters (page 82) or Shrimp and Avocado Salad (page 208). I've even chopped them into egg and tuna salads.

1 small watermelon
2 tablespoons kosher salt
6 cups water
2 cups cider vinegar
2 cups packed light brown sugar
1 teaspoon coriander seeds
2 bay leaves
1 3-inch cinnamon stick
6 allspice berries
1 arbol chili

Cut the watermelon into large wedges, and slice off the flesh. Cover the fruit and refrigerate it for another use (like snacking). Using a spoon, scrape any remaining flesh from the rind. Peel the outermost layer of the rind with a vegetable peeler and discard it. Rinse the rind under cold water and cut it into large dice. You should have 5 to 6 cups of watermelon rind.

Place the salt and water in a 2- or 3-quart stainless-steel saucepan and bring to a boil over high heat. Add the watermelon rind and let return to a boil. Then set the pan aside and allow to cool.

serving accompaniments

When the rind is cool, transfer it to a container, pour the liquid over it, cover, and store overnight. (This step will remove any bitterness in the rind.)

Drain the watermelon rind and rinse it under cold water.

Prepare an ice bath.

Place the vinegar and brown sugar in a 2- or 3-quart stainless-steel saucepan and bring to a boil.

Meanwhile, place the coriander, bay leaves, cinnamon stick, allspice, and chili in a skillet over medium heat and cook, stirring often, until the spices darken and are very fragrant, 2 to 3 minutes. Set aside to cool. When they are cool enough to handle, wrap the toasted spices in a cheesecloth bag and add it to the vinegar mixture. Bring back to a boil and add the watermelon rind. Stir once and let return to a boil.

Transfer the pan to the ice bath, and allow to cool completely. Then transfer the watermelon rind and the liquid to a container, cover, and refrigerate for up to 4 weeks.

About 2 quarts

Watermelon: Watermelons are available from May to September, but they're at their best from mid-June to late August. Look for nicely shaped melons—round or oval—without any flat sides. To test for ripeness, give the melon a whack with your hand—if it makes a hollow sound, it's probably ripe. The rind should be dull and should just barely yield to pressure. Cut watermelons should reveal a brightly colored, juicy-looking flesh. An abundance of small white seeds means the melon is immature. If you buy a whole watermelon, store it in the refrigerator if there's room; if not, store it in a cool, dark place. In either case, keep it no longer than a week.

starters

The best parties are the ones with great hors d'oeuvres and fun music. The trick to the hors d'oeuvres part is variety, presentation, and timing. Don't put all your selections out in the beginning. To start, pick a few things that are light, chilled, or easy to eat, like Vegetable Nori Rolls or Vietnamese Summer Rolls. As your guests arrive, these few dishes will become a point of conversation and enjoyment and will receive extra attention. Then later start bringing on the variety. Each new dish will create a buzz of excitement and anticipation! One more tip: If you organize things well in advance, even down to the serving platters, you can finish these starters in the kitchen quickly and easily—even with guests coming and going.

Everyone loves spring rolls, from the littlest kids to their grandparents. These crunchy, crispy, savory snacks are as fun to make as they are to eat. It just takes a little practice to roll them good and tight. The filling can vary widely. Keep in mind, however, that if the filling is too wet, the wrapper will get soggy and may not cook up as crisp as we all like.

Serve these with Hoisin and Spice Dipping Sauce (page 48), Citrus Dipping Sauce (page 50), Cool Lime Dip (page 51), and assorted pickles.

4 cups Wonton Filling (page 86)
1 large egg
¼ cup cold water
18 (2 packages) spring roll wrappers
2 tablespoons soy oil

Squeeze out any excess liquid from the Wonton Filling.

Place the egg and water in a small bowl and mix to combine.

All those wrappers: Spring roll wrappers—also called egg roll skins—are made of wheat flour, and are soft and malleable when fresh. Lumpia wrappers, the Philippines version, are thinner and cook up crisper than egg roll skins. Rice paper wrappers are made with rice flour and are dried; they are rehydrated before using, and are often eaten without any further cooking. Wonton wrappers are made of wheat flour, and sometimes egg, and are soft like fresh pasta dough; wontons are served steamed, fried, or boiled.

Place one spring roll wrapper on a flat, dry surface or on a clean kitchen towel, and position it so that one point is toward you, creating a diamond shape. Brush the wrapper with a thin coating of the egg mixture. Place about 3 to 4 tablespoons of the filling in the center of the wrapper. Fold the sides in over the filling to close off the ends, and then fold the edge once around the filling. Roll the wrapper up tightly until you get to the pointed end. Place the roll, pointed end down, on a platter or baking sheet. Repeat with the remaining wrappers and filling. Cover with plastic wrap and refrigerate for at least 1 hour or up to 6 hours.

Place a cast-iron skillet or a wok over medium-high heat. When it is hot, add the oil. When the oil is hot, add three or four spring rolls and cook, turning occasionally, until they are golden brown on all sides, 4 to 5 minutes. Using a slotted spoon, transfer the rolls to paper towels to drain. Repeat with the remaining rolls. Serve immediately.

18 rolls

spring roll wrapper

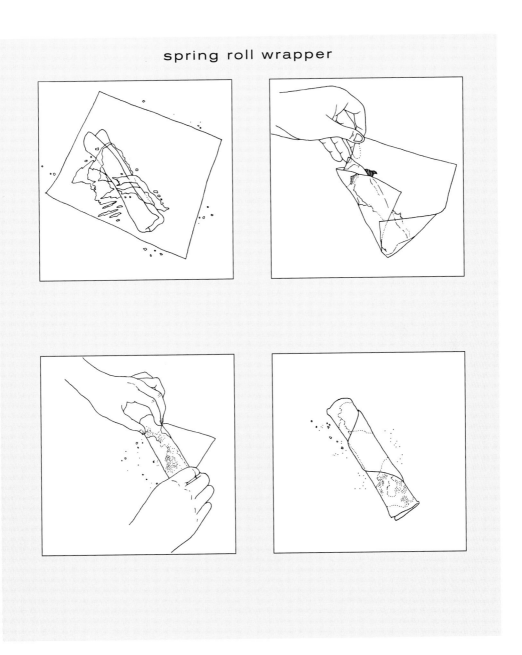

Also called "fresh" or "salad" rolls, these treats are lighter than spring rolls, which are fried. These Vietnamese rolls highlight a different combination of ingredients and feature rice noodles, crisp raw vegetables, and fragrant Asian herbs. They are not cooked, so they are great for hot weather and for low-fat diets.

Taking the time to organize your ingredients is critical in helping this process go smoothly and in making the finished roll prettier (you will be able to see through the wrapper).

If you want, you can add 1 poached shrimp or about 1 tablespoon crabmeat, lobster, beef, or pork to each summer roll.

Serve the rolls with Cool Lime Dip (51), Hoisin and Spice Dipping Sauce (48), or Spicy Peanut Sauce (49).

8 ounces (½ package) rice vermicelli
3 quarts cold water
18 rice paper wrappers (1 package)
18 red-leaf lettuce leaves (about 1 small head)
1½ cups loosely packed fresh mung bean sprouts
2 red or yellow bell peppers, julienned
4 small carrots, julienned
⅓ cup packed fresh mint leaves
⅓ cup packed fresh cilantro leaves
Kosher salt
Black pepper

Place the rice vermicelli and the cold water in a large bowl and let sit until the noodles are al dente, about 20 minutes.

Fill a large bowl with hot tap water.

Place one rice paper wrapper in the hot water and remove it when it becomes pliable, about 30 seconds.

Place the wrapper on a clean, flat surface and place one lettuce leaf in the center, with the center rib up. Cover the center of the leaf with about ⅓ cup of the rice noodles. Top the rice noodles with one portion ($\frac{1}{18}$) of each of the vegetables and herbs. Sprinkle with salt and pepper.

Fold the bottom third of the rice paper over the ingredients, making sure they are completely captured. Fold and tuck the sides in, envelope style, to close off the ends; then fold the wrapper once around the filling. Continue rolling and tightening until you get to the end. Place the roll, seam side down, on a baking sheet and cover with a moist dish towel. Repeat with the remaining wrappers and filling. Refrigerate for at least 1 hour and up to 6 hours. Serve at room temperature.

18 rolls

Rolling Vietnamese Summer Rolls

The more often you make these, the more proficient you'll get at it and the better you'll know what filling you like. If you are thinking of serving these to guests, I recommend a practice round. Or two. These rolls, also called *maki,* lend themselves to lots of variations: In addition to the fillings here, try adding tofu, cold roasted mushrooms, or raw fish (or sashimi). Do not add zucchini or big pieces of raw vegetables. For a nice presentation, cut the rolls into different shapes, slicing them at different angles or in thin and thick pieces.

Variation Serve with Spicy Daikon (page 62), Hoisin and Spice Dipping Sauce (page 48), and the traditional accompaniments of wasabi paste and gari (pickled ginger, available at Asian markets).

You will need a sushi mat (available in Asian markets or by mail order; see page 21)—it is essential for shaping and tightening.

2 tablespoons wasabi powder
2 tablespoons cold water
6 sheets nori
6 cups Sushi Rice (recipe follows)
1 tablespoon mixed white and black sesame seeds, toasted

For the vegetable filling:
1 yellow or red bell pepper, julienned
2 small carrots, julienned
½ English (hothouse) cucumber, julienned
1 bunch (about 8) scallions, white and green parts, cut diagonally
    into 1½-inch pieces
1 avocado, thinly sliced (optional)
⅔ to ¾ pound thin asparagus, blanched, cut diagonally into 1½-inch pieces (optional)

Sushi mats: Sushi mats, which can be found in Asian markets, make it easy to prepare maki rolls. These simple bamboo mats allow you to compose your maki by first laying out the nori (sheets of seaweed) and seasoned rice and then arranging all the other ingredients over them. The mat is then used to aid in rolling a tight, consistent, easily sliceable maki.

nori rolls

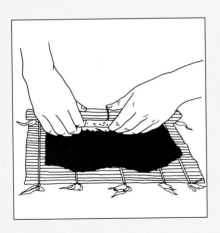 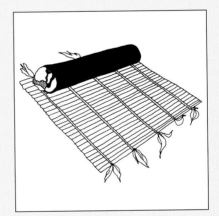

Soak a sushi mat in hot water for at least 20 minutes or up to 1 hour.

Have a small bowl of cold water available for dipping your fingers, so the rice and wrappers don't stick to you.

Place the wasabi and cold water in a small bowl, and mix well to form a thick paste. Set aside.

Place one nori sheet, shiny side down (the other side is grainier) on the sushi mat. Place 1 cup loosely packed rice on the lower two-thirds of the nori sheet, and spread it out evenly to the edges. Using your finger, swipe about one sixth of the wasabi paste on the rice. Sprinkle with about ½ teaspoon of the sesame seeds. Pile about one sixth of each vegetable across the center of the rice in individual piles, being sure they reach all the way to the side edges.

Fold the bottom of the sushi mat up, surrounding the filling with the first fold and pinching the mat as you tighten the roll. Lightly moisten the top edge of the nori with water. Spread your fingers across the mat so that they cover as much width as possible, and continue rolling—but be careful not to roll in the sushi mat. Tighten the roll by placing it in the center of the mat so that the top edge is shorter than the bottom edge. Hold the bottom of the mat firmly in one hand and pull down the bottom of the sushi mat toward you.

Repeat with the remaining nori, rice, and vegetables.

Cover the rolls and refrigerate for no more than 4 hours. Then trim the ends, cut each roll into six pieces, and serve.

36 pieces

salmon variation:

6 ounces raw, cured, or smoked salmon
½ English (hothouse) cucumber, julienned
1 bunch (about 8) scallions, white and green parts, cut diagonally
  into 1½-inch pieces

Substitute the salmon, cucumber, and scallions for the vegetable filling, and proceed as directed.

crabmeat variation:

8 ounces crabmeat
1 ripe avocado, cut into ¼-inch-thick slices
1 red bell pepper, julienned (about 1 cup)

Substitute the crabmeat, avocado, and bell pepper for the vegetable filling, and proceed as directed.

Wasabi powder: Like its American counterpart, this Japanese version of horseradish comes from a plant root. The most common form of wasabi is powder, although some specialty stores do carry fresh wasabi, which can be grated like fresh horseradish. Wasabi powder can be added to soups or sauces; most often it is mixed with a small amount of water or soy sauce to create wasabi paste, which is a popular condiment with sushi.

sushi rice

Similar to short-grain, high-starch arborio rice, sushi rice should cook up as individual grains surrounded by thick creaminess. It should double in size.

2¼ cups new crop sushi rice (preferably Rose new crop by Kokuno brand), rinsed in cold water
¼ cup rice vinegar
6 tablespoons mirin
½ teaspoon kosher salt

Place the rice in a bowl, add cold water to cover by 2 inches, and let sit for at least 15 minutes and up to 30 minutes.

Stovetop method:

Drain and rinse the rice, and transfer it to a large pot. Add 2⅓ cups water and bring to a boil over high heat. Cover, reduce the heat to the lowest possible setting, and cook until tender and fluffy, about 18 minutes.

Rice cooker method:

Drain and rinse the rice, and transfer it to the cooker. Add 2½ cups water and cook until your cooker turns off, about 30 minutes.

Assorted nori rolls

To season the rice:

While it is hot, transfer the rice to a large platter and add the rice vinegar, mirin, and salt. Stir gently, being careful not to smash the rice.

6 cups

pork and tofu steamed buns

I look for these starters on the menu at every Chinese restaurant I go to—they are a good test of the kitchen. These wonderful treats really are quite simple to make. Assemble the dough a day ahead to make prep as easy as possible. If you start two days ahead, you can keep the buns (uncooked) in the fridge overnight.

I like these with a fairly spicy dipping sauce, such as the Spicy Sesame Sauce or the Spicy Peanut Sauce (pages 52, 49).

For the dough:

1 ounce (4 envelopes) dry yeast
1 cup warm water (105° to 110°F)
4 cups all-purpose flour
3 tablespoons sugar
1 cup cold water
1 teaspoon baking powder
1 bunch (about 8) scallions, green and white parts minced separately
1 teaspoon dark sesame oil, for oiling the bowl

For the filling:

3 teaspoons dark sesame oil
2 small onions, minced
1 tablespoon minced fresh ginger
6 garlic cloves, minced
4 leaves napa cabbage, diced
1 pound ground pork
1 tablespoon Sweet Spice Mix (recipe follows)
1 cup diced firm tofu
2 tablespoons hoisin sauce
1 teaspoon chili garlic paste (see page 82)
1 tablespoon soy sauce
1 teaspoon tomato paste
Reserved minced scallion whites
1 tablespoon cold water
1 tablespoon cornstarch
1 teaspoon kosher salt
½ teaspoon black pepper

Chinese steamers: A Chinese steamer is a stackable bamboo (or sometimes metal) steamer that fits over a wok or a pot. You can often stack three to five layers to serve a large number of people. An alternative is to set up a double boiler, but that will allow you to steam only one layer at a time. Steamers are available in Asian markets.

Prepare the dough: Combine the yeast and the warm water in a mixing bowl and let sit until foamy, 6 to 8 minutes.

Stir in ½ cup of the flour and 1 tablespoon of the sugar and let sit until foamy, about 10 minutes. Then add 2½ cups of the flour, the remaining 2 tablespoons sugar, and the cold water, baking powder, and scallion greens. Stir to form a soft dough.

Sprinkle the remaining 1 cup flour on a flat work surface, and place the dough on the flour. Knead the flour into the dough until it is smooth and elastic (the dough will still be soft). Lightly oil a clean mixing bowl with the dark sesame oil. Place the dough in the bowl, cover, and refrigerate for at least 2 hours or overnight.

Prepare the filling: Place a skillet over medium heat and when it is hot, add 2 teaspoons of the oil. Add the onions, ginger, and garlic and cook until lightly caramelized, 3 to 5 minutes. Add the cabbage, ground pork, and Sweet Spice Mix, and continue cooking until the pork is fully cooked, 4 to 5 minutes. Transfer the mixture to a mixing bowl, and add the tofu, remaining 1 teaspoon dark sesame oil, hoisin sauce, chili garlic paste, soy sauce, tomato paste, and scallion whites. Stir to combine.

In a separate bowl, stir together the cold water and cornstarch to form a slurry. Add the slurry to the pork mixture. Season with the salt and pepper. This filling may be made ahead and held, covered, in the refrigerator for up to 24 hours.

Assemble the buns: Divide the dough into twelve equal pieces, and shape each roughly into a ball. On a lightly floured work surface, roll out each piece of dough to form a round approximately ⅛ inch thick and 4 inches in diameter.

Place ⅓ cup of the filling in the center of each dough round, and gather the dough together, enclosing the filling completely and pinching the dough together.

Arrange the buns in steamer, and steam for 14 to 15 minutes. (Or arrange the buns on a nonstick baking sheet and bake in a preheated 375°F oven for 12 to 15 minutes.) Serve immediately.

Serves 6

sweet spice mix

Easy to assemble, this stores well in an airtight glass or plastic container for up to 3 months.

2 tablespoons coriander seeds
1 tablespoon star anise pods
1 tablespoon Szechuan peppercorns

Place the spices in a dry skillet and cook over medium heat until they are lightly toasted, 2 to 3 minutes. Allow to cool, and then transfer to a spice grinder. Grind until smooth.

These are the most delicious shrimp fritters ever. Punctuated by ginger, lemongrass, cilantro, and Thai basil (some of my favorite flavors) and just the right amount of heat, they are a must for the summer cookout as an hors d'oeuvre, appetizer, or accompaniment. They are especially delicious with Spicy Grilled Lobster (pg. 108).

A great fritter is a test of a good cook: It must be light, savory, and not greasy. The secret to the texture lies in using egg whites and very cold water. You also need to be sure of your frying temperature: Use a deep-frying thermometer. For those who deep-fry with regularity, an electric countertop fryer is a great purchase.

Serve these fritters with Tropical Fruit Pickles (page 61), Watermelon Pickles (page 68), and Cool Lime Dip (page 51).

Chili garlic paste: A paste made of chili peppers, garlic, salt, and oil that is used as both a cooking ingredient and a condiment. It's available in gourmet stores and Asian markets.

2 teaspoons light sesame oil
1 pound shrimp, peeled, deveined, and minced
2 teaspoons minced fresh ginger
2 garlic cloves, minced
1 stalk lemongrass, outer husk discarded, inner heart minced
2 teaspoons shrimp paste (see page 187)
1 teaspoon chili garlic paste
2 teaspoons Sweet Spice Mix (page 81)
1 cup rice sticks
2 egg whites
⅓ cup ice-cold water
2 tablespoons cornstarch
1 teaspoon kosher salt
½ teaspoon cracked black pepper
3 to 4 tablespoons sliced fresh cilantro leaves
2 tablespoons sliced fresh Thai basil leaves

1 scallion, white and green parts, thinly sliced

1 cup soy oil

Place a skillet over medium-high heat, and when it is hot, add the oil. Add the shrimp, ginger, garlic, and lemongrass, and stir-fry until the mixture is fragrant and the shrimp have turned pink and are firm to the touch, 1 to 2 minutes. Stir in the shrimp paste, chili garlic paste, and spice mix. Transfer to a mixing bowl and set aside to cool.

Fill a bowl with 4 cups of warm water, add the rice sticks, and soak until they are al dente, 10 to 15 minutes. Drain well and cut into 1-inch lengths.

In another bowl, beat the egg whites with a whisk until lightened and frothy. Then whisk in the cold water, cornstarch, salt, and pepper until smooth. Add the shrimp mixture, rice sticks, cilantro, basil, and scallions. Stir until well combined.

Place a cast-iron skillet over medium-high heat and add the oil. When it has heated to 360°F, or when the surface of the oil is shimmering, drop small spoonfuls of the batter into the oil and cook until browned, 1 to 2 minutes on each side.

Using a slotted spoon, transfer the fritters to paper towels to drain. Serve immediately.

Serves 6

chicken and peanut lettuce cups

I guess I never really liked the restraints of a knife and fork, which is one reason I like these pretty hors d'oeuvres so much. You can use any kind of small lettuce leaves including Bibb, buttercup, or baby romaine, and it's a great way to use leftover chicken, pork, turkey, or beef. You can also substitute roasted cashews or pine nuts for the peanuts. The variations are limited only by your imagination!

⅓ cup sliced fresh cilantro leaves
½ cup unsalted peanuts, toasted and finely ground
2 cups shredded or diced cooked chicken
1 small red onion, minced
2 scallions, white and green parts, thinly sliced
¼ cup Hoisin and Spice Dipping Sauce (page 48)
2 heads Bibb lettuce, inner leaves separated, rinsed, and patted dry

Set aside 1 tablespoon each of the cilantro and peanuts to use as garnish.

Place the chicken, red onion, scallions, remaining cilantro and peanuts, and the dipping sauce in a mixing bowl. Toss to combine.

Divide the mixture among the lettuce leaves, and arrange them on a platter. Sprinkle with the reserved peanuts and cilantro.

Serves 6

scallion popovers

One evening a friend, a regular customer who travels frequently to Japan, came into the restaurant carrying something very heavy: cast-iron *tako-yaki* pans from Osaka, a gift for our kitchen. *Tako yaki,* savory octopus popovers, are a popular Japanese street food. Here we have a simplified vegetarian version. You can bake these tasty treats in nonstick mini muffin tins (I like the ones made by Calphalon). Serve them with Hoisin and Spice Dipping Sauce (page 48) or as an accompaniment to any fish or chicken dish.

Kosher salt: We always use kosher salt because it is milder than table salt, has none of that metallic taste, and is easier to use effectively without overdoing.

1 cup all-purpose flour
1 teaspoon baking powder
½ teaspoon kosher salt
3 large eggs
¼ cup whole milk
1 tablespoon dark sesame oil
4 scallions, white and green parts, thinly sliced

Preheat the oven to 425°F.

Sift the flour, baking powder, and salt into a large bowl.

In a separate bowl, whisk together the eggs, milk, oil, and scallions. Add the egg mixture to the flour, and whisk gently.

Heat the muffin tins in the oven for 2 to 3 minutes. Then quickly add the batter, filling each cup three quarters full. Bake until firm and golden brown, 7 to 8 minutes. Serve immediately.

Serves 6 (30 to 32 mini popovers)

wontons:
filling and variations

Everyone loves wontons—including kids! This filling can be used for wontons that are fried, steamed, or pan-seared. Wontons are a great place to use up the end of a roast or a leftover chicken breast. Of course they can be made vegetarian as well. I have frozen wontons successfully for up to 2 months.

1 tablespoon light sesame oil
2 tablespoons minced fresh ginger
6 garlic cloves, minced
1 red onion, finely diced
1 small carrot, finely diced
1 red bell pepper, finely diced
1 small zucchini, cored and finely diced
1 cup diced napa cabbage
½ bunch (about 4) scallions, white and green parts, thinly sliced
⅓ cup thinly sliced fresh cilantro leaves
2 tablespoons soy sauce
1 teaspoon dark sesame oil
1 teaspoon coriander seeds, ground
1 teaspoon kosher salt
½ teaspoon black pepper
1 cup finely diced cooked chicken breast, pork loin, roast beef, tofu, or shiitake mushrooms
1 package wonton wrappers, round or square
1 egg beaten with 1 tablespoon water, for egg wash
¼ cup soy oil, for pan-frying

Place a skillet over medium-high heat, and when it is hot, add the light sesame oil. Add the ginger and garlic and cook until lightly caramelized, 2 to 3 minutes. Then add the onion, carrot, bell pepper, zucchini, and cabbage. Sauté until the vegetables are tender but still a little crisp, 2 to 4 minutes.

Remove the skillet from the heat and add the scallions, cilantro, soy sauce, dark sesame oil, coriander, salt, and pepper. Add the chicken, and toss thoroughly. Allow to cool completely before using.

Fill the wonton wrappers, using one of the methods described below.

Four-corner fold:

Lay four to six wonton wrappers on a work surface, and paint the edges with egg wash. Place 1 heaping teaspoon of the filling in the center of each wrapper. Gather all four corners by lifting them above the center, and press the edges together with your fingertips. Repeat with the remaining wrappers and filling.

Simple triangle fold:

Lay four to six wonton wrappers on a work surface, and paint the edges with egg wash. Place 1 heaping teaspoon of the filling slightly off center. Fold the far corner over the filling and down to meet the near corner, forming a triangle. Press the seams together to seal. Repeat with the remaining wrappers and filling.

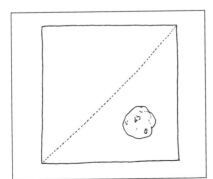 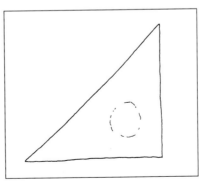

Classic soup fold:

Lay four to six round wonton wrappers on a work surface, and paint the edges with egg wash. Place 1 level teaspoon of the filling (slightly less than for the other folds) just off center. Fold the far corner over the filling and down to meet the near other side. Press the seams together to seal. Brush the two points of the half-circle with more egg wash and bring them together, forming a traditional "hat" shape. Press them together to seal, or crimp edges gyoza-style. Repeat with the remaining wrappers and filling.

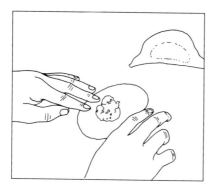

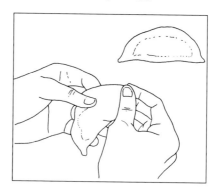

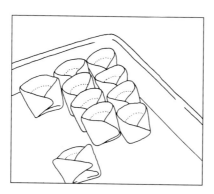

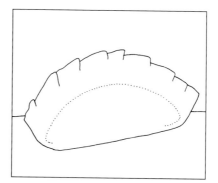

Two-piece ravioli:

Lay all the wonton wrappers out on a work surface, and paint the edges with egg wash. Place 1 heaping teaspoon of the filling in the center of half of the wrappers. Place the empty wrappers over the filled ones, matching up the edges. Press down on all four sides to seal.

To steam: Bring a pot of water to a boil over high heat. Place the filled wontons, in a single layer, in a bamboo steamer and place over the pot. Cover and steam until the wrappers tighten and become opaque, 5 to 6 minutes. Serve immediately.

To pan-fry: Place a large skillet over medium heat, and when it is hot, add ¼ cup soy oil to the pan. Allow the oil to heat until it shimmers, 1 to 2 minutes. Then add the wontons in a single layer, and pan-fry until browned, 2 minutes on each side. Remove to paper towels, blot off the oil, and serve immediately.

48 wontons

savory rice noodle and tofu pancake

Jam-packed with herbs, rice sticks, tofu, and sprouts, this is an intriguing and delicious vegetarian hors d'oeuvre or appetizer. In Western cuisines, you almost never see a pancake batter with this kind of texture—silky but not smooth. Best cooked on a griddle or in a nonstick pan, these little pancakes—they're about the size of a silver dollar—can also be served as a base for grilled vegetables or even floated in a soup. I enjoy varying them by adding julienned mushrooms or zucchini to the mixture.

Serve these with Sweet Cucumber Pickles (page 65) and Spicy Daikon (page 62), and with Spicy Peanut or Hoisin and Spice Dipping Sauce (pages 49, 48).

1 ounce rice sticks
1 cup finely diced firm tofu
⅓ cup thinly sliced fresh cilantro leaves
¼ to ⅓ cup thinly sliced fresh mint leaves
½ bunch (about 4) scallions, white and green parts,
   thinly sliced
½ cup fresh mung bean sprouts
1 cup tempura flour; or ½ cup all-purpose flour and
   ½ cup rice flour or cornstarch
1 large egg
⅓ cup cold water
1½ teaspoons kosher salt
1 teaspoon black pepper
2 teaspoons coriander seeds, toasted and cracked
1 tablespoon light sesame oil

Tofu: Made from yellow soybeans that have been soaked, ground, mixed with water, and briefly cooked, *tofu* is the Japanese term for bean curd. Firm bean curd is usually used for frying or sautéing, whereas soft bean curd is generally used in soups. Once it has been opened, tofu can be kept in the refrigerator for up to 3 days, as long as it is covered in fresh cold water. Tofu is a great source of protein.

Place the rice sticks in a large bowl, and add warm water to cover by 2 inches. Soak until al dente, 5 to 8 minutes. Drain well.

Place the noodles, tofu, cilantro, mint, scallions, and sprouts in a bowl. Toss to combine.

Prepare the batter: Place the flour, egg, cold water, salt, pepper, and coriander in a bowl and whisk together. Add the noodle mixture and stir to combine. This batter can sit, covered and refrigerated, for up to 2 hours before cooking.

Place a large griddle or nonstick skillet over medium heat. When it is hot, add the oil. Drop tablespoons of the batter onto the griddle and cook until golden and cooked through, 1 to 2 minutes per side. Drain on paper towels.

Serve immediately.

36 pancakes

Similar to hummus and other bean spreads, this earthy, Indian-spiced dip has a satisfying, comforting appeal. It is excellent on cheese or roasted-vegetable sandwiches, or alongside grilled or roasted chicken. Vary the cheese according to taste and availability: I like Pyrenees, Pecorino Romano, and feta. You can also use other dried legumes or beans, such as white beans, flageolets, or yellow split peas.

2 teaspoons light sesame oil
1 tablespoon minced garlic
2 small onions, finely diced
1 small fennel bulb, finely diced
1 carrot, finely diced
1 teaspoon coriander seeds, coarsely cracked
1 teaspoon cumin seeds, coarsely cracked
1 teaspoon fennel seeds, coarsely cracked
½ cup dry white wine
1 cup canned diced tomatoes, drained
½ pound (about 1½ cups) red lentils, well rinsed
4 cups Vegetable Stock (page 37) or water
2 teaspoons kosher salt
1 teaspoon black pepper
2 tablespoons sesame tahini
2 tablespoons coarsely chopped fresh parsley leaves
2 tablespoons coarsely chopped fresh cilantro leaves
¼ cup lemon juice
1 baguette or foccacia, thinly sliced and toasted, or
 4 pita breads, cut into wedges and toasted
½ pound sheep's milk cheese, such as
 Pecorino Romano, Pyrenees, or feta

Parsley and cilantro sprigs, for garnish (optional)
Lemon wedges, for garnish (optional)
Olives, for garnish (optional)

Place a 2½- to 3-quart saucepan over medium heat, and when it is hot, add the oil. Add the garlic and cook until caramelized, 1 to 2 minutes. Add the onions, fennel, and carrot, and cook until lightly caramelized, 3 to 4 minutes. Add the coriander, cumin, and fennel seeds. Stir to combine, and cook until the spices are lightly toasted and fragrant, 1 to 2 minutes.

Add the white wine and tomatoes, and bring to a boil. Reduce the heat and simmer for 5 minutes. Then add the lentils, stock, salt, and pepper, and simmer until the lentils begin to fall apart, 20 to 25 minutes.

Remove the pan from the heat, and stir in the tahini, parsley, cilantro, and lemon juice.

Serve warm or at room temperature, accompanied by the toasts and cheese. Garnish the platter with the herb sprigs, lemon wedges, and olives if you wish.

Serves 6

These yummy little Indian-spiced treats are full of wonderful herbs and spices and are delicious as an appetizer, hors d'oeuvre, or side dish. They are especially good when served with Sweet and Hot Pepper Relish (page 55) or Spicy Eggplant Chutney (page 59). I like to include these when I am serving a variety of savory snacks, or on a buffet loaded with accompaniments and chutneys.

The batter can be made a day ahead.

1 cup lentils
2 cups Vegetable Stock (page 37) or water
1 small onion, coarsely chopped
1 small carrot, coarsely chopped
2 teaspoons kosher salt
1 red onion, finely diced
1 red bell pepper, finely diced
1 small zucchini, finely diced
½ bunch (about 4) scallions, white and green parts, finely diced
⅓ to ½ cup sliced fresh parsley leaves
⅓ to ½ cup sliced fresh cilantro leaves
1 egg
¼ cup whole milk
¼ cup chickpea flour
¼ cup all-purpose flour
1 tablespoon baking powder
1 teaspoon coriander seeds, toasted and cracked
1 teaspoon cumin seeds, toasted and ground
1 teaspoon fennel seeds, toasted and ground
1 teaspoon black pepper
2 tablespoons soy oil

Place the lentils, stock, onion, carrot, and 1 teaspoon of the salt in a saucepan and bring to a boil over medium-high heat. Reduce the heat to low and simmer until the lentils are tender, 15 to 20 minutes. Drain, and spread the mixture out in a single layer on a baking sheet or plate; set aside to cool. Remove and discard the chunks of onion and carrot.

When they are cool, transfer the lentils to a mixing bowl. Add the red onion, bell pepper, zucchini, scallions, parsley, and cilantro. Mix to combine.

Place the egg and milk in a small bowl and whisk together.

Place the chickpea and all-purpose flours, baking powder, coriander, cumin, fennel, remaining 1 teaspoon salt, and pepper in a bowl and mix to combine. Add the egg mixture and the lentil mixture, and stir to combine.

Place a large skillet over medium heat, and when it is hot, add the oil. Drop tablespoons of the lentil batter into the oil and cook until deeply golden and cooked through, 2 minutes per side. Drain on paper towels, and serve immediately.

36 fritters

Chickpea flour: Also known as *besan* and *gram flour,* this pale yellow flour is made from ground dried chickpeas (garbanzo beans). The high-protein, gluten-free flour is commonly used in Indian and Asian preparations of doughs, flatbreads, and noodles and can be found in most Indian and Asian markets.

glazed grilled shrimp
with peanut coating

Sweet and sour, spicy and nutty. I love the look, aroma, and taste of this shrimp dish. The shiny, sticky glaze, charred exterior, and fabulous fragrance remind me of shrimp I ate in Thailand in the early 1990s.

Wooden skewers are just fine, but if you can use lemongrass, it is well worth it: The shrimp pick up a great deal of flavor from the lemongrass skewers. Be sure to reduce the glaze until it becomes sticky enough for the peanuts to adhere. These are good hot or at room temperature.

18 skewers cut from fresh lemongrass, or 18 6-inch bamboo skewers
18 extra-large shrimp (about 1 pound), peeled and deveined
1 to 2 tablespoons light sesame oil
Kosher salt
Black pepper
½ cup honey
½ cup rice vinegar
¼ cup chili garlic paste, preferably Red Rooster (see page 82)
½ cup unsalted peanuts, toasted and finely chopped
2 limes, each cut into 4 wedges
Cilantro sprigs, for garnish
1 ripe pineapple or melon, cut into wedges, for garnish

How to toast nuts: Place a heavy-bottomed skillet over medium to medium-high heat, and add the nuts. Cook, stirring occasionally, until the nuts are fragrant and lightly browned, 3 to 8 minutes, depending upon the type of nut. Transfer to a plate or baking sheet and set aside to cool.

Soak the lemongrass or bamboo skewers in cold water to cover for 20 minutes to 1 hour.

Place one shrimp on each skewer. Brush the shrimp lightly with the oil, and sprinkle with salt and pepper to taste. Place the skewers on a plate, cover, and refrigerate until ready to use.

Place the honey, rice vinegar, and chili garlic paste in a small stainless steel–lined saucepan and cook over medium heat until reduced by half, about 10 minutes.

Prepare a charcoal, gas, or stovetop grill. Put the peanuts in a shallow dish.

Place the skewers on the grill and cook over medium-high heat until the shrimp are firm and bright red, 1 to 2 minutes per side.

Transfer the skewers to a baking sheet, brush both sides of the shrimp with the honey mixture, and then immediately roll them in the peanuts. Arrange the skewers on plates, garnish with the lime, cilantro, pineapple, and serve immediately.

Serves 6

starters

scallion and oyster popovers

When I first created this recipe—essentially a savory Asian-flavored popover—my chefs looked at me as if I were nuts. Soon after, they couldn't stop eating them. In fact, during the first week these were offered as a menu special, more of the popovers went into our bellies than out the kitchen door! The secret is to really preheat your muffin tins well so that the batter literally gets a jump-start. This is a great appetizer, or it can be an accompaniment to Crispy Sole Fillets with Wild Mushroom Stew (page 148) or your favorite grilled or roasted tuna dish.

For the filling:
1½ teaspoons light sesame oil
1 shallot, minced
2 teaspoons minced fresh ginger
1 garlic clove, minced
6 fresh shiitake mushrooms, sliced
1 bunch (about 8) scallions, white and
    green parts, cut into ½-inch lengths
2 teaspoons soy sauce
1 pint shucked oysters (24 to 30 oysters,
    depending on size)

For the batter:
1 cup all-purpose flour
½ teaspoon kosher salt
1 teaspoon sugar
1 cup milk
2 eggs, lightly beaten
4 tablespoons (½ stick) unsalted butter, melted

For the sauce:
1½ teaspoons light sesame oil
1 tablespoon minced fresh ginger
4 garlic cloves, minced

Shucking an oyster

2 shallots, minced

½ to ¾ pound mixed wild mushrooms (chanterelle, shiitake, morel, oyster)

1 cup Shellfish Stock (page 41)

3 tablespoons very cold unsalted butter, cut into pieces

½ teaspoon kosher salt

½ teaspoon cracked black pepper

Garnish:

1 bunch (about 8) scallions, white and green parts, cut into diagonal pieces or julienned

Prepare the filling: Place a 10-inch skillet over medium-high heat. When it is hot, add the oil. Add the shallot, ginger, and garlic, and cook until lightly caramelized, 1 to 2 minutes. Add the shiitake mushrooms and the scallions, and cook an additional 1 to 2 minutes. Add the soy sauce and oysters, and cook until the oysters are just barely firm to the touch and the edges have curled, 2 minutes. Transfer the mixture to a plate or baking sheet and place in the refrigerator to cool.

Prepare the batter: Place the flour, salt, and sugar in a bowl and mix well.

Place the milk, eggs, and melted butter in another bowl, and mix well. Add the milk mixture to the flour mixture and whisk until smooth.

Preheat the oven to 500°F. Place two muffin pans (twelve muffin cups) in the oven to preheat.

When the muffin pans are hot, carefully brush the muffin cups generously with soy or light sesame oil. (If you brush the cups with oil before preheating the pans, the oil will burn.) Spoon ¼ cup batter and 2 tablespoons oyster filling into each muffin cup, and bake until the popovers rise above and pull away from the muffin pan and are golden brown, 10 to 12 minutes.

While the popovers are baking, prepare the sauce: Place a 1½-quart saucepan over medium-high heat, and when it is hot, add the oil. Add the ginger, garlic, and shallots and cook until lightly caramelized, 2 minutes. Add the mushrooms and cook until they are very aromatic, 2 to 3 minutes. Add the Shellfish Stock and bring to a boil. Reduce the heat to low and simmer until reduced by one fourth, 5 to 6 minutes. Remove the pan from the heat, and gradually whisk in the cold butter until smooth and fully incorporated. Season with the salt and pepper.

Serve the pancakes over pools of sauce, and garnish with the scallions.

Serves 6 (12 popovers)

miso soup

Fortifying and comforting, light in weight and rich in flavor: I like broth-based soups better than pureed or cream soups. Whether chicken noodle, matzoh ball, consommé, or miso, broth soups are all mothers' cure for colds.

Never boil miso: The flavor and nutritive value diminish at high temperatures. Simply spoon a heaping teaspoon of miso into the bottom of each bowl and then ladle broth over it. Try different types of miso, including barley and a long-aged miso, and judge the differences for yourself.

Miso Vegetable Pickles (page 66) are a nice accompaniment for the soup.

2 teaspoons light sesame oil
1 tablespoon minced fresh ginger
2 garlic cloves, minced
1 onion, julienned
1 small carrot, finely julienned
6 medium to large fresh shiitake mushrooms, julienned
1 teaspoon coriander seeds
6 cups Dashi Chicken Stock (page 34) or Vegetable Stock (page 37)
2 teaspoons dark sesame oil
1 tablespoon soy sauce
1 tablespoon rice vinegar
1 teaspoon kosher salt
½ teaspoon black pepper
4 ounces firm tofu, diced
6 rounded teaspoons white or red miso (see page 67)

Place a large saucepan over medium-high heat, and when it is hot, add the light sesame oil. Add the ginger and garlic and cook until lightly caramelized, 1 to 2 minutes. Add the onion, carrot, and shiitake mushrooms, and sauté until lightly colored, 2 to 3 minutes. Add the coriander and sauté until fragrant, about 1 minute.

Add the stock and bring to a boil. Add the dark sesame oil, soy sauce, vinegar, salt, and pepper and stir to combine.

Divide the tofu and miso among six soup bowls. Ladle the soup into the bowls, and encourage each guest to stir their soup.

Serves 6

shellfish

Lobsters, oysters, crabs, and clams: Shellfish lovers love them all! From briny mussels to creamy scallops to shrimp and prawns, these delicate and delectable proteins from the sea are eaten raw, marinated, steamed, stir-fried, and grilled. Do take care not to overcook them, because the lean flesh will become dry and toughened if cooked too long. Good tests for doneness are when oysters curl or lobster meat becomes opaque and can be gently pulled away from the shell. Shrimp are fully cooked when they feel firm to the touch and are bright in color.

Take precautions when buying shellfish. Go to a reputable fishmonger, and inquire about freshness, date received, and place of origin. Truly fresh shellfish look moist, have a clean ocean smell, and do not have cracked or broken shells. Always keep seafood well refrigerated or on ice prior to cooking it or eating it raw. Always serve raw shellfish ice-cold.

coriander-spiced diver scallops with pear glaze

I created this dish in the fall as a way of showing my appreciation for both the creamy, rich scallop and the crisp, sweet pear. The glaze brings them together perfectly.

I am not a big fan of poached scallops and always prefer to either sear or grill them. To ensure a good char and a crunchy, crispy exterior, be sure to get your pan nice and hot.

For the pear glaze:

1½ teaspoons light sesame oil
1 tablespoon minced fresh ginger
2 garlic cloves, minced
2 shallots, minced
1 Bartlett or Anjou pear, diced
1½ cups pear nectar
½ cup water or Chicken Stock (page 34)
2 tablespoons honey
2 tablespoons rice vinegar
2 teaspoons soy sauce

For the vinaigrette:

¼ cup reserved pear glaze
⅓ cup soy oil
1 teaspoon dark sesame oil
¼ teaspoon coriander seeds, toasted and ground
Juice of 1 lime
1 tablespoon rice vinegar
½ teaspoon kosher salt
½ teaspoon cracked black pepper

Mizuna: A Japanese salad green, mizuna is crisp, delicate, and feathery; it is often included in mesclun mixtures. It is available in specialty markets.

Diver scallops: If you can find diver scallops, use them. Diver scallops are hand-harvested sea scallops that are of amazing size and flavor. Given the current state of the scallop supply, harvesting them without dredging is probably the most sustainable method. They are perfect for grilling, roasting, and pan-searing. Ask your fishmonger for them. Or buy "dry packed" scallops.

For the salad:

1 large head frisée (also known as curly endive)

¼ pound mizuna, or 1 small bunch arugula

1 bunch watercress, stems well trimmed

¼ to 1 cup packed fresh cilantro leaves

2 Asian pears, julienned

For the scallops:

18 jumbo or extra-large sea scallops (1¼ to 1½ pounds)

2 teaspoons light sesame oil

1 teaspoon kosher salt

½ teaspoon cracked black pepper

3 tablespoons coriander seeds, toasted and cracked

1 tablespoon soy oil

Prepare the glaze: Place a small saucepan over medium-high heat, and when it is hot, add the oil. Add the ginger, garlic, and shallots and cook until lightly caramelized, 2 minutes. Add the pear, pear nectar, water, and honey, and bring to a boil. Reduce the heat to low and simmer until the mixture is reduced and the pears are very tender, 5 to 6 minutes. Transfer to a blender, add the rice vinegar and soy sauce, and puree. Cover and refrigerate for at least 1 hour. Measure ¼ cup of the glaze for the vinaigrette.

Prepare the vinaigrette: Place all the vinaigrette ingredients in a food processor or blender, and blend well.

Just prior to serving, place the salad ingredients in a large mixing bowl and lightly dress with the vinaigrette. Divide among six plates.

Prepare the scallops: Place the scallops in a bowl and toss with the sesame oil. Then toss with the salt, pepper, and coriander.

Place a cast-iron skillet over medium-high heat, and when it is hot, add the soy oil. Add the scallops in a single layer and cook for 1 to 2 minutes on each side, searing them well. Add the remaining pear glaze and toss well.

Distribute the scallops evenly over the salads, and serve immediately.

Serves 6

char-grilled shrimp satay with tamarind barbecue sauce

Satay. Ah, it sounds so exotic, but really it is just food grilled on a stick. At the new Salamander on Copley Square we have installed custom-made grills in our bar so that customers can watch as our satay chefs pull these spicy sweet nibbles off the grills.

Tamarind may seem unfamiliar, but you know the flavor: It is an overwhelmingly sour and tangy fruit in the mango family that frequently flavors chutneys, steak sauces, and barbecue glazes.

This barbecue sauce can be prepared as much as 2 weeks in advance. Use it with pork chops, chicken, and strongly flavored grilled fish, such as mahi-mahi and tuna.

Serve the shrimp with additional sauce and Miso Vegetable Pickles (page 66).

For the barbecue sauce:

1½ teaspoons light sesame oil
1 tablespoon minced fresh ginger
4 garlic cloves, minced
2 medium onions, finely diced
1 14-ounce can diced tomatoes
1 tablespoon tomato paste
1 cup Tamarind Juice (page 54)
2 teaspoons coriander seeds, toasted and cracked
½ teaspoon Szechuan peppercorns, toasted and cracked
1 star anise pod
1 teaspoon chili garlic paste (see page 82)
2 tablespoons rice vinegar
2 tablespoons molasses
1 teaspoon dark sesame oil

Shrimp

2 teaspoons soy sauce
½ teaspoon kosher salt
½ teaspoon cracked black pepper

For the shrimp:
18 skewers cut from fresh lemongrass, or 18 6-inch bamboo skewers
18 jumbo shrimp (about 1½ pounds), peeled and deveined
1½ teaspoons light sesame oil
1 teaspoon kosher salt
½ teaspoon cracked black pepper

Garnish:
Herb sprigs, such as cilantro

Prepare the barbecue sauce: Place a 1½-quart saucepan over medium-high heat, and when it is hot, add the oil. Add the ginger and garlic and cook until lightly caramelized, 1 to 2 minutes. Add the onions and cook until they are lightly caramelized, 3 to 5 minutes. Add the tomatoes and tomato paste and cook, stirring often, until the mixture is nearly dry, 7 to 8 minutes. Add the tamarind juice, coriander, peppercorns, star anise, chili garlic paste, vinegar, and molasses. Stir to combine. Simmer until the mixture is reduced and thickened, 7 to 8 minutes. Remove the pan from the heat, and add the dark sesame oil, soy sauce, salt, and pepper. Allow to cool. Then transfer to a container, cover, and refrigerate until ready to use. (The sauce may be served warm or chilled.)

Soak the lemongrass or bamboo skewers in cold water to cover for 20 minutes to 1 hour.

Prepare the shrimp: Prepare a charcoal, gas, or stovetop grill. When it has reached medium-high heat, brush the grill rack with oil.

Place the shrimp in a bowl, and toss with the sesame oil, salt, and pepper. Thread the shrimp on the skewers, lay them on the rack, and grill, brushing with the barbecue sauce, until they are bright red and firm throughout when pressed with your finger, about 2 minutes per side. Serve immediately, with the remaining barbecue sauce alongside.

Serves 6

Tart, gingery, and sweet spicy (as opposed to hot spicy), this dish demands U15s or U12s (restaurant talk for fifteen or twelve shrimp per pound)—the biggest shrimp you can find and the best for brining and grilling. This flavorful and incredibly versatile brine can also be used for pork, bass, snapper, scallops, and chicken. You should mark this page: You will be back here often.

Serve these shrimp with rice or Pan-Seared Somen Noodle Cake (page 242).

For the brine:
1 tablespoon light sesame oil
1½ cups sliced galangal (see page 30) or fresh ginger
1 head garlic, halved horizontally to expose the cloves
3 tablespoons coriander seeds
2 tablespoons star anise pods
⅓ cup sugar
⅓ cup packed light brown sugar
½ cup kosher salt
12 cups water
1 lemon, quartered
2 oranges, quartered
1 lime, quartered
3 stalks lemongrass, sliced

For the shrimp:
3 pounds jumbo shrimp, split through back and deveined, peel left on

Garnish:
Scallion Oil (page 45)

Prepare the brine: Place a large saucepan over medium heat, and when it is hot, add the oil. Add 1 cup of the galangal and the garlic, and cook until lightly browned, 2 to 3 minutes. Add the coriander and star anise, and cook until lightly toasted, about 2 minutes. Add both sugars and the salt, and cook until melted and lightly caramelized, about 5 minutes. Carefully and gradually add the water (to prevent splattering). Raise the heat to high and bring to a boil.

Remove the pan from the heat, and add the lemon, orange, and lime quarters, the lemongrass, and the remaining ½ cup sliced galangal. If you are saving the brine for later use, transfer the mixture to a 1-gallon container (it will make that much). Cover and refrigerate for at least 1 hour or up to 2 weeks.

To brine the shrimp: Place the shrimp in a very large container and cover with cold brine by 1 to 2 inches. Cover and refrigerate for at least 2 hours and up to 6 hours. Remove the shrimp and discard the brine.

To cook the shrimp: Prepare a gas, charcoal, or stovetop grill.

Place the shrimp on the grill (with the shells still on) and cook over medium-high heat until bright red, firm when gently pressed, and well charred, 2 to 3 minutes on each side. Serve immediately, garnished with Scallion Oil.

Serves 6

Brining: A brine is a liquid used to pickle, preserve, tenderize, and flavor foods. While by definition consisting of only water and salt, brines are in fact often flavored with herbs, fruits, spices, sweeteners, or almost anything to impart a unique and flavorful tang to the food being brined.

spicy grilled lobster with corn and sweet potato curry

Spicy and lush, this innovative lobster dish is perfect for Indian Summer, those long dusky days approaching autumn.

If you haven't grilled lobster before, don't shy away from this recipe. It is a great cooking method that can be mastered easily—but if it seems too arduous, or if it's snowing or raining, you can also cook it in a sauté pan or under the broiler. And like almost all grilled foods, the lobster pairs well with the curry.

If you're not ready to butcher your own lobsters, have the fish market prepare them for you. The lobsters must be cooked as soon as possible after they've been killed.

You can substitute shrimp or scallops for the lobster.

For the curry:

2 teaspoons light sesame oil
2 onions, diced
2 carrots, diced
1 red bell pepper, diced
½ fennel bulb, diced
¼ cup Yellow Curry Paste (page 31)
1 large sweet potato, diced
2 cups Fish Fumet (page 40)
1 14-ounce can unsweetened coconut milk
1 cup corn kernels (2 to 3 ears), fresh or frozen (do not substitute
  canned corn)
2 fresh or frozen kaffir lime leaves (see page 32)
1 tablespoon rice vinegar
2 tablespoons soy sauce
1 teaspoon kosher salt
½ teaspoon cracked black pepper

Coconut milk: Coconut milk should always be unsweetened. My favorite brand is Chaokoh. It is richly flavored and has the smooth, lush consistency I like. (Sweetened coconut milk is generally sold as coconut cream and is usually used for desserts or beverages.) Most good supermarkets carry canned coconut milk.

For the lobster:

Six 1¼-pound lobsters, split in half lengthwise through the head, claws and knuckles
  removed

8 tablespoons (1 stick) unsalted butter, at room temperature

1 tablespoon Red Curry Paste (page 32)

Kosher salt

Black pepper

½ to ¾ cup sliced fresh cilantro leaves

6 cilantro sprigs, for garnish

Lime wedges, for garnish

Spicy Grilled Lobster with Corn and Sweet Potato Curry and Scallion Noodle Cake

Prepare the curry: Place a 3½- to 4-quart saucepan over medium-high heat, and when it is hot, add the oil. Add the onions, carrots, bell pepper, and fennel and cook until lightly caramelized, 3 to 4 minutes. Add the curry paste and stir to combine. Reduce the heat to medium and stir-fry, stirring often, until the curry is richly aromatic and darkened in color, 1 to 2 minutes. Then add the sweet potatoes, fumet, and coconut milk, and bring to a boil. Reduce the heat to low and simmer until the sweet potatoes are tender, 10 to 12 minutes. Remove the pan from the heat, and add the corn, lime leaves, rice vinegar, soy sauce, salt, and pepper. (You can make curry to this point up to 2 days in advance; be sure to keep it refrigerated. Reheat to serve.)

When you are ready to cook the lobsters, bring a large pot of water to a boil over high heat. Add the lobster claws and knuckles, and cook for 4 minutes. Remove and cool under cold running water. Crack the shells and remove the meat. Set it aside.

Prepare a gas or charcoal grill. When it reaches medium-high heat, brush the grill rack clean.

In a small bowl, stir together the butter and Red Curry Paste. Brush the cut side of the split lobsters with this curry butter. Season with salt and pepper to taste, and carefully place, cut side down, on the hot grill. Do not try to move the lobsters for at least a full minute or even two; you want the lobster to get well seared and charred and for the flesh to feel firm under gentle pressure. Turn the lobster and allow it to cook on the shell side. Baste the meat with the rest of the curry butter. Total cooking time is approximately 5 minutes.

Just before serving, gently reheat the curry sauce. Stir in the cilantro leaves and the meat from the lobster claws. Ladle the curry into six large flat soup plates, and top with the grilled lobster halves. Garnish with cilantro sprigs and lime wedges.

Serves 6

shellfish

lobster tempura

Tempura is a Japanese specialty: lightly battered, perfectly fried, moderately small pieces of lobster, chicken, shrimp, or vegetable. The tempura flour and carbonated water help produce a finished dish that is much lighter than the more familiar fritters, onion rings, or fried chicken. As soon as you lift the tempura out of the simmering oil, you can tell whether it has been cooked perfectly or not: The succulent morsels should be perfectly enrobed in their crisp, airy shells.

Do buy tempura flour, a premeasured mixture of rice and soft wheat flours. Many varieties are available at Asian markets.

This dish is a great way to serve an expensive ingredient to a large number of people—especially if you cook the lobsters yourself. Or you can buy freshly steamed lobster and avoid the work, if not the cost. Tempura is traditionally served with a dipping sauce, in soup broth over Udon noodles. Serve this tempura with Hoisin and Spice Dipping Sauce (page 48) or the Citrus Dipping Sauce (page 50).

1 pound steamed lobster meat (4 pounds whole lobsters)
1¼ cups tempura flour
1 teaspoon kosher salt
½ teaspoon black pepper
1¼ cups cold unflavored carbonated water
2 cups vegetable oil, for frying

Divide the lobster into twelve equal pieces, and dust them with ¼ cup of the tempura flour.

Place the remaining 1 cup tempura flour, salt, pepper, and carbonated water in a bowl and whisk together; a few lumps may remain. Cover and refrigerate until ready to use.

Place the oil in a 1-quart saucepan and heat over medium heat to 360°F or until the surface is shimmering. (If you are using a deep-fryer, fill to the minimum line and heat to 360°F.)

Using chopsticks or tongs, dip a chunk of lobster into the tempura batter, covering it completely. Lift the lobster from the batter and allow the excess to run back into the bowl. Carefully drop the individual pieces into the hot oil. For best results, do this in three or four batches.

The tempura should quickly float (if it doesn't, it's a sign that the oil is probably not hot enough). Allow the tempura to turn straw gold in color, approximately 2 minutes. Remove, and place on a paper towel–lined plate to drain.

Serve immediately.

Serves 6

pan-roasted clams and mussels with fragrant lime leaves

I can't get enough of this dish and can easily eat two portions, so if you're a big fan of mussels, you may want to double the recipe! This appetizer or luncheon entree dish is perfect for mussel lovers who may not know what to do with them other than steaming them with garlic. Mussels and clams (saltier, chewier) work well together because they bring different flavors to the dish. I do not like to stew the shellfish in their broth, but favor instead "blistering" them by placing them directly on a grill or a dry pan and blistering or scorching the shells so the tasty mollusks steam themselves open. The result is a more tender and flavorful morsel.

36 mussels
24 littleneck clams
2 teaspoons light sesame oil
1 onion, julienned
2 carrots, julienned
1 red bell pepper, julienned
1 yellow bell pepper, julienned
1 bunch (about 8) scallions, white and green parts, cut into 1-inch lengths
¼ cup Southeast Asian Green Curry Paste (page 29)
3 cups Shellfish Stock (page 41)
4 fresh or frozen kaffir lime leaves (see page 32), cut into fine julienne
½ cup coarsely chopped fresh cilantro leaves
1 teaspoon kosher salt
Several cilantro sprigs, for garnish
2 limes, cut into wedges, for garnish

Wash, debeard, and scrub the mussels and clams under cold water. Cover and refrigerate.

Place a skillet over medium-high heat until the rim is hot to the touch. Do not add oil! Add the shellfish in a single layer and watch them pop open. As they cook through, remove them to a platter or a large bowl. Repeat until all the mussels and clams are cooked, 2 to 4 minutes per batch.

Place a 1½- to 2-quart saucepan over medium-high heat, and when it is hot, add the oil. Add the onion, carrots, bell peppers, and scallions, and stir-fry until lightly caramelized, 3 to 4 minutes. Add the curry paste and reduce the heat to medium. Cook, stirring, until very fragrant, 1 to 2 minutes. Then add the Shellfish Stock and bring to a boil. Skim off any foam, reduce the heat to low, and simmer for 5 minutes. Add the lime leaves.

Divide the mussels and clams evenly among six shallow bowls. Add the cilantro leaves and salt to the curry, and ladle the sauce over the blistered shellfish. Garnish with cilantro sprigs and lime wedges.

Serves 6

Pan-
Roasted
Clams and
Mussels
with
Fragrant
Lime
Leaves

indonesian-style
red seafood curry

Spicy, exotic, and rich, this Asian-style seafood chowder is a great one to add to your repertoire. The salty, sweet, and sour flavors of the broth go equally well with tuna, bluefish, and
many other seafoods, singly or in combination. You can prepare this one-pan dish in an easy
45 minutes from start to finish.

*How to crack seeds
and peppercorns:*

"Cracked" seeds and
peppercorns are very
coarsely ground—
just broken, really.
You can do this in a
spice mill or a coffee
grinder if you are very
careful not to over-
process them. Other,
more controllable,
methods are to use a
mortar and pestle, or
to press them with
the flat bottom of a
heavy skillet.

24 mussels
18 littleneck clams
1½ pounds jumbo shrimp, peeled and deveined
1 pound jumbo sea scallops, muscle removed
4 teaspoons light sesame oil
1 teaspoon cracked coriander seeds
1 teaspoon kosher salt
2 onions, diced
2 carrots, diced
1 fennel bulb, diced
2 leeks, halved lengthwise and sliced into ¼-inch-thick half-moons
*2 to 3 tablespoons Red Curry Paste (page 32; 2 for very spicy, 3 for
     way hot!)*
1 14-ounce can diced tomatoes
4 cups Shellfish Stock (page 41)
¼ cup fish sauce
½ cup sliced fresh cilantro leaves
6 cilantro sprigs, for garnish
Cilantro Oil (page 46), for garnish

Wash, debeard and scrub the mussels and clams under cold running water. Cover
and refrigerate.

Place the shrimp, scallops, 2 teaspoons of the sesame oil, coriander, and salt in a
bowl and toss to combine.

Place a roasting pan or a deep sauté pan over medium-high heat until the rim is hot to the touch. Do not add oil! Add the mussels and clams in a single layer and watch them pop open. As they cook through, remove them to a platter or a large bowl. Repeat until all are cooked, 2 to 4 minutes per batch.

Reheat the braiser, and when it is hot, add 1 teaspoon of the sesame oil. Add the shrimp and scallops in a single layer and sear well, about 1 minute on each side (you may need to do this in batches, depending on the size of the

Indonesian-Style Red Seafood Curry

pan). Remove to the platter with the clams and mussels.

Once all of the seafood is cooked, add the remaining 1 teaspoon sesame oil to the brasier. When it is hot, add the onions, carrots, fennel, and leeks, and stir-fry until lightly caramelized, 3 to 4 minutes. Stir in the curry paste and cook until fragrant, 1 to 2 minutes. Add the tomatoes and cook until the mixture is dry and thick, 5 to 6 minutes. Add the Shellfish Stock and bring to a boil. Skim off any foam that rises. Reduce the heat to medium, and simmer for about 7 minutes. Add the fish sauce, cilantro leaves, and reserved seafood. Cover and cook 2 to 3 minutes.

Ladle the chowder into deep soup plates, and garnish with the cilantro sprigs and Cilantro Oil.

Serves 6

shellfish

curry-basted grilled jumbo scallops with cashew sauce

The spicy curry basting liquid integrates beautifully with the sweet, rich scallops and cashews in this dish.

We are very fortunate in New England to be able to get large diver scallops. I mean huge—sometimes weighing 2 to 3 ounces apiece! These are great hot off the grill, but since they are delicate, be sure to baste them throughout the cooking period with the red curry butter. Remember: a hot, clean grill is needed to gain the best results. I find it easiest to thread the scallops onto long bamboo or metal skewers for ease of handling. Soak the skewers for 20 minutes to 1 hour in cold water before using them.

Serve the scallops with Sweet Curried Mango Chutney (page 58), Exotically Spiced Basmati Rice Pilaf (page 251), Yang Chow Fried Rice (page 252), and/or Spicy Eggplant Chutney (page 59).

For the scallops:
3 pounds jumbo sea scallops, muscle removed
2 teaspoons light sesame oil
2 teaspoons kosher salt
2 teaspoons cracked coriander seeds
1 teaspoon cracked black pepper

For the basting sauce:
1 to 2 tablespoons Red Curry Paste (page 32), depending on how spicy you like it
1 cup (2 sticks) unsalted butter, at room temperature
1 teaspoon kosher salt
1 teaspoon black pepper

For the cashew sauce:

2 teaspoons light sesame oil

1 tablespoon minced fresh ginger

4 garlic cloves, minced

1 cup unsalted cashews, toasted

¼ cup mango juice

1 tablespoon mirin

2 tablespoons soy sauce

2 tablespoons rice vinegar

1 tablespoon chili garlic paste (see page 82)

1 teaspoon kosher salt

½ teaspoon black pepper

Prepare the scallops: Place the scallops, sesame oil, salt, coriander, and pepper in a bowl and toss to combine. Keep refrigerated for 1 to 4 hours, until ready to grill.

Prepare the basting sauce: Place the curry paste, butter, salt, and pepper in a bowl and mix to combine thoroughly. Set aside at room temperature.

Prepare the cashew sauce: Place a 1-quart saucepan over medium-high heat, and when it is hot, add the oil. Add the ginger and garlic and cook until caramelized, 1 to 2 minutes. Add the cashews and stir for 1 minute. Add the mango juice and mirin, and bring to a boil.

Transfer the mixture to a blender. Pulse a few times to combine, and then add the soy sauce, rice vinegar, chili garlic paste, salt, and pepper. Puree until smooth. Set aside at room temperature.

Prepare a gas or charcoal grill.

When the grill is good and hot, lay the scallops on the grill rack (threaded on skewers if you like). Grill, basting often with the basting sauce until the scallops are firm but still yield slightly to gentle pressure, about 2 minutes on each side.

Divide the cashew sauce among six plates, and top with the scallops.

Serves 6

shellfish

chilled jumbo shrimp with asparagus and cucumber mango relish

This appetizer or summer lunch dish is bursting with tropical flavors. Seek out some truly jumbo shrimp for this dish, and poach them gently (do not boil) in the spice-laden liquid. This beautiful, colorful dish is quick to prepare, and the cucumber-mango relish is extremely versatile—try it on grilled tuna, chicken, or pork.

For the shrimp:
18 jumbo shrimp (about 1¼ pounds—15 count or larger), peeled and deveined
2 teaspoons light sesame oil
1 small onion, quartered
3 inches fresh ginger, sliced
1 head garlic, halved horizontally to expose the cloves
2 tablespoons coriander seeds
6 star anise pods
4 arbol chilies
1 tablespoon kosher salt
4 cups cold water

For the asparagus:
1 pound asparagus, woody ends trimmed
½ teaspoon kosher salt

For the cucumber-mango relish:
1 ripe mango, cut into small dice
1 cucumber, cut into small dice
1 red bell pepper, cut into small dice
1 red onion, cut into small dice
2 teaspoons minced fresh ginger
1 garlic clove, minced
2 teaspoons soy oil
1 teaspoon dark sesame oil

1 teaspoon chili garlic sauce (see page 82)
¼ cup rice vinegar
2 scallions, white and green parts, thinly sliced
⅓ cup sliced fresh cilantro leaves
¼ cup sliced fresh mint leaves
1 teaspoon kosher salt
½ teaspoon black pepper

Garnish:
Cilantro and mint sprigs
Cilantro Oil (page 46)

Prepare the shrimp: Place a 2- or 3-quart saucepan over medium-high heat, and when it is hot, add the oil. Add the onion, ginger, and garlic and cook until lightly caramelized, 3 to 4 minutes. Add the coriander, star anise, and chilies, and toast, stirring often, about 1 minute. Add the salt and water and bring to a boil. Boil for 5 minutes. Reduce the heat to barely a simmer, and add the shrimp. Poach until they are firm to the touch, 4 to 6 minutes, never allowing the poaching liquid to boil. Remove the shrimp from the liquid, cover, and refrigerate.

Prepare the asparagus: Fill a saucepan or a deep skillet with water and bring to a boil. Add the salt and the asparagus, and cook until bright green and barely tender, 3 to 4 minutes. Drain, and then cool in an ice bath. Drain again, cover, and refrigerate.

Prepare the relish: Place the mango, cucumber, bell pepper, and red onion in a mixing bowl and stir to combine. Add the ginger and garlic, soy and sesame oils, chili garlic sauce, rice vinegar, scallions, cilantro, mint, salt, and pepper. Toss well, cover, and refrigerate.

To serve, arrange the asparagus in bundles on chilled plates. Spoon large dollops of the relish over the asparagus, and arrange the shrimp on top. Garnish with cilantro and mint sprigs and Cilantro Oil.

Serves 6

fish

Many people tell me that they have trouble cooking fish at home, with the worst offense being that the fillets often stick to the pan or fall apart on the grill. Here are my four top tips for cooking fish:

- When sautéing, use a nonstick pan.
- When broiling, drizzle a little sesame oil over the fish and broil for 10 minutes per inch of thickness.
- Buy an inexpensive Chinese steamer and steam the fish over a saucepan of simmering water.
- When grilling, make sure the grill surface is very clean, well seasoned, and very hot. Choose a solid-flesh fish like snapper, bluefish, or tuna, and be sure to oil either the grill or the fish first.

High-quality fresh fish is delicious. Always shop the market: Look the fish case over. Ask the fishmonger what he or she suggests or what arrived that day. One of the best freshness checks is the sniff test—your purchase should smell sweet and somewhat like the sea. If the shop reeks of fish, walk out.

honey tamari—brined striped bass

The characteristic Thai flavors in this recipe should taste distinct and harmonious at the same time, making sense in some delightful composition on your palate. The honey (sweet), fish sauce (salty), tamari (malty), and lime leaf (perfume and acidity) create a wonderful and melodious expression of flavors in balance.

The brine is also good on seafood like bass (but not the flavorless Chilean sea bass), snapper, shrimp, lobster, or scallops and on lighter meats such as pork. Serve with Curried Rice Sticks, page 247.

1 tablespoon light sesame oil
½ cup thinly sliced fresh ginger
½ cup thinly sliced galangal (see page 30) or ½ additional cup fresh ginger
3 heads garlic, halved horizontally to expose the cloves
3 tablespoons coriander seeds
1 cup honey
12 cups water
⅓ cup kosher salt
1 cup fish sauce
5 fresh or frozen kaffir lime leaves (see page 32)
1 cup tamari
6 6- to 8-ounce striped bass fillets
1 tablespoon soy oil
Cilantro Oil (page 46) or Curry Oil (page 47), for garnish
Spicy Daikon (page 62), for garnish

Place a large saucepan over medium heat, and when it is hot, add the sesame oil. Add the ginger, galangal, and garlic and cook until lightly browned, 2 to 3 minutes. Add the coriander and cook until lightly toasted, about 2 minutes. Add the honey and cook until caramelized, about 3 minutes. Carefully and gradually add the water (to avoid splattering). Then add the salt and bring to a boil.

Remove the pan from the heat and add the fish sauce, lime leaves, and tamari. Stir to combine. If saving the brine for later use, transfer it to a container. Cover and refrigerate for at least 1 hour and up to 2 weeks.

Place the fillets in a large container and cover with the cold brine by 1 to 2 inches. Cover, and refrigerate for at least 3 and up to 6 hours.

Remove the bass and discard the brine. Place a large skillet over medium-high heat, and when it is hot, add the soy oil. Add the bass in batches, waiting about 30 seconds after each addition so the pan reheats, and cook until the exterior is golden brown and the fish flakes under gentle pressure, 4 to 5 minutes per side. Serve immediately, garnished with Cilantro Oil or Curry Oil, and Spicy Daikon.

Serves 6

I started making this dish about twenty years ago, while cooking my way through college in Athens, Georgia. The owner of the cafe where I was working called it *Beau Séjour,* or "beautiful day." I hadn't made it for quite a while until the day I prepared lunch for our fabulous editor, Sydny Miner. When she tasted this salmon ceviche flavored with Thai basil, lemongrass, ginger, and lime leaves, Sydny flipped. She demanded that it be in the book, and I'd give her just about anything she wants. Really.

Serve the salmon with crisps, shrimp crackers, lettuce leaves, or fancy cress and sprouts.

Asian
Marinated
Salmon

For the salmon:

1 pound boneless, skinless wild salmon fillet, cut into ⅓-inch dice

1 small red onion, finely diced

1 cucumber, finely diced

1 red bell pepper, finely diced

3 scallions, white and green parts, sliced

¼ cup sliced fresh Thai basil leaves

¼ cup sliced fresh mint leaves

2 teaspoons Sweet Spice Mix (page 81)

1 teaspoon kosher salt

½ teaspoon cracked black pepper

For the marinade:

1 tablespoon minced fresh ginger

4 garlic cloves, minced

1 stalk lemongrass, outer husk discarded, inner heart minced

2 tablespoons fish sauce

¾ cup lime juice (4 to 6 limes)

½ cup rice vinegar

1 tablespoon dark sesame oil

2 teaspoons chili garlic paste (see page 82)

2 kaffir lime leaves (see page 32), bruised

Prepare the salmon: Place the salmon, diced vegetables, scallions, basil, mint, Sweet Spice Mix, salt, and pepper in a large bowl and toss to mix well.

Prepare the marinade: Place the ginger, garlic, lemongrass, fish sauce, lime juice, vinegar, oil, chili garlic paste, and lime leaves in a bowl and whisk until smooth. Pour the marinade over the salmon salad, and toss well. Place a sheet of plastic wrap directly on top of the salmon, pressing down lightly to submerge all the salmon and vegetables in the marinade.

Refrigerate for at least 8 hours and up to overnight. Before serving, drain off and discard half the marinade.

Serves 6

hot and sour soup with ginger tamari-glazed seafood

This is the best hot and sour soup anywhere on earth, and well worth the effort! Unlike the Szechuan-style soup served in Chinese restaurants, this light Vietnamese-style soup is made hot and sharp with ginger, lemongrass, and chili; made sour with tamarind and lime; and given sweetness with pineapple and tomato. It's finished with the characteristic taste of fish sauce as a seasoning. I love to add the seafood to dress it up a bit, but you certainly don't have to.

Like almost all soups, for the best results, make this 1 or 2 days before serving.

1 tablespoon light sesame oil
2 tablespoons minced fresh ginger
2 tablespoons minced galangal (see page 30), or 2 additional tablespoons fresh ginger
4 to 6 garlic cloves, minced
2 stalks lemongrass, outer husk discarded, inner heart minced
2 small onions, diced
2 teaspoons chili garlic paste (page 82)
1 cup canned diced tomatoes, drained
½ cup Tamarind Juice (page 54)
2½ cups Fish Fumet (page 40)
2½ cups Shellfish Stock (page 41), Chicken Stock (page 34), or Vegetable Stock (page 37)
¼ cup fish sauce
¼ cup lime juice (about 2 limes)
1 cup diced pineapple
2 teaspoons coriander seeds, toasted and cracked
2 star anise pods, toasted

For the glaze:
2 tablespoons honey
2 tablespoons mirin
¼ cup tamari
¼ cup cold water
¼ cup minced fresh ginger

Lemongrass: I use lots of lemongrass. Its fragrance and subtle lemon oil flavor are integral to the cuisines of Southeast Asia. You can find lemongrass in most grocery stores; during the summer months, I buy mine from a local organic farmer. You can use lemongrass as an infusion (in a soup stock or brine) or in a stir-fry.

To prepare lemongrass, peel away any dried or browning outer layers. Lay the stalk flat on your cutting board, and using the back (as opposed to the sharp side) of a heavy knife or cleaver—or even a small hammer—bruise the lemongrass by hitting it repeatedly to expose the inner layers. You will smell the wonderful fragrance immediately, and it will be easy to pull the woody bottom off the stalk. Discard it, and you're ready to proceed. You can use the bruised stalk as is for an infusion, or you can slice it crosswise for transferring to your food processor or for mincing by hand.

Be careful when bruising the lemongrass—it is easy to get overzealous. My friend and sous chef Michael McEwen almost took his ear off when the tip of his knife broke off and came flying past his head. You could actually hear a *voo-voo-voo* boomerang sound as it flew by!

Lemongrass

For the seafood:

1 tablespoon soy oil

4 to 6 ounces monkfish tail

6 ounces salmon fillet

6 jumbo (11–15 count) shrimp, split through the back of the shell and deveined

Garnish:

6 cilantro sprigs

6 mint sprigs

1 cup fresh mung bean sprouts

2 limes, cut into wedges

Place a 3½- to 4-quart saucepan over medium-high heat, and when it is hot, add the oil. Add the ginger, galangal, garlic, and lemongrass and cook until lightly caramelized, 3 to 4 minutes. Reduce the heat, add the onions, and cook until deeply caramelized, 4 to 5 minutes. Add the chili garlic paste and the tomatoes, and cook until the mixture is nearly dry, 4 to 5 minutes. Add the tamarind juice, fumet, and Shellfish Stock, and bring to a boil. Reduce the heat to low and simmer for 10 minutes. Remove the pan from the heat and stir in the pineapple, fish sauce, lime juice, coriander, and star anise. (If you are making this in advance, cool and refrigerate until ready to serve.)

Prepare the glaze: Place the honey and mirin in a small saucepan and bring to a boil over medium heat. Cook until caramelized, 2 to 3 minutes. Add the tamari, cold water, and ginger and bring to a boil. Remove from the heat and allow to steep until cool. Strain.

Place the seafood in the cooled glaze, cover, and refrigerate for at least 1 and up to 4 hours.

Place a skillet over medium-high heat, and when it is hot, add the oil. Remove the seafood from the glaze (reserve the glaze for basting). Add the fish and shrimp to the pan in batches; cook the fish about 4 minutes on each side per inch of thickness, and cook the shrimp for 2 minutes per side.

Bring the soup back to a quick boil over medium-high heat.

Divide the soup among six bowls. Slice the monkfish and salmon into six pieces, and place in the soup, along with one shrimp in each bowl. Garnish with the cilantro and mint sprigs, sprouts, and lime wedges.

Serves 6

sweet tamari-glazed salmon fillet

Salmon lends itself to many flavors—dill, horseradish, and tamari, to name a few—and to many different cooking methods, including broiling, steaming, poaching, curing, and smoking. This recipe demonstrates a flavor and technique combination that is one of my favorites. The ebony color of this dish is especially lovely when served with the backdrop of Sesame Parsnips (page 235).

This recipe can be adapted for chicken, pork, tuna, eggplant slices, and portobello mushrooms.

1 cup tamari
1 tablespoon minced fresh ginger
2 garlic cloves, minced
½ cup honey
2 teaspoons coriander seeds, toasted and ground
3 pounds salmon fillet, cut into 6 portions
2 teaspoons coarsely cracked black pepper
2 teaspoons vegetable oil
1 cup Fish Fumet (page 40) or Vegetable Stock (page 37)
1 tablespoon unsalted butter (optional)
Scallion Oil (page 45) or Fragrant Chili and Spice Oil (page 44), for garnish
Miso Vegetable Pickles (page 66), for garnish

Place the tamari, ginger, garlic, honey, and coriander in a shallow plastic or glass container, and mix to combine. Add the salmon, cover, and refrigerate for 15 minutes, turning once. Drain off the marinade, pouring it into a small saucepan. Leave the salmon in the container; cover, and refrigerate for up to 24 hours.

Place the reserved tamari marinade over medium heat and bring to a boil. Cook until reduced to 2 tablespoons, 8 to 10 minutes. Set aside to cool.

Sprinkle the salmon fillets with the pepper. Place a skillet over high heat, and when it is very hot, add the oil. Place the salmon, skin side down, in the pan and cook for 3 minutes on each side.

Meanwhile, place the reduced tamari marinade and the fumet in a 1-quart saucepan and bring to a quick boil over medium-high heat. Whisk in the butter, if desired.

Divide the salmon fillets and sauce among six plates. Drizzle with Scallion Oil, and garnish with Miso Vegetable Pickles.

Serves 6

I enjoy being playful and creative with soups. This savory tomato-vegetable soup can be served hot or cold, as is or enhanced with the addition of a beautiful snapper fillet.

You can substitute mackerel, tuna, bluefish, or tilapia for the snapper.

For the tomato soup:

1 tablespoon light sesame oil

1 onion, diced

½ fennel bulb, diced

1 carrot, diced

2 or 3 garlic cloves, minced

1 teaspoon minced fresh ginger

1 tablespoon tomato paste

1 teaspoon coriander seeds, toasted and cracked

1 28-ounce can diced tomatoes

4 cups Vegetable Stock (page 37), Fish Fumet (page 40), or Chicken Stock (page 34)

¼ to ½ teaspoon kosher salt

½ teaspoon black pepper

For the red snapper:

1 to 2 teaspoons coriander seeds, toasted and cracked

1 teaspoon cumin seeds, toasted and cracked

½ teaspoon kosher salt

¼ to ½ teaspoon black pepper

1 tablespoon olive oil

6 4-ounce red snapper fillets, scaled and pin bones removed

Garnish:

Thai basil or cilantro sprigs

Cilantro Oil (page 46)

Prepare the soup: Place a heavy soup pot over medium heat, and when it is hot, add the oil. Add the onion, fennel, carrot, garlic, and ginger and cook until the mixture is a deep caramel color and fragrant, 8 to 10 minutes.

Add the tomato paste, coriander, tomatoes, and stock, and bring to a boil. Reduce the heat to low and simmer until the vegetables are tender, about 10 minutes. Add the salt and pepper. Keep the soup warm, or cover and refrigerate for up to 3 days.

Prepare the red snapper: Place the coriander, cumin, salt, and pepper in a shallow dish, and stir well. Roll the snapper fillets in the spice mixture. Place a 10- or 12-inch sauté pan over medium-high heat, and when it is hot, add the oil. Add the fillets and cook until firm to the touch, about 1½ minutes per side. (Alternatively, the red snapper can be cooked over a medium-hot grill for the same amount of time.)

Ladle the hot or chilled soup into six flat soup plates, and "float" a fillet in the center of each one. Garnish with basil sprigs, and drizzle with Cilantro Oil.

Serves 6

Thai basil: The flavor of Thai basil is somewhat mintier and less anise-like than other varieties of basil. It is also more fragrant. Thai basil is available in Asian markets and at farm stands—or, better yet, you can grow your own.

teriyaki glazed halibut
with sake pine-nut sauce

Teriyaki is a dish consisting of a food that is marinated in a sweet soy glaze and then grilled or cooked on a griddle. As well as using the glaze as a marinade, you can also use it as a basting liquid to brush on shrimp, chicken, pork, or scallops while grilling. This halibut dish is a beautiful marriage of flavors: creamy white fish, sweet tamari, and the rich sake-accented butter sauce.

Serve the halibut with seared Vegetable Wontons (page 86) or Scallion Noodle Cakes (page 244).

For the teriyaki:

½ cup honey

½ cup mirin

½ cup water

½ cup tamari

¼ cup sake

6 6- to 8-ounce halibut fillets

For the sauce:

1 teaspoon light sesame oil

2 shallots, minced

1 tablespoon minced fresh ginger

2 garlic cloves, minced

½ cup Versatile Dashi (page 38)

¼ cup sake

2 tablespoons rice vinegar

1 tablespoon mirin

1 tablespoon tamari

8 tablespoons (1 stick) unsalted butter

½ cup sliced fresh sorrel or watercress leaves (cut into chiffonade, or thin ribbons)

¼ cup pine nuts, toasted

1 teaspoon kosher salt

1 teaspoon black pepper

For the fish:

1 tablespoon light sesame oil

Prepare the teriyaki glaze: Place the honey and mirin in a small saucepan and bring to a boil over medium heat. Boil until caramelized, fragrant, and thick, 6 to 8 minutes. Carefully and gradually add the water, tamari, and sake, and bring back to a boil. Transfer the glaze to a shallow dish and refrigerate until completely cooled.

Add the halibut to the glaze, cover, and refrigerate for at least 2 and up to 6 hours. Turn the fish occasionally so it marinates evenly.

Prepare the sauce: Place a small saucepan over medium heat, and when it is hot, add the oil. Add the shallots, ginger, and garlic and cook until lightly caramelized, 2 to 3 minutes. Add the dashi, sake, vinegar, mirin, and tamari and bring to a boil. Reduce the heat to low and simmer until reduced to ⅓ to ½ cup, 10 to 12 minutes. Set aside until ready to cook the halibut. Just prior to using, reheat the sauce and add the butter, whisking it in one tablespoon at a time. Then stir in the sorrel, pine nuts, salt, and pepper.

Drain the halibut and discard the marinade.

Place a large skillet over medium-high heat, and when it is hot, add the oil. Add the halibut, one fillet at a time, allowing the pan to reheat for a few seconds after each addition. Cook until well seared and brown, no more than 3 to 4 minutes on each side.

Divide the sauce among six plates, and top each with a halibut fillet.

Serves 6

Sake: This Japanese wine is made from fermented rice and has a relatively low alcohol content of 12 to 16 percent. Sake is typically served cold but may be served warm (especially in the United States) in small cups. It is used in cooking to impart a heady, slightly sweet flavor.

grilled salmon steaks with fresh oyster sauce

Oysters are very precious, and in truth I enjoy them best on the half-shell in their own liquor. Because they hold so much richness and so much flavor in so small a package, they are used with entrees either to add even more richness or to provide a counterpoint to another ingredient. In this case, I am pairing the rich and creamy oyster with the strong flavor and charred, crispy texture of grilled salmon.

There is nothing quite like wild salmon; you certainly can't beat the flavor. I always recommend it over farmed salmon.

Serve the salmon steaks with Ginger Garlic Spinach (page 232) and the Pan-Seared Somen Noodle Cake (page 242). (If you can find fresh pea tendrils, use those as a substitute for the spinach in the Ginger Garlic Spinach recipe.)

Grilled Salmon Steaks with Fresh Oyster Sauce

This dish is also great when made with trout, cod, or halibut.

For the marinade:

¼ *cup minced fresh ginger*

12 garlic cloves, minced

1 tablespoon coriander seeds, toasted and cracked

2 star anise pods, toasted and ground

1 teaspoon Szechuan peppercorns, toasted and ground

2 tablespoons light sesame oil

1 orange, zested and then juiced

6 8-ounce salmon steaks

For the sauce:
2 teaspoons light sesame oil
1 tablespoon minced fresh ginger
4 garlic cloves, minced
½ cup dry white wine
2 cups Fish Fumet (page 40)
½ cup heavy cream
18 to 24 large oysters, shucked
⅓ cup fresh Thai basil leaves
Kosher salt
Black pepper

Garnish:
Thai basil sprigs

Woodbury's Wellfleet littlenecks

Prepare the marinade: Place the ginger, garlic, coriander, star anse, peppercorns, sesame oil, orange zest, and orange juice in a shallow bowl and mix to combine.

Rub both sides of the salmon steaks with the marinade. Keep refrigerated until ready to grill.

Prepare the sauce: Place a 1-quart saucepan over medium-high heat, and when it is hot, add the oil. Add the ginger and garlic and cook until caramelized, 1 to 2 minutes. Add the wine and cook until reduced to 1 tablespoon, 4 to 5 minutes. Add the fumet and reduce again for about 10 minutes. Then add the cream and reduce for 5 minutes longer. Reduce the heat to very low, and keep the sauce hot.

Prepare a gas or charcoal grill.

When the grill is good and hot, lay the salmon on the rack. Grill for 3 minutes on each side per inch of thickness for medium, 5 minutes per inch of thickness for well done.

Poach the oysters in the sauce over low heat until their edges curl and the centers are just firm to the touch. Add the basil leaves, and season with salt and pepper.

Divide the salmon and oyster sauce among six plates. Garnish with the basil sprigs, and serve immediately.

Serves 6

Skate is a light, sweet fish that takes well to many flavors and cooking methods. I prefer to pan-roast the skate wing with the bone in because any time you roast or sauté something closer to its whole state (on the bone), it cooks more evenly and retains more moisture—but of course you can always use a fillet. I think the flavor of the skate with these lightly pickled vegetables is as delicious as the presentation is beautiful. The light fireworks of the spices in the marinade add tremendous flavor but no heat.

For the marinade:

2 tablespoons coriander seeds, toasted and cracked
1 teaspoon Szechuan peppercorns, toasted and cracked
½ cup fresh cilantro leaves
2 tablespoons dark sesame oil
1 tablespoon minced fresh ginger
2 garlic cloves

6 6- to 8-ounce portions skate wing, bone in

For the pickled vegetables:

1 tablespoon light sesame oil
1 tablespoon minced fresh ginger
2 garlic cloves, minced
1 red onion, diced
1 red bell pepper, diced
2 carrots, diced
½ cup rice vinegar
1 tablespoon mirin
1 tablespoon palm sugar
1 tablespoon tamari
2 teaspoons coriander seeds, toasted and cracked

1 pound asparagus, woody ends trimmed, cut into 1-inch lengths
1 cup corn kernels (2 or 3 ears), fresh or frozen
1 cup peas, fresh or frozen
1½ cups Fish Fumet (page 40), or half clam juice and half water
4 scallions, white and green parts, sliced into thin rings
2 tablespoons chopped fresh cilantro leaves
1½ teaspoons kosher salt
½ teaspoon black pepper

1 tablespoon soy oil
1½ teaspoons kosher salt
1 teaspoon black pepper

Garnish:
Cilantro sprigs

Prepare the marinade: Place the coriander, Szechuan peppercorns, cilantro, sesame oil, ginger, and garlic in the bowl of a food processor and process until smooth.

Rub the marinade into the skate wing. Cover, and refrigerate until ready to cook, but not more than 24 hours.

Prepare the pickled vegetables (this can be done while the skate is marinating): Place a skillet over high heat, and when it is hot, add the oil. Add the ginger and garlic and cook until lightly browned, 2 to 3 minutes. Add the red onion, bell pepper, and carrots and cook until lightly caramelized, 2 to 3 minutes. Add the vinegar, mirin, palm sugar, tamari, and coriander and bring to a boil. Then add the asparagus, corn, and peas. Add the fumet and bring to a boil. Remove the skillet from the heat, and stir in the scallions, cilantro, salt, and pepper.

To cook the skate, place a large skillet over medium-high heat. When it is hot, add the soy oil. Sprinkle the skate with the salt and pepper. Add the skate to the skillet, one fillet at a time, allowing the pan to reheat after each addition, and cook until well seared and brown, 3 to 4 minutes on each side per inch of thickness.

Divide the pickled vegetables among six shallow bowls, showing off as many colors and shapes of the vegetables as you can. Top each bowl with a portion of skate. Garnish with cilantro sprigs, and serve immediately.

Serves 6

seared tuna in dashi with chewy fat noodles

This light dish is delicious, easy, fun to prepare, and healthy. Unlike the classic French flour-based or cream-and-butter-enriched sauces, in a lot of Asian cooking the sauce is a broth. Here the aggressively spiced tuna sits in dashi broth that's flavored with soy and ginger. If your kids won't eat tuna, they will still love the veggies and udon noodles.

Serve this with Ginger Garlic Spinach (page 232). If you have some seaweed, such as wakame, use that for a garnish instead of the cilantro sprigs.

For the tuna:

6 8-ounce tuna steaks, 1 to 1½ inches thick
2 tablespoons Korean Chili Spice Blend (page 28)
1½ teaspoons kosher salt
½ teaspoon black pepper

For the vegetable udon:

2 teaspoons light sesame oil
1 tablespoon minced fresh ginger
2 garlic cloves, minced
2 small or 1 large red onion, julienned
2 carrots, julienned
2 red bell peppers, julienned
2 leeks, white parts only, halved lengthwise and cut into ¼-inch-thick half-moons
4 scallions, white and green parts, cut into 1-inch lengths
1 pound frozen udon noodles, cooked al dente
Kosher salt
Black pepper

Wash those leeks! Trim the roots off the leeks and remove all but 2 inches of the green parts. Slice the leeks lengthwise and wash in several changes of cold water, being sure to get rid of any sand. Drain well in a colander.

For the dashi:

4 cups Versatile Dashi (page 38), Fish Fumet (page 40), or Vegetable Stock (page 37)
1 tablespoon tamari
2 teaspoons rice vinegar

1 tablespoon light sesame oil

Garnish:

Cilantro sprigs or slivered scallions

Place the tuna on a baking sheet and sprinkle both sides evenly with the Korean Chili Spice Blend, salt, and pepper. Set aside.

Prepare the vegetable udon: Place a large skillet over medium-high heat, and when it is hot, add the oil. Add the ginger and garlic and cook until lightly browned, about 2 minutes. Add the onions, carrots, bell peppers, leeks, and scallions, and cook until the vegetables start to soften, about 2 minutes. Remove the skillet from the heat, and add the udon. Season with salt and pepper. Cover, and set aside.

Place the dashi, tamari, and vinegar in a 2- or 3-quart saucepan and heat to a simmer (but not a boil) over medium heat. Cover, and set aside.

When you are ready to cook the tuna, place a large skillet over medium-high heat. When it is hot, add the oil. Add the tuna steaks and cook until seared on all four sides, 1 to 2 minutes on each side for medium-rare, 3 to 4 minutes for medium-well.

Divide the vegetable udon mixture among six shallow bowls or deep plates, and top each with a piece of tuna. (For a more dramatic presentation, try slicing the tuna and fanning the slices over the noodles.) Divide the dashi among the bowls. Garnish with herb sprigs, and serve immediately.

Serves 6

tuna steaks in saffron broth
with spicy pepper puree

In this combination of Indian and Middle Eastern flavors, the rich tuna steaks pair well with the spices and heat of the pepper puree. The broth is the perfect bridge between the two.

When buying tuna, look for the thickest portions you can get. You could even buy double-thick pieces and divide them in half after cooking.

Try this with East Indian Chickpea Smash (page 230) or Yogurt Whipped Potatoes (page 234).

For the pepper puree:

1 tablespoon olive oil
1 tablespoon minced fresh ginger
4 garlic cloves, minced
4 shallots, minced
1 small fennel bulb, cut into small dice
3 small or 2 large red bell peppers, roasted (see page 57), cored, seeded, and peeled
½ cup Vegetable Stock (page 37)
2 tablespoons cider vinegar
1 teaspoon coriander seeds
½ teaspoon cumin seeds
½ teaspoon mustard seeds
½ teaspoon cayenne pepper
½ cup panko or plain dry bread crumbs
¼ cup extra-virgin olive oil
1 teaspoon kosher salt

For the saffron broth:

1 tablespoon olive oil
2 tablespoons minced fresh ginger
6 garlic cloves, minced
4 shallots, minced
1 small fennel bulb, cut into small dice

Panko: One of the few Western-style breads used in Asian cuisines, panko is white, spiky, coarse bread crumbs that create a lighter breading than other types of commercial bread crumbs. It is sold in Asian and specialty markets.

½ cup dry white wine

12 saffron threads

4 cups Fish Fumet (page 40), Vegetable Stock (page 37), or 2 cups clam juice
    and 2 cups water

1½ teaspoons kosher salt

½ teaspoon black pepper

For the tuna:

6 8-ounce tuna steaks, about 1 to 1½ inches thick

1½ teaspoons kosher salt

1 teaspoon black pepper

1 tablespoon soy oil

Garnish:

Julienned scallions

Fragrant Chili and Spice Oil (page 44)

Prepare the pepper puree: Place a 1-quart saucepan over medium heat, and when it is hot, add the oil. Add the ginger, garlic, shallots, and fennel. Cook, stirring occasionally, until deeply browned and caramelized, 5 to 6 minutes. Add the roasted peppers, stock, and vinegar, and bring to a boil. Reduce the heat to low and simmer until all the liquid has evaporated, 6 to 8 minutes. Transfer the mixture to a food processor or blender, and process. Add the remaining puree ingredients and process until smooth. Pour into a glass or plastic container, cover, and refrigerate for up to 7 days. (Leftovers make a great sandwich spread!)

Prepare the broth: Place a 2- or 3-quart saucepan over medium-high heat, and when it is hot, add the oil. Add the ginger, garlic, shallots, and fennel and cook until lightly browned, 2 to 3 minutes. Add the wine and saffron, bring to a boil and cook until reduced by half, about 5 minutes. Add the fumet, salt, and pepper, and let return to a boil. Set aside.

Sprinkle both sides of the tuna evenly with the salt and pepper. Place a large skillet over medium-high heat, and when it is hot, add the oil. Add the tuna and cook until seared on all sides, 1 to 2 minutes per side for medium-rare.

Divide the tuna among six large shallow soup bowls or deep plates, and ladle the saffron broth around the fish. Top each serving with a dollop of Spicy Pepper Puree. Garnish with julienned scallions and a drizzle of Fragrant Chili and Spice Oil, and serve immediately.

Serves 6

rich and poor man's lobster

In New England, monkfish was commonly caught by fishermen trawling for other more marketable fish like haddock and cod. To try to sell more monkfish, also called angler fish, purveyors started calling it "the poor man's lobster" because the shape and texture of the filleted monkfish tail (the only real salable part) are reminiscent of a lobster tail. In this dish I combine both ingredients. The rich sauce, lush texture, and lightly curried spices make this unusual dish mild on the tongue. I believe pan-roasting is one of the best techniques for cooking monkfish.

Serve this with the Pan-Seared Somen Noodle Cake (page 242) or steamed jasmine rice.

For the lobster curry:

1 tablespoon minced fresh ginger

4 garlic cloves, minced

1 stalk lemongrass, outer husk discarded, inner husk minced

1 tablespoon minced galangal (see page 30), or 1 additional tablespoon fresh minced ginger

1 shallot, minced

1 tablespoon plus 2 teaspoons light sesame oil

1 star anise pod, toasted and ground

1 cardamom pod, toasted and ground

½ teaspoon coriander seeds, toasted and ground

½ teaspoon ground turmeric

¼ teaspoon cumin seeds, toasted and ground

¼ teaspoon fennel seeds, toasted and ground

1 cup pearl onions; or 2 small red onions, diced

12 fresh shiitake mushrooms

4 cups Shellfish Stock (page 41)

1 14-ounce can unsweetened coconut milk

1 tablespoon lime juice

⅓ cup sliced fresh cilantro leaves

1 pound cooked lobster meat, diced

For the monkfish:

6 6- to 8-ounce monkfish tail fillets
2 teaspoons kosher salt
1 teaspoon black pepper
1 tablespoon soy oil

Garnish:

Cilantro sprigs

Place the ginger, garlic, lemongrass, galangal, shallot, and 1 tablespoon of the sesame oil in a food processor or blender. Add the star anise, cardamom, coriander, turmeric, cumin, and fennel. Process to a smooth paste. Set aside.

Place a 4-quart saucepan over medium heat, and when it is hot, add the remaining 2 teaspoons sesame oil. Add the onions, mushrooms, and reserved spice paste, and cook until lightly browned and very aromatic, 5 to 6 minutes.

Then add the stock and bring to a boil. Cook until reduced by half, about 15 minutes. Add the coconut milk and bring to a boil. Remove the pan from the heat, and add the lime juice and cilantro. (Hold the lobster meat aside until just prior to serving.) Keep the sauce warm.

To cook the monkfish, season the fillets on both sides with the salt and pepper. Place a skillet over medium-high heat, and when it is hot, add the oil. Add the monkfish and cook for 4 minutes on each side per inch of thickness.

Add the lobster meat to the curry, and let it heat briefly. Divide the lobster curry among six deep plates, and top with the monkfish. Garnish with the cilantro sprigs, and serve.

Serves 6

cod fillet with curry tomato sauce

Sweet codfish, joyous cod. One can argue that cod was the most significant reason why explorers kept returning to the New World and settled it—cod seemed to be a never-ending resource. Unfortunately this is no longer true, but the population is in recovery through conservation methods. To help, look to buy hook and line—caught cod (check with your fishmonger). This dish plays a mellow curry and tomato sauce against the large moist white flakes of the fish. Try it with the Exotically Spiced Basmati Rice Pilaf (page 251).

For the curry tomato sauce:
1 tablespoon olive oil
¼ cup minced fresh ginger
8 garlic cloves, minced
1 small fennel bulb, diced
4 carrots, diced
2 small onions, diced
2 leeks, white parts only, halved lengthwise and cut into ¼-inch-thick slices
2 teaspoons curry powder
1 cup dry white wine
1 28-ounce can diced tomatoes, undrained
1 cup Fish Fumet (page 40), Vegetable Stock (page 37), or clam juice
1 tablespoon coarsely chopped fresh mint leaves
2 tablespoons coarsely chopped fresh cilantro leaves
1 teaspoon kosher salt
½ teaspoon black pepper

6 8-ounce cod fillets (preferably the thick center-cut portions)
2 tablespoons East Indian Spice Blend (page 26)
2 teaspoons kosher salt
1 teaspoon black pepper
1 tablespoon soy oil

Garnish:
Mint and cilantro sprigs
Fragrant Chili and Spice Oil (page 44) or Curry Oil (page 47)

Prepare the curry tomato sauce: Place a 4-quart saucepan over medium-high heat, and when it is hot, add the oil. Add the ginger and garlic and cook until lightly browned, 2 to 3 minutes. Add the fennel, carrots, onions, and leeks and cook until all the vegetables are deeply browned, caramelized, and fragrant, 6 to 8 minutes. Stir in the curry powder and wine, and bring to a boil. Cook until the liquid has almost evaporated, 8 to 10 minutes. Then add the tomatoes and their liquid, and bring to a boil. Reduce the heat to low and cook until thick, 5 to 6 minutes. Add the fumet, mint, cilantro, salt, and pepper, and bring to a boil. Immediately remove from the heat; keep warm.

Meanwhile, prepare the cod: Rub the fillets on both sides with the East Indian Spice Blend, salt, and pepper. Place a skillet over medium-high heat, and when it is hot, add the oil. Add the cod and cook until seared on all sides, about 4 minutes on each side per inch of thickness.

Divide the curry tomato sauce among six plates, and top each serving with a piece of cod. Garnish with the mint and cilantro sprigs. Drizzle with the Fragrant Chili and Spice Oil, and serve immediately.

Serves 6

This rich, buttery dish was so popular at Salamander that I thought I was going to have to take it off the menu—it just sold too well! Why? Because in a restaurant you need your staff to have a balanced workload, and when one dish is overwhelmingly popular, one guy works too hard and the other people are not able to help balance the load.

However, you can make this at home anytime! Cook the salmon gently so as not to brown the nuts too quickly. Try substituting peanuts, almonds, or pine nuts for variety. Serve the salmon with steamed rice and a simple vegetable like broccoli, asparagus, or watercress.

For the marinade:
6 8-ounce salmon fillets
1 cup Coconut Five-Spice Marinade (page 152)

For the sauce:
2 teaspoons light sesame oil
¼ cup Yellow Curry Paste (page 31)
2 tablespoons tomato paste
2 14-ounce cans coconut milk
½ teaspoon kosher salt
¼ teaspoon black pepper
Juice of 1 lime
⅓ cup sliced fresh cilantro leaves

For the salmon:
2 cups panko or plain dry bread crumbs
¼ cup chopped raw cashews
½ teaspoon kosher salt
¼ teaspoon black pepper
1 tablespoon soy oil

Garnish:
Cilantro sprigs
Cilantro Oil (page 46)

Marinate the salmon: Place the salmon and the marinade in a flat plastic or glass container, cover, and refrigerate for at least 2 and not more than 12 hours.

While the salmon is marinating, make the sauce: Place a large saucepan over medium heat, and when it is hot, add the oil. Add the curry paste and tomato paste. Cook, stirring often, until fragrant, 2 to 3 minutes. Add the coconut milk, stir to combine, and bring to a boil. Simmer until reduced by half, 14 to 16 minutes. Then remove the pan from the heat and add the salt, pepper, lime juice, and cilantro. (The sauce will keep, covered and refrigerated, for 24 hours.)

When you are ready to cook the salmon, place the panko, cashews, salt, and pepper on a plate and mix to combine. Drain the salmon and discard the marinade. Dredge the salmon in the crumb mixture to cover completely.

Place a large skillet over medium heat, and when it is hot, add the oil. Add the fillets and cook until golden, 3 to 4 minutes on each side.

If necessary, reheat the sauce very gently over low heat. Divide the sauce among six plates, and top each serving with a piece of salmon. Garnish with cilantro sprigs and drizzle with Cilantro Oil. Serve immediately.

Serves 6

crispy sole fillets with wild mushroom stew

Living in Boston, I am able to enjoy many varieties of the local sole and flounder: blackback, grays, dab, and lemon. The sweet and delicate fillets seem destined for a quick pan-fry. This recipe includes a delicate tempura batter to complement the fish and protect it during cooking. Choose milder mushrooms, such as oyster or shiitake, to pair best with the light fish fillets.

You can substitute trout, a thin slice of salmon, and even chicken breast for the sole. Serve the fillets accompanied by Pan-Seared Somen Noodle Cake (page 242) or steamed rice.

For the mushroom stew:
1 tablespoon light sesame oil
4 shallots, julienned
1 tablespoon minced fresh ginger
4 garlic cloves, minced
1 pound mixed fresh wild mushrooms (shiitake, oyster, chanterelle, portobello),
  chopped if large
2 small carrots, diced
1 small fennel bulb, diced
1 small red bell pepper, diced
1 14-ounce can unsweetened coconut milk
2 cups Fish Fumet (page 40) or Chicken Stock (page 34)
1 tablespoon soy sauce
1 teaspoon coriander seeds, toasted and cracked
About ¼ pound spinach, cut into chiffonade (very thin strips)

For the sole:
6 large egg whites
¼ cup tempura flour; or 2 tablespoons all-purpose flour and 2 tablespoons
  cornstarch or rice flour
2 teaspoons coriander seeds, toasted and cracked

2½ to 3 pounds sole fillets, trimmed
1 teaspoon kosher salt
1 teaspoon black pepper
2 tablespoons soy oil

Garnish:
4 scallions, white and green parts, cut into 1-inch diagonal pieces
⅓ cup thinly sliced fresh cilantro leaves

Prepare the mushroom stew: Place a saucepan over medium heat, and when it is hot, add the oil. Add the shallots, ginger, and garlic and cook until lightly caramelized, 2 to 3 minutes. Add the mushrooms and cook for 2 to 3 minutes. Add the carrots, fennel, and bell pepper, and cook for another 2 to 3 minutes. Add the coconut milk and cook until reduced by half or more, 10 to 12 minutes. Add the fumet and reduce by half again, 10 to 12 minutes. Remove the pan from the heat and add the soy sauce, coriander, and spinach. Keep warm.

Preheat the oven to 250°F.

Place the egg whites in a medium-size bowl and whip until they form soft peaks. Gently fold in the tempura flour and coriander.

Sprinkle the sole fillets with the salt and pepper. Place a large skillet over medium-high heat, and when it is hot, add the oil. Dip the fillets, one at a time, into the tempura batter and then carefully lay them in the skillet. Cook until golden, about 2 minutes on each side. Drain on paper towels. (Cook the fish in small batches and hold the finished pieces in the oven to keep warm.)

Divide the mushroom stew among six plates, and top with the sole fillets. Garnish with the scallions and cilantro, and serve.

Serves 6

149

poultry

Everyone's eating more and more chicken at home (although, it so happens, we aren't selling more in restaurants). This chapter will add to your repertoire of chicken dishes—and duck, quail, and Rock Cornish game hens as well. Small birds like quail and game hens make a festive dish, and allow you to serve each person his or her own bird. That way there's no jealousy or, as in my house, fighting over the dark meat!

I always cook poultry on the bone because cooking it in its most intact form yields the best results: moist, tender chicken with better flavor. Skinless, boneless chicken breasts are a great time-saver, but they will never be as flavorful. Try it my way.

coconut five-spice chicken

The five-spice powder provides the entire flavor palate for this dish: sweet, hot, fragrant, and tingly.

When working with lime leaves, look for fresh, shiny, supple leaves. Cut both sides of the leaf away from the tough stem that runs through the center, and then slice according to the recipe directions.

You can substitute pork for the chicken here. If you would like to use salmon, cod, or halibut, marinate the fish for at least 1 hour and up to 4 hours.

6 bone-in chicken breast halves or 12 bone-in thighs, trimmed of excess fat
Five-Spice Marinade (recipe follows)
1 teaspoon kosher salt
½ teaspoon black pepper
2 teaspoons light sesame oil

Place the chicken in a large nonreactive bowl, and cover with the marinade. Cover and refrigerate for at least 4 hours and up to 24 hours.

Preheat the oven to 400°F.

When you are ready to cook the chicken, drain off as much marinade as possible. Season the chicken with the salt and pepper. Place a large ovenproof skillet over medium-high heat, and when it is hot, add the oil. Add the chicken, skin side down, and cook until it is golden brown, 3 to 4 minutes. Turn the chicken pieces over, and transfer the skillet to the oven. Cook until the chicken is firm to the touch throughout and the skin is crisp, 12 to 14 minutes (18 to 20 minutes for thighs). Serve immediately.

Serves 6

five-spice marinade

1 13.5- or 14-ounce can (about 1⅔ cups) unsweetened coconut milk
2 tablespoons five-spice powder
2 tablespoons tamari or soy sauce
2 tablespoons minced fresh ginger
2 or 3 garlic cloves, minced
4 kaffir lime leaves, julienned, or zest of 2 limes

Place all the ingredients in a blender or food processor and process until they form a well-blended, homogeneous mixture. Transfer to a plastic or glass container, cover, and refrigerate for up to 2 weeks.

2 cups

black tea—brined chicken

One of my signature dishes, this amazingly moist and beautiful ebony-colored chicken was inspired by the classic Chinese tea-smoked duck. I've been serving this dish in the restaurant and to friends for 12 years now. The preparation is actually quite easy: Just be sure to start 2 to 3 days in advance in order to give the brine a chance to cool and the chicken plenty of time to soak. In spite of its ease, I suggest you practice the dish once for yourself before sharing it with friends—who will soon start begging you for more. (This recipe can be doubled easily for a crowd.)

Serve this with Glazed Sweet Potatoes (page 236) or Scallion Noodle Cakes (page 244).

Szechuan peppercorns: Taking its name from the province of China where it is grown, the Szechuan peppercorn resembles more familiar black peppercorns but is not technically a member of the same family. It's available whole or ground. Toasting the whole berries before grinding them brings out the characteristic anise flavor and aroma.

For the brine:
1 tablespoon light sesame oil
1 cup sliced fresh ginger
1 head garlic, halved horizontally to expose the cloves
3 tablespoons coriander seeds
2 tablespoons star anise pods
2 tablespoons Szechuan peppercorns
½ cup kosher salt
8 cups cold water
4 cups soy sauce
1 cup black tea leaves, tied in a cheesecloth bag
About 16 ice cubes

For the chicken:
1 3½- to 4-pound chicken, trimmed of excess fat

Prepare the brine: Place a large saucepan over medium heat, and when it is hot, add the oil. Add the ginger and garlic and cook until lightly browned, 2 to 3 minutes. Add the coriander, star anise, and peppercorns, and cook until the spices are toasted and very fragrant, 2 to 3 minutes. Then raise the heat to high, add the salt, cold water, and soy sauce, and bring to a boil. Remove the pan from the heat and add the tea. Let steep for 10 minutes. Then discard the tea.

Add the ice cubes and allow the brine to cool completely. If you are saving this for later use, transfer the brine to a 1-gallon container, cover, and refrigerate for up to 2 weeks.

Brine the chicken: Place the chicken in a very large container and cover it with the brine by 1 to 2 inches. Cover and refrigerate for at least 24 and up to 48 hours.

When you are ready to cook the chicken, preheat the oven to 400°F. Remove the chicken from the brine and discard the brine.

Place the chicken, breast side up, in a roasting pan, and cook until the exterior is mahogany and the juices run clear when a thigh is pierced with a sharp knife, 40 to 45 minutes.

After removing the chicken from the oven, let it rest for 6 to 10 minutes. Serve it on a platter, or cut it into eight pieces and serve on individual plates.

Serves 4

Black Tea–Brined Chicken

cashew-crusted chicken breasts with coconut curry sauce

I like this recipe not only for its flavor, which combines sweet, nutty coconut with fragrant, punchy curry and rich, buttery cashews, but also for its foolproof ease of preparation. The glaze acts as the glue that makes this possible, but it also adds another layer and a wonderful dimension of flavor. Adding the crust at the last minute ensures that the coconut and cashews will not burn during sautéing.

You can substitute pork loin or shrimp for the chicken.

Serve this with Scallion Noodle Cakes (page 244).

Guava paste: A thick, sweet paste made of guava, sugar, and other ingredients, guava paste is a Latin American favorite, often served in slices alongside cheeses. The paste dissolves easily in soups and sauces, making it a deliciously different sweetener. It's available in cans and tubes, in gourmet and Latin markets.

For the lemongrass glaze:
1 cup orange juice
1 cup guava paste, or 2 cups mango or pineapple juice
½ cup rice vinegar
2 tablespoons coriander seeds
2 tablespoons minced fresh ginger
2 stalks lemongrass, outer husk discarded, inner heart sliced

For the cashew crust:
½ cup unsalted cashews, toasted
¼ cup shredded unsweetened coconut, toasted and cooled
¼ cup panko or plain dry bread crumbs
2 teaspoons curry powder
2 teaspoons minced fresh ginger
½ teaspoon kosher salt
½ teaspoon black pepper

For the coconut curry sauce:
2 teaspoons soy oil
2 red bell peppers, coarsely chopped

1 onion, coarsely chopped

6 garlic cloves, coarsely chopped

1 inch fresh ginger, coarsely chopped

3 arbol chilies, coarsely chopped

1 cup Red Curry Paste (page 32)

1 14-ounce can unsweetened coconut milk

1 cup Chicken Stock (page 34)

¼ cup lime juice (2 to 3 limes)

1 teaspoon kosher salt

¼ teaspoon black pepper

For the chicken:

6 8-ounce boneless or bone-in chicken breast halves, trimmed of excess fat

2 teaspoons coriander seeds, toasted and ground

1 teaspoon kosher salt

½ teaspoon black pepper

2 teaspoons vegetable oil

Garnish:

Curry Oil (page 47)

Cilantro Oil (page 46)

Tropical Fruit Pickles (page 61)

Toasting coconut: Place a large non-stick skillet over medium heat, and when it is hot, add the coconut. Cook, shaking the pan occasionally, until the coconut is golden, about 10 minutes. Set aside until ready to use.

Prepare the glaze: Place the orange juice, guava paste, vinegar, coriander, ginger, and lemongrass in a 1½-quart stainless steel–lined saucepan and simmer over medium heat until reduced by two thirds, 15 to 20 minutes. Strain, and discard the solids. Set the glaze aside to cool. If you are preparing the glaze ahead of time, transfer it to a glass or plastic container, cover, and refrigerate for up to 2 weeks.

Prepare the cashew crust: Place the cashews, coconut, panko, curry powder, ginger, salt, and pepper in a food processor and pulse six to eight times to form a coarse, well-blended mixture. Set aside.

Prepare the sauce: Place a large heavy saucepan over medium heat, and when it is hot, add the oil. Add the bell peppers, onion, garlic, ginger, and chilies and cook until lightly caramelized, 4 to 5 minutes. Add the curry paste and cook, stirring constantly so it does not scorch, until it is very aromatic, about 2 minutes. Then add the coconut milk and stock, and bring to a boil. Cook until slightly reduced and thickened, 10 to 15 minutes. Puree the sauce with an immersion blender or in a food processor or blender, and strain it. Add the lime juice, salt, and pepper. Keep warm.

Sprinkle the chicken breasts with the coriander, salt, and pepper. Place a 10- or 12-inch sauté pan over medium heat, and when it is hot, add the oil. Add the chicken breasts, skin side down, and sauté until deep golden brown, 4 to 5 minutes per side for boneless, 6 to 8 minutes per side for bone-in. Transfer to a platter and brush liberally on all sides with the glaze. Pat the cashew crust onto the chicken.

To serve, divide the curry sauce among six plates, and top each serving with a chicken breast. Drizzle with Curry Oil and Cilantro Oil, and garnish with Tropical Fruit Pickles.

Serves 6

cider lemongrass-brined chicken wings

The interplay of sweet and savory makes this autumn-flavored brine perfect for chicken, turkey, pheasant, game hens, rabbit, and pork. It echoes the spirit of the long, cool evenings of fall, when there is a wisp of wood smoke in the air and the aromas of baked goods and roasts are wafting through the kitchen. I love those special evenings as the season turns toward the cold winter ahead.

Tropical Fruit Pickles (page 61) and Spicy Peanut Sauce (page 49) are natural accompaniments.

1 tablespoon light sesame oil
1 cup sliced fresh ginger
1 head garlic, halved horizontally to expose the cloves
2 3-inch cinnamon sticks
10 whole cloves
6 allspice berries
5 arbol chilies
2 tablespoons coriander seeds
½ cup kosher salt
6 cups apple cider
6 cups water
1 lemon, quartered
1 apple, quartered
1 pear, quartered
3 stalks lemongrass, outer husk discarded, inner heart sliced
3 pounds chicken wings, cut into individual sections

Place a large saucepan over medium heat, and when it is hot, add the oil. Add the ginger and garlic, and cook until lightly browned, 2 to 3 minutes. Add the cinnamon sticks, cloves, allspice, chilies, coriander, and salt and cook until lightly toasted, about 2 minutes. Add the cider and water, raise the heat to high, and bring to a boil.

Allspice: While many believe it to be a spice blend, allspice is in fact the tiny berry of the ever-green pimiento tree. It tastes like a blend of cinnamon, nutmeg, and cloves—hence its name. Allspice may be used in both sweet and savory cooking and is available whole and ground.

Remove the pan from the heat and add the lemon, apple, and pear quarters and the lemongrass. If you are saving the brine for later use, transfer it to a 1-gallon container. Cover and refrigerate for at least 1 hour and up to 2 weeks.

Brine the chicken wings: Place the chicken in a very large container and cover with the cold brine by 1 to 2 inches. Cover and refrigerate for at least 24 and up to 48 hours.

When you are ready to cook the chicken, preheat the broiler. Remove the chicken from the brine and discard the brine. Place the chicken wings in a single layer in a roasting pan, and broil, turning at least once, until golden caramel brown, 10 to 12 minutes. Serve immediately.

Serves 6

Chinese pears

Malaysian cooking is a crossroads of Indian, Thai, Chinese, and Muslim influences: very spicy, very hearty, and typically with strong hits of galangal, lemongrass, turmeric, coriander, and black pepper. This rub really shines through on the chicken, but it can also be used on beef, shrimp, or fish, including tuna, snapper, and bass. If you are using fish, leave the rub on for no longer than 4 hours. And if you want to use boneless chicken breasts, cook them for just 4 to 6 minutes on each side.

For the spice rub:

2 tablespoons coriander seeds
1 tablespoon star anise pods
1 tablespoon ground turmeric
1 tablespoon coarsely cracked black peppercorns
1 tablespoon minced galangal (see page 30) or fresh ginger
2 garlic cloves, minced
1 stalk lemongrass, outer husk discarded, inner heart minced
2 tablespoons chili garlic paste (see page 82)
¼ cup dark sesame oil

6 bone-in chicken breast halves, trimmed of excess fat
1 tablespoon soy oil
1 teaspoon kosher salt
½ teaspoon black pepper

Prepare the rub: Place the coriander, star anise, turmeric, and peppercorns in a skillet and cook over low heat until the spices darken and are very fragrant, 2 to 3 minutes. Set aside to cool.

Place the cooled spices in a spice grinder and process to form a coarse powder. Transfer it to a large stainless-steel or glass bowl, add the remaining rub ingredients, and stir to combine completely. Add the chicken and toss well. Cover and refrigerate for at least 2 and up to 24 hours.

When you are ready to cook the chicken, place a large skillet over medium-high heat. When it is hot, add the oil. Sprinkle the chicken breasts with the salt and pepper, and add them to the skillet, one at a time, allowing about 30 seconds between additions. Sauté until fully cooked, 8 to 10 minutes on each side. There should be no pink remaining when the chicken is fully cooked, and the chicken will feel firm when gently pressed. Serve immediately.

Serves 6

pan-roasted chicken breasts with japanese eggplant and mushrooms

The sauce here is basically a vegetable-and-mushroom stew flavored with oyster sauce. Don't let on how easy this one is—it *tastes* time-consuming!

Serve Exotically Spiced Basmati Rice Pilaf (page 251) or Yang Chow Fried Rice (page 252) alongside.

For the chicken:

6 8-ounce bone-in breast halves, trimmed of excess fat

2 tablespoons cracked coriander seeds

1 tablespoon Sweet Spice Mix (page 81)

2 teaspoons kosher salt

½ teaspoon cracked black pepper

2 teaspoons light sesame oil

For the sauce:

2 teaspoons light sesame oil

1 tablespoon minced fresh ginger

4 garlic cloves, minced

1 onion, diced

2 cups mixed fresh mushrooms (shiitake, portobello, oyster), sliced

3 or 4 small Japanese eggplants (about 1 pound), chopped

1 red bell pepper, diced

½ cup diced canned tomatoes

2 tablespoons oyster sauce

2 cups Chicken Stock (page 34)

1½ teaspoons coriander seeds

1 star anise pod
3 scallions, white and green parts, sliced into thin rings
⅓ cup sliced fresh cilantro leaves

Garnish:
Scallion Oil (page 45)

Sprinkle the chicken breasts with the coriander, Sweet Spice Mix, salt, and pepper. Cover and refrigerate for at least 2 and up to 24 hours.

Place a large skillet over medium-high heat, and when it is hot, add the oil. Add the chicken breasts, skin side down, one at a time, allowing about 30 seconds between additions, and reduce the heat to medium. Cook until golden brown, 4 to 5 minutes on each side. Set the chicken breasts aside.

Prepare the sauce: Place a large skillet over medium-high heat, and when it is hot, add the oil. Add the ginger and garlic and cook until lightly caramelized, 1 minute. Add the onion and cook until caramelized, 2 to 3 minutes. Add the mushrooms and eggplants, and cook until deeply browned and aromatic, 4 to 5 minutes (add a little more oil if necessary). Add the bell pepper, tomatoes, and oyster sauce and cook until slightly thickened, 2 to 3 minutes. Add the stock, coriander, and star anise, and bring to a boil. Reduce the heat to low. Add the scallions and the reserved chicken breasts. Cover and simmer for 10 to 12 minutes to finish cooking the chicken. When the chicken is ready, stir in the cilantro.

Divide the sauce among six plates, and top each serving with a piece of chicken. Drizzle with Scallion Oil, and serve.

Serves 6

163

stir-fried chicken with sesame and spiced walnuts

Basically a tastier version of the Cantonese stir-fry you get in your neighborhood Chinese restaurant, this easy dish is quick, colorful, and classic-looking. Scented with orange and walnuts, this is my favorite way of using boneless chicken breasts.

The trick to stir-frying lies in the temperature of the pan: It should be consistently medium-hot, which means you should wait for a moment to let the pan reheat between additions of ingredients and do not overcrowd them. Show a little patience the first couple of times you try this—the results will be worth the extra minute or two.

Serve the stir-fry with plain rice and Miso Vegetable Pickles (page 66).

You can certainly substitute whatever vegetables you have on hand for the ones listed here.

For the chicken:
1 to 1½ pounds boneless, skinless chicken breasts, trimmed of excess
   fat and cut into 1-inch-wide strips
2 teaspoons kosher salt
1 teaspoon cracked black pepper
1½ cups all-purpose flour
⅓ cup white sesame seeds
4 large eggs
¼ cup cold water

For the stir-fry liquid:
¼ cup soy sauce
2 teaspoons dark sesame oil
½ cup orange juice
2 teaspoons walnut oil
½ cup Chicken Stock (page 34)
3 tablespoons hoisin sauce

2 teaspoons light sesame oil, or more as needed
1 tablespoon minced fresh ginger
4 garlic cloves, minced
1 onion, julienned
2 small carrots, roll-cut (see page 67)
1 cup tiny broccoli florets
2 red bell peppers, diced
½ cup sliced fresh shiitake mushrooms (sliced ¼ inch thick)
1 cup finely slivered napa cabbage (chiffonade)
3 scallions, white and green parts, cut into 1-inch lengths
1 bunch watercress, stems trimmed
½ cup fresh mung bean sprouts
⅔ cup Spiced Walnuts (recipe follows)

Sprinkle the chicken with the salt and pepper.

Place the flour and sesame seeds in a shallow bowl. Place the eggs and water in another shallow bowl, and stir to combine. Dip the chicken strips in the egg wash and then dredge them in the flour mixture, coating all the pieces well. Arrange the chicken strips in a single layer on a plate or cookie sheet, cover, and refrigerate for 1 hour. Discard excess egg and flour.

While the chicken is chilling, combine all the ingredients for the stir-fry liquid in a bowl, and set aside.

Place a wok or skillet over medium-high heat, and when it is hot, add 1 teaspoon of the light sesame oil. Add the chicken, in batches, in one layer and cook until deeply browned, 1 to 2 minutes per side, adding more oil if necessary. Remove the chicken from the wok.

Reheat the wok over medium-high heat, and when it is hot, add the remaining 1 teaspoon oil. Add the ginger and garlic and cook until lightly caramelized, 1 minute. Add the onion and stir-fry for 2 minutes. Add the carrots, broccoli, bell peppers, and mushrooms and stir-fry for 3 to 4 minutes, until just tender.

Return the chicken to the wok, add the reserved stir-fry liquid, and bring to a boil. Cook until the liquid evaporates, 2 to 3 minutes. Add the cabbage, scallions, watercress, sprouts, and walnuts, and serve immediately.

Serves 6

spiced walnuts

We always serve this with Stir-Fried Chicken, and making it ahead of time saves work. I suggest you double the recipe—the walnuts are also really good with cheese, on their own as a savory snack, or sprinkled on a salad. You can freeze them for up to 2 months.

1 cup walnut halves
1 tablespoon unsalted butter, melted
2 teaspoons Korean Chili Spice Blend (page 28)

Preheat the oven to 375°F.

Place the walnut halves, melted butter, and spice blend in a bowl, and toss well. Spread the nuts in a single layer on a baking sheet, and toast until browned and aromatic, 5 to 6 minutes. Set aside to cool.

1 cup

twice-cooked philippines-style chicken with papaya relish

This dish is punctuated by the strong, piquant flavors of vinegar, garlic, and soy, characteristic of Filipino cooking. The papaya relish is equally delicious cold and is great with beef or grilled or steamed shellfish. While the relish is an essential component, if you don't have the time or energy, you can certainly purchase a bottle of chutney instead. Or you can prepare the relish a day ahead and refrigerate it; stir in the cilantro and mint at the last minute.

Choose a large skillet or braising pan to cook the chicken in the first time. The second time, the chicken can be crisped in a sauté pan or even under the broiler. Make plenty—this is one the chef will love to snack on!

Serve this chicken with Exotically Spiced Basmati Rice Pilaf (page 251). Note that you need to start preparing the chicken a day ahead.

For the chicken, stage 1:
3 pounds bone-in chicken thighs, trimmed of excess fat
1 tablespoon kosher salt
1 tablespoon cracked black pepper
1 tablespoon cracked coriander seeds
1 tablespoon soy oil
1 large onion, coarsely chopped
1 head garlic, cloves coarsely chopped
1½ cups soy sauce
1½ cups balsamic vinegar

For the chicken, stage 2:
1 cup all-purpose flour
4 large eggs, beaten with ¼ cup water
2 cups panko or plain dry bread crumbs
2 tablespoons soy oil

For the papaya relish:

1½ teaspoons light sesame oil

1 tablespoon minced fresh ginger

2 garlic cloves, minced

3 shallots, minced

1 small red bell pepper, finely diced

1 tablespoon sugar

3 tablespoons rice vinegar

½ cup pineapple juice

2 ripe papayas, cut into small dice

1 teaspoon Sweet Spice Mix (page 81)

1 teaspoon dark sesame oil

½ teaspoon kosher salt

2 teaspoons lime juice

¾ cup coarsely chopped fresh cilantro leaves

¾ cup coarsely chopped fresh mint leaves

Garnish:

Cilantro sprigs

Mint sprigs

1 bunch scallions (about 8), white and green parts, sliced paper-thin

1 or 2 limes, cut into wedges

One or 2 days before you plan to serve the chicken, do the first stage of cooking: Rinse the chicken thighs and pat them dry with paper towels. Sprinkle with the salt, pepper, and coriander. Place a heavy skillet or braising pan over medium-high heat, and when it is hot, add the oil. Add the chicken, skin side down, and cook until browned, 3 to 4 minutes per side. Remove the chicken from the pan, and drain off all but about 1 tablespoon of the fat from the skillet. Add the onion and garlic to the skillet, and cook until lightly browned and richly aromatic, 3 to 4 minutes. Return the chicken to the skillet, and add the soy sauce and balsamic vinegar. (The chicken should be covered by 1 inch of liquid; if necessary, add a little water to cover.) Bring to a boil. Then reduce the heat to low, cover, and simmer for 15 minutes. Remove the skillet from the heat, and allow the chicken to cool in the pan. Then cover and refrigerate overnight or for up to 2 days in the cooking liquid.

Papayas

When you are ready to serve the chicken, carefully remove the chicken thighs from the braising liquid. Place the flour, egg mixture, and panko in separate shallow dishes. Bread the chicken by first dredging it in the flour, then dipping it in the egg mixture, and finally rolling it in the crumbs, patting the panko firmly onto the thighs.

Place a large skillet over medium-high heat, and when it is hot, add the oil. Add the chicken in a single layer, and reduce the heat to medium. Cook until crisp, 3 to 4 minutes per side.

Prepare the papaya relish: Place a 1½-quart saucepan over medium-high heat, and when it is hot, add the oil. Add the ginger, garlic, and shallots and cook until lightly caramelized, 2 minutes. Add the bell pepper and cook for 1 minute. Then add the sugar, rice vinegar, and pineapple juice and bring to a boil. Reduce the heat and simmer until thickened and syrupy, 6 to 8 minutes. Add the papaya and quickly bring back to a boil. Immediately remove the pan from the heat and stir in the Sweet Spice Mix, oil, salt, and lime juice. Stir in the chopped cilantro and mint.

Top the chicken with the papaya relish, and garnish with the cilantro and mint sprigs, scallions, and lime wedges.

Serves 6

"Deviled" is a great old-fashioned expression for a dish in which the main ingredient has been rubbed with mustard or another hot seasoning and then breaded. In this recipe we use Rock Cornish game hens, cousins to the more common domesticated chicken. They typically average around 1 pound each and are served one per person. This recipe calls for removing the backbone and flattening the bird. You can also remove the breastbone, a butchering technique called spatchcocking. If you don't feel up to this, your butcher can do it for you. This dish is quick and flavorful.

Chinese hot mustard powder: This is a spicy mustard powder that packs a punch. Typically used for appetizers and egg rolls, it can be rehydrated with water—or, for a sweeter tropical twist, with mango juice. It is available at Asian markets.

Serve the game hens with Spicy Eggplant Chutney (page 59), Sweet and Hot Pepper Relish (page 55), and steamed rice.

6 fresh Rock Cornish game hens, wings trimmed at the second joint, backbone cut out, breastbone removed, and breast pressed flat with the palm of your hand

1 teaspoon kosher salt

1 teaspoon black pepper

½ cup Chinese hot mustard powder

½ cup mango juice

4 cups panko or plain dry bread crumbs

Preheat the oven to 375°F.

Sprinkle the hens with the salt and pepper. Place the mustard powder and mango juice in a small bowl and mix together to form a thick paste. Place the panko crumbs in a large shallow dish. Rub the paste all over the hens, and then coat the hens with the panko crumbs.

Place the hens, breast up, in a roasting pan and cook until they are golden brown and the thigh juices run clear, 30 to 35 minutes. Serve immediately.

Serves 6

grilled quail with caramel garlic sauce and cilantro

This dish is inspired by Vietnamese cooking—and by my own love for combining toasted garlic, fish sauce, and caramel. Sound strange? Maybe, but I guarantee you'll be hooked, and so will your family and friends. Try the sauce with other grilled poultry, such as turkey or chicken. Buy sleeve-boned quail for ease of eating and quicker cooking (the butcher bones everything except the drumstick and wing).

Serve the quail with Ginger Garlic Spinach (page 232) and Scallion Popovers (page 85) or Exotically Spiced Basmati Rice Pilaf (page 251).

For the quail:
¼ cup light sesame oil
2 tablespoons coarsely chopped fresh ginger
8 garlic cloves, coarsely chopped
1 stalk lemongrass, outer husk discarded, inner heart coarsely chopped
½ cup fish sauce
1 tablespoon sugar
1 tablespoon lime juice
1 tablespoon soy sauce
¼ to 1 cup sliced fresh cilantro leaves
12 fresh quail, sleeve-boned

For the sauce:
1 tablespoon light sesame oil
6 garlic cloves, minced
1 tablespoon palm sugar or white sugar
¼ cup Chicken Stock (page 34), Veal Stock (page 36), or water
2 tablespoons lime juice
½ to 1 teaspoon chili garlic paste (see page 82)
2 tablespoons fish sauce

⅓ cup sliced fresh cilantro leaves
½ teaspoon kosher salt

1 teaspoon kosher salt
1 teaspoon black pepper

Garnish:
Cilantro sprigs

Place a small saucepan over medium-high heat, and when it is hot, add the oil. Add the ginger, garlic, and lemongrass and cook until browned and aromatic, 2 to 3 minutes. Remove the pan from the heat and add the fish sauce, sugar, lime juice, soy sauce, and cilantro. Stir to combine, and set aside to cool.

Lay the quail in a shallow baking dish and top with the cooled marinade. Make sure the quail are completely covered. Cover and refrigerate for at least 1 but not more than 2 hours.

While the quail is marinating, prepare the sauce: Place a small saucepan over medium-high heat, and when it is hot, add the oil. Add the garlic and cook until browned and aromatic, 1 to 2 minutes. Add the sugar and cook until it caramelizes to a honey-brown color, 1 to 2 minutes. Slowly and carefully add the stock, and bring to a boil. Remove the pan from the heat and add the lime juice, chili garlic paste, fish sauce, cilantro, and salt. Stir to combine.

Prepare a gas, charcoal, or stovetop grill, and when it is good and hot, brush it clean. Remove the quail from the baking dish and discard the excess marinade. Sprinkle the quail with the salt and pepper, and place on the grill, breast side down. Grill until well charred, 2 to 3 minutes per side. Garnish with the cilantro sprigs, and serve.

Serves 6

slow-roasted tamarind duck

Duck is one of the most succulent birds. I like to roast it very slowly so that the duck renders most of its fat and essentially bastes itself. The result is meat that is falling apart, tender, rich, and delicious. The brine infuses the duck with subtle hints of tamarind, spices, and sweet, smoky molasses. This is a great winter dish and is perfect with Yang Chow Fried Rice (page 252) and with Watermelon Pickles (page 68) or Tropical Fruit Pickles (page 61) alongside.

For the brine:
1 tablespoon light sesame oil
4 inches fresh ginger, thinly sliced
1 head garlic, halved horizontally to expose the cloves
¼ cup coriander seeds
8 star anise pods
4 dried arbol chilies
¼ cup molasses
¼ cup Tamarind Juice (page 54)
3 tablespoons kosher salt
12 cups cold water
1 orange, quartered
2 tablespoons dark sesame oil
1 tablespoon chili oil
2 tablespoons soy sauce

2 fresh ducks, about 5 pounds each, trimmed of excess fat
2 onions, coarsely chopped
3 carrots, coarsely chopped
4 inches fresh ginger, coarsely chopped
2 heads garlic, halved horizontally to expose the cloves

For the sauce:

1 tablespoon tomato paste
¼ cup dry sherry
¼ cup rice vinegar
¼ cup orange juice
2 cups Chicken Stock (page 34) or Veal Stock (page 36)
1 tablespoon soy sauce
1 tablespoon honey
1 teaspoon Sweet Spice Mix (page 81)
½ teaspoon kosher salt
½ teaspoon black pepper

Place an 8-quart soup pot over medium-high heat, and when it is hot, add the oil. Add the ginger and garlic and brown well, 2 to 3 minutes. Add the coriander, star anise, and chilies, and toast, stirring constantly, until strongly aromatic, 1 to 2 minutes. Add the molasses, tamarind juice, salt, and water, and bring to a boil. Reduce the heat to low and simmer for 10 minutes. Remove the pot from the heat and add the orange quarters, sesame oil, chili oil, and soy sauce. Set aside to cool completely.

Place the ducks in a large container and cover with the brine by 1 to 2 inches. Cover and refrigerate for at least 2 days but not more than 3 days.

Fifteen minutes prior to cooking the duck, preheat the oven to 325°F.

Spread the onions, carrots, ginger, and garlic on the bottom of a roasting pan and lay the ducks on top, breast side up. Transfer the pan to the oven and roast, basting with the pan drippings every 30 minutes, for 2½ hours. Then increase the oven temperature to 425°F and roast for an additional 20 minutes to crisp the skin. Transfer the ducks to a platter.

Prepare the sauce while the ducks are resting: Carefully pour off all of the rendered fat from the roasting pan, keeping the vegetables in the pan. Place the roasting pan on two burners over medium heat. Add the tomato paste to the roasted vegetables and cook for 2 minutes to remove the raw flavor of the paste. Add the sherry, rice vinegar, and orange juice. Cook, stirring and scraping up the cooked bits from the bottom of the pan, until nearly dry, about 4 minutes. Add the stock, soy sauce, honey, Sweet Spice Mix, salt, and pepper. Bring to a boil, and then strain into a sauceboat.

Cut the ducks into six pieces each—separating the breast, thigh, and leg—and transfer to a serving platter. Serve immediately, with the sauce alongside.

Serves 4 to 6

meats

One of the truly American restaurant concepts is the steakhouse. Americans love red meat, whether it's steak, lamb chops, or venison. The flavor of the meat depends primarily on how it is raised for market: Smart, sustainable production methods always ensure the best quality, so look for naturally raised or organic meats. The texture and flavor are worth the premium price.

I always season meats well, using lots of spices and often marinades or brines. I also always cook meat at a high temperature on a hot grill, or with the oven at 425°F and the sauté pan over medium-high heat. The result is greater caramelization, deeper color in the pan sauces, and richer flavors overall. And if you like your steaks or chops or roast medium-rare, cooking them at a good high heat sears that exterior and cooks the outer layer while leaving that rosy red center. Mmmm . . .

indian-spiced leg of lamb
with creamy yogurt sauce

I love cooking lamb: The earthy red meat and the caramelized exterior, laden with craggy bits of garlic and spices, are great gastronomic pleasures. In this dish, the creamy sauce contrasts with and nicely complements the strong flavor of the lamb.

Other fruit-and-nut combinations you might try in the sauce include cashews and golden raisins, almonds and black raisins, or walnuts and apricots.

I try to buy Stonyfield Farm organic yogurt. You can use whole-fat, low-fat, or even nonfat yogurt for this dish.

Accompany the lamb with Exotically Spiced Basmati Rice Pilaf (page 251).

For the lamb:
1 boneless leg of lamb (5 to 6 pounds) butterflied and cleaned of excess
   fat and silver skin (your butcher can do this)
6 whole cloves
6 cardamom pods
2 teaspoons coriander seeds
2 teaspoons cumin seeds
1 teaspoon anise seeds
1 teaspoon ground turmeric
2 teaspoons kosher salt
1 teaspoon black pepper

For the sauce:
1 tablespoon unsalted butter
2 small onions, diced
1 fennel bulb, diced
2 carrots, diced
1½ teaspoons minced fresh ginger
4 garlic cloves, minced
½ cup unsalted pistachios, toasted
2 tablespoons tomato paste

1 cup mango or pineapple juice
1½ cups Veal Stock (page 36)
¼ cup golden raisins
1½ cups plain yogurt
½ teaspoon kosher salt
½ teaspoon black pepper
⅓ cup sliced fresh cilantro leaves

Garnish:
Fragrant Chili and Spice Oil (page 44) or Curry Oil (page 47)

Spread the lamb out on a cutting board. The butterflied leg should be about the same thickness all across. If necessary, pound the meat with a mallet to achieve this.

Place the cloves, cardamom pods, coriander, cumin, anise seeds, and turmeric in a spice grinder and grind to a fine powder. Rub half of the spice mixture into the lamb, and sprinkle with 1 teaspoon of the salt and ½ teaspoon of the pepper. Roll the meat up tightly and tie it with butcher's twine. Sprinkle the exterior of the lamb with the remaining 1 teaspoon salt and ½ teaspoon pepper. Reserve the remaining spice mix for the sauce.

Preheat the oven to 400°F.

Place the lamb on a rack in a roasting pan, and place it in the oven. Lower the heat to 350° to 360°F and roast until the internal temperature reaches 110° to 115°F for medium-rare to medium, about 2 to 2½ hours. Every 30 minutes, turn the meat a quarter turn and baste it with the pan drippings. Set the lamb aside for 10 to 15 minutes before slicing.

While the lamb is resting, prepare the sauce: Place the butter in a saucepan over medium heat, and when it is melted, add the onions, fennel, and carrots. Cook until lightly caramelized, 3 to 5 minutes. Add the ginger and garlic and cook for 1 to 2 minutes. Add the reserved spice mixture and the pistachios, and toast until fragrant, about 1 to 2 minutes. Add the tomato paste and cook, stirring constantly, for 2 minutes. Add the mango juice, bring to a boil, and boil until the mixture is reduced by half, 5 minutes. Then add the stock and reduce by half again, 6 to 8 minutes. Stir in the raisins and yogurt, and simmer until heated through. Stir in the salt, pepper, and cilantro.

Slice the lamb. Spoon the sauce onto six plates, arrange slices of lamb on top, and drizzle the lamb with Fragrant Chili and Spice Oil or Curry Oil. Serve immediately.

Serves 6

ginger-and-mustard-braised rabbit with wild mushrooms

Sweet and tender, rabbit is wonderful; I don't know why anyone says it tastes like chicken breast. Fuller in character and much leaner (so be sure not to overcook it), rabbit is by far the tastier of the two. This recipe is an excellent and straightforward approach to cooking rabbit at home. Try it when you want to spend a day in the kitchen. Take your time—there can be no rushing here. Assume one rabbit for two people, and unless you are a pro, ask your butcher to divide the rabbit in half for you. This dish pairs well with either a white or a red burgundy, perhaps to be determined by the season of the year.

Serve this as a stew over steamed rice, Pan-Seared Somen Noodle Cake (page 242), or Yogurt Whipped Potatoes (page 234).

3 rabbits, dressed, about 1½ pounds each, split in half lengthwise
2 teaspoons kosher salt
1 teaspoon cracked black pepper
¼ cup Dijon mustard
2 tablespoons minced fresh ginger
6 garlic cloves, minced
1 cup chickpea flour or all-purpose flour
12 bacon slices (about ½ pound)
1 tablespoon light sesame oil
1 large onion, diced
2 carrots, diced
2 celery stalks, diced
2 cups (about 1 pound) mixed fresh wild mushrooms, such as chanterelles, morels, and
*   shiitakes, sliced*
1 tablespoon tomato paste
1 teaspoon brown or yellow mustard seeds
½ teaspoon cumin seeds

1 cup dry white wine
6 cups Veal Stock (page 36) or Chicken Stock (page 34)
½ cup sliced fresh cilantro leaves

Divide the rabbits into six pieces: forelegs, hind legs, and the saddles cut in half laterally. Sprinkle with the salt and pepper.

Combine the mustard, ginger, and garlic in a large bowl. Add the rabbit pieces, and toss to coat them well. Cover and refrigerate for at least 6 hours or overnight.

Dust the marinated rabbit with the flour. Wrap the six saddle pieces with the bacon, using bamboo skewers or wooden toothpicks if needed to keep them rolled tightly.

Place a large Dutch oven over medium-high heat, and when it is hot, add the oil. Add the rabbit, three or four pieces at a time, and sear until deeply golden, 2 to 3 minutes per side. Repeat until all the rabbit is seared. Remove the rabbit from the pan.

Add the onion, carrots, celery, and mushrooms to the braising pan and cook until lightly caramelized and aromatic, 4 to 5 minutes. Add the tomato paste, mustard seeds, cumin seeds, and wine, and bring to a boil. Cook until reduced by half, 3 to 5 minutes. Add the stock and the rabbit legs (reserve the saddles), and bring to a boil. Reduce the heat to low and simmer, covered, skimming off the foam when necessary, for about 20 minutes. Add the rabbit saddles, cover, and simmer for another 20 minutes. Stir in the cilantro just prior to serving.

Serves 6

grilled soy-soaked flank steak over crispy noodles

As a kid, I ate a lot of flank steak, always soaked in very strong Mediterranean-style marinades. I love the flavor and texture of flank steak and believe that it must be grilled: grilling will give the hottest cooking surface. The charred quality of the meat is a perfect complement to this classic Asian-flavored marinade. (I don't use strong vinegars or wine in my marinades because I believe they affect the meat in an adverse manner.)

You can make this more kid-friendly by leaving the spices out of the marinade and substituting chicken drumsticks for the flank steak.

For the marinade:
2 tablespoons coriander seeds
2 tablespoons star anise pods
1 tablespoon Szechuan peppercorns
3 arbol chilies
4 garlic cloves, smashed
2 inches fresh ginger, sliced
1 cup soy sauce
1 cup water
⅓ cup honey
½ cup orange juice

3 pounds flank steak, cleaned and trimmed

For the sauce:
2 teaspoons dark sesame oil
1 teaspoon minced fresh ginger
2 cloves garlic, minced
1 teaspoon chili garlic paste (see page 82)
1 tablespoon oyster sauce

Fresh yellow Chinese noodles: These are wheat noodles, prepared with eggs. They are similar in cut to spaghetti and are easy to prepare: Simply drop the fresh noodles into boiling water, and when the water returns to a boil, drain them. They are available at Asian markets.

1 tablespoon hoisin sauce

1 tablespoon mushroom soy sauce

2 teaspoons Sweet Spice Mix (page 81)

1 tablespoon tomato paste

½ cup orange juice

2 cups Veal Stock (page 36)

For the noodle cake:

1 teaspoon dark sesame oil

1 pound fresh yellow Chinese noodles

½ cup water

For the stir-fry:

2 teaspoons light sesame oil

1 tablespoon minced fresh ginger

4 garlic cloves, minced

2 red onions, julienned

1 red bell pepper, julienned

1 green or yellow bell pepper, julienned

4 scallions, white and green parts, cut into 1-inch lengths

2 cups (1 pound) mixed fresh mushrooms, including a combination of oyster, shiitake,
   and portobello, sliced

1 teaspoon kosher salt

½ teaspoon cracked black pepper

At a Chinese noodle shop

Prepare the marinade: Place the coriander, star anise, Szechuan peppercorns, and chilies in a skillet over medium heat and toast, stirring often, until dark and aromatic, 1 to 2 minutes. Set aside to cool for 5 minutes. Then grind the spices to a coarse powder in a spice grinder.

Place the garlic, ginger, ground toasted spices, soy sauce, water, honey, and orange juice in a large plastic or glass container or bowl and mix well. Add the flank steak, cover, and refrigerate for at least 1 hour on each side but not more than 4 hours.

Prepare the sauce: Place a 1½-quart saucepan over medium-high heat, and when it is hot, add the oil. Add the ginger and garlic and cook until lightly caramelized, 1 to 2 minutes. Add the chili garlic paste, oyster sauce, hoisin, soy sauce, Sweet Spice Mix, tomato paste, and orange juice. Bring to a boil and cook until reduced by half, 4 to 5 minutes. Add the stock and reduce by half again, 10 to 12 minutes. Keep warm. (The sauce can be prepared up to 2 days ahead and gently reheated.)

Prepare the crispy noodle cakes: Place a 12- or 14-inch nonstick skillet over medium-high heat, and when it is hot, add the oil. Add the noodles and press them firmly into the pan to form a cake. Allow the noodles to brown lightly, and then add the water. (The water will steam the noodles and cook them through.) Allow all the water to evaporate and the cake to become crisp again before flipping it over. Cook the second side until crisp, 3 to 4 minutes (without any water). Leave the cake in the skillet and keep it warm while you grill the steak.

Prepare a gas or charcoal grill, and get it good and hot.

Drain the flank steak well, and place on the grill. Cook for 3 to 4 minutes per side for medium-rare; 4 to 5 minutes per side for medium. Remove the steak from the grill and let it rest on a cutting board for 3 to 5 minutes.

While the steak is resting, prepare the stir-fry: Place a wok or skillet over medium-high heat, and when it is hot, add the oil. Add the ginger and garlic and cook until lightly caramelized, 1 to 2 minutes. Add the red onions, bell peppers, scallions, and mushrooms. Stir-fry, tossing often, until the vegetables are light brown, tender, and fragrant, 2 to 3 minutes. Season with the salt and pepper.

Remove the crisp noodle cake from the skillet and cut it into six wedges. Place one wedge on each plate. Thinly slice the flank steak, and arrange the slices over the noodle cake. Drizzle with the sauce, and top it all with the stir-fry.

Serves 6

beef short ribs braised
with sweet and sour onions

Sweet and sour with just a touch of fragrant star anise, these ribs are a big favorite of mine; they are succulent, rich, and falling off the bone. If there is any drawback to this recipe, it is that short ribs are no longer as inexpensive as they once were.

Serve the ribs over Sesame Parsnips (page 235) or Yang Chow Fried Rice (page 252).

For the ribs:

4 pounds beef short ribs
1 tablespoon kosher salt
1 tablespoon cracked black pepper
3 teaspoons soy or canola oil
1 large onion, coarsely chopped
2 carrots, coarsely chopped
2 celery stalks, coarsely chopped
1 head garlic, halved horizontally to expose the cloves
3 inches fresh ginger, sliced
1 cup dry red wine
8 cups Veal Stock (page 36)

For the sauce:

2 teaspoons light sesame oil
3 large onions, julienned
1 tablespoon minced fresh ginger
4 garlic cloves, minced
¼ cup rice vinegar
1 cup pineapple or mango juice
2 tablespoons tomato paste
2 tablespoons hoisin sauce
⅓ cup Tamarind Juice (page 54)
3 tablespoons soy sauce
1 tablespoon star anise pods, toasted and ground

¼ cup fresh Thai basil leaves, stems removed and leaves sliced
1 teaspoon kosher salt
1 teaspoon black pepper

Sprinkle the ribs with the salt and pepper. Place a 3½- to 5-quart Dutch oven over medium-high heat, and when it is hot, add 1½ teaspoons of the oil. Add the ribs and sear on all sides until deeply browned, 2 to 3 minutes per side. Transfer the seared ribs to a platter. Discard the fat from the pan and reheat the pan over medium-high heat. When it is hot, add the remaining 1½ teaspoons oil. Add the onion, carrots, celery, garlic, and ginger and cook until caramelized, brown and fragrant, 4 to 5 minutes. Add the wine and cook until it is reduced to 2 tablespoons, 3 to 5 minutes. Add the stock, return the ribs to the pan, and bring to a boil over medium-high heat. Reduce the heat to low and simmer, skimming off the foam when necessary, until the meat is tender and pulling away from the bone, about 1½ hours. Remove the pan from the heat and allow the ribs to cool in the cooking liquid, 30 to 60 minutes.

Remove the ribs from the liquid (cover and refrigerate if not serving the same day). Strain the braising liquid (there should be 6 to 8 cups); discard the solids.

Prepare the sauce: Place a 3-quart saucepan over medium-high heat, and when it is hot, add the oil. Add the onions, ginger, and garlic and cook until deeply caramelized, 6 to 8 minutes. Add the rice vinegar, pineapple juice, tomato paste, hoisin, and tamarind juice. Cook until reduced by half, 3 to 5 minutes. Add the reserved braising liquid and bring to a boil. Cook until reduced to 3 cups, about 20 minutes. Remove the pan from the heat and add the soy sauce, star anise, Thai basil, salt, and pepper. Keep warm.

While the sauce is cooking, preheat the oven to 375°F.

Place the short ribs in a roasting pan and place it in the oven. Roast until heated through, 14 to 16 minutes (depending on starting temperature of ribs).

Divide the ribs among six plates, top with the sauce, and serve.

Serves 6

szechuan peppercorn–rubbed rib-eye steak with ginger demi-glace

To me, the rib-eye is a noble steak. I love the richness of the well-marbled meat and the tenderness of this premier cut. By any other name, this is Chinese *steak au poivre*.

Instead of buying six 12-ounce steaks, I recommend that you buy three 24-ounce steaks. This way you will have a thicker steak to grill, which will give you a great crusty seared surface for the peppercorns and a juicier, more tender, and more rare interior. Smaller rib-eyes will be too thin and just won't be as good—take my word for it!

Serve Yogurt Whipped Potatoes (page 234) and a plain green vegetable or Ginger Garlic Spinach (page 232) with the steaks.

For the steaks:
3 24-ounce rib-eye steaks
1 tablespoon minced fresh ginger
6 garlic cloves, minced
½ cup light sesame oil
2 tablespoons Szechuan peppercorns
2 tablespoons black peppercorns
2 tablespoons coriander seeds
2 teaspoons kosher salt

For the demi-glace:
2 teaspoons dark sesame oil
4 shallots, minced
½ cup dry red wine
½ cup port
2 cups Veal Stock (page 36)
2 teaspoons minced fresh ginger
1 tablespoon cold unsalted butter

Place the steaks in a large bowl and toss with the ginger, garlic, and oil. Cover and refrigerate for at least 4 and up to 24 hours.

Remove the steaks from the marinade and drain them well.

Place the Szechuan peppercorns, black peppercorns, and coriander seeds in a small skillet and toast over medium heat, stirring often, until darker and very fragrant, 1 to 2 minutes. Allow the spices to cool. Then place them in a spice grinder and pulse to a coarse grind. Combine the ground spices with the salt. Rub the spice mixture onto the steaks.

Prepare a gas or barbecue grill, and when it is good and hot, put the steaks on it. Cook the steaks for 3 to 4 minutes per side for medium-rare. Transfer the steaks to a platter and allow to rest for 10 to 15 minutes.

While the steaks are resting, prepare the sauce: Place a 1-quart saucepan over medium-high heat, and when it is hot, add the oil. Add the shallots and cook until lightly caramelized, 2 to 3 minutes. Add the red wine and port, and bring to a boil. Cook until reduced to ¼ cup, 5 to 8 minutes. Then add the stock and bring to a boil. Reduce the heat to low and simmer for 5 minutes. Stir in the ginger and butter.

Ladle the sauce over the steaks, and serve immediately.

Serves 6

Szechuan
Peppercorn—
Rubbed
Rib-Eye
Steak with
Ginger
Demi-Glace,
Yogurt
Whipped
Potatoes,
and Spicy
Daikon

grilled sirloin steak with spicy stir-fried shrimp and watercress

A few years ago, two huge New England Patriots football players came into Salamander, accompanied by their girlfriends and two very big appetites. They stopped by the open grill, and as we chatted, they tried to impress upon me how hungry they were and how much they were going to eat. Basically, their question was a challenge: Are you going to be able to fill me up?

I told them that I had never sent anyone away hungry and we would create a dish especially for them—but I wasn't taking any chances. I made each of them a large steak (of a size to normally feed two) and then topped each steak with about half a pound of stir-fried shrimp in a moderately spicy butter. It's since become a signature dish. Essentially a surf-and-turf, this steak will appeal to the most "meat and potatoes" person you know!

Serve the steaks over Scallion Noodle Cakes (page 244) or steamed rice.

Shrimp paste: With its dark color and funky aroma, shrimp paste may be considered the ugly duckling of Asian cuisine. Made by grinding up salted fermented shrimp, it has a strong salty, fishy flavor and is used (sparingly) in many Asian preparations, including soups, sauces, and rice dishes. The pungent odor dissipates somewhat during cooking.

For the flavored butter:

1 tablespoon dark sesame oil
1 tablespoon minced fresh ginger
2 or 3 garlic cloves, minced
1 tablespoon soy sauce
2 teaspoons chili garlic paste (see page 82)
1 teaspoon shrimp paste
8 tablespoons (1 stick) unsalted butter, at room temperature

6 12-ounce sirloin steaks
1 tablespoon light sesame oil
2 teaspoons kosher salt
1 teaspoon black pepper
1 tablespoon Sweet Spice Mix (page 81)

1 pound jumbo (15 count) shrimp, peeled and deveined
3 bunches watercress, bottom inch of stems removed
1 cup Veal Stock (page 36)

Prepare the flavored butter: Place a small skillet over medium-high heat, and when it is hot, add the oil. Add the ginger and garlic and cook until lightly caramelized, 1 to 2 minutes. Transfer the mixture to a bowl, and add the soy sauce, chili garlic paste, and shrimp paste. Stir to combine. Add the butter and stir until fully blended. Set aside. (This can be prepared 2 to 3 days in advance and refrigerated, or frozen for up to 3 months.)

Prepare a gas or charcoal grill and get it good and hot.

Rub the steaks with the oil and sprinkle with the salt, pepper, and Sweet Spice Mix. Place the steaks on the grill and cook for 3 to 4 minutes per side for medium-rare. Transfer the steaks to a serving platter and allow them to rest for 10 to 15 minutes.

While the steaks are resting, place a large skillet over medium-high heat, and when it is hot, add half of the reserved flavored butter. Add the shrimp and cook for 2 minutes. Add the watercress and cook until just barely wilted, about 1 minute. Spoon the watercress and shrimp over the steaks. Add the stock to the skillet and bring to a boil. Remove the skillet from the heat, swirl in the remaining flavored butter, and pour the sauce over the steaks.

Serves 6

pork tenderloin with guava glaze

I could definitely eat pork every day. There's a wide range of quality in the market, and I suggest you buy the best you can find: Niman Ranch is great. What I like so much about this recipe is that it is easy to prepare and so yummy with its tropical guava-laced glaze. Versatile, sweet and tangy, the glaze works well as a marinade, as a glaze, and as a sauce. Try it with chicken breasts, turkey cutlets, or spare ribs.

Serve the pork with steamed rice. Sweet Curried Mango Chutney (page 58) or Spicy Daikon (page 62) makes a great accompaniment.

For the guava glaze:
1 tablespoon light sesame oil
2 shallots, minced
4 garlic cloves, minced
1 tablespoon minced fresh ginger
2 teaspoons Sweet Spice Mix (page 81)
⅓ cup rice vinegar
¼ cup orange juice
1 tablespoon tomato paste
1 cup guava paste (see page 155)
½ cup water
1 teaspoon chili garlic paste (see page 82)
2 teaspoons kosher salt
½ teaspoon black pepper

For the pork:
4 pork tenderloins (about 2½ to 3 pounds total), trimmed of silver skin
1 tablespoon light sesame oil
1 teaspoon kosher salt
1 teaspoon black pepper

Pork Tenderloin with Guava Glaze and Sweet Curried Mango Chutney

Prepare the glaze: Place a saucepan over medium-high heat, and when it is hot, add the oil. Add the shallots, garlic, and ginger and cook until lightly caramelized, 2 minutes. Add the Sweet Spice Mix and toast for 1 minute. Add the rice vinegar, orange juice, and tomato paste and bring to a boil. Cook until reduced by two thirds, 5 to 6 minutes. Add the guava paste, water, chili garlic paste, salt, and pepper, and bring to a boil. Reduce the heat to low and simmer until the mixture is thick and coats the back of a spoon, 15 to 20 minutes. Allow to cool completely. (This will keep in the refrigerator for up to 2 weeks.)

Cut the pork tenderloins into 1 to 1½-inch-thick medallions and place them in a singer layer in a glass container. Add about half of the cooled guava glaze, and toss to combine. Cover, and refrigerate for at least 6 and up to 24 hours. (Reserve the remaining glaze.)

Preheat a gas or charcoal grill, a stovetop grill pan, or a skillet until very hot. Drain the pork, and toss it with the oil, salt, and pepper. Place the pork slices on the grill and cook for 2 to 3 minutes per side, brushing them with the remaining glaze.

Serve immediately, with additional guava glaze as a sauce.

Serves 6

honey and five-spice barbecued pork ribs

Don't you just love ribs? Once in a while we like to beat the winter blues and get the grill going in the snow! You could be a little adventurous and serve these ribs with grilled bananas or pineapple brushed with a savory glaze. For this recipe, you first brine the pork in order to get the deepest flavor and to retain as much moisture as possible during grilling. Start 1 or 2 days ahead of time and have fun. You can double or triple this recipe for a party.

These ribs are great with Tamarind Fruits (page 53) and Yang Chow Fried Rice (page 252) and/or Watermelon Pickles (page 68).

For the brine:
1 tablespoon light sesame oil
2 inches fresh ginger, sliced
6 garlic cloves, smashed
2 tablespoons star anise pods
1 teaspoon anise seeds
2 tablespoons coriander seeds
1 3-inch cinnamon stick
½ teaspoon whole cloves
3 arbol chilies
2 teaspoons annato seeds
1 cup honey
¼ cup kosher salt
¼ cup soy sauce
8 cups water

4 to 5 pounds pork rib racks (about 2 large racks)

Annatto seeds: More than fifty seeds grow inside each prickly orange pod at the end of the branches of the annatto tree. The seeds are covered with a reddish aril that is the source of an orange-yellow dye, used as a natural source of food coloring for margarine, cheeses, and other yellow or orange foods. If you use annatto in a spice rub or in a stew, the dish will pick up that orange hue. Annatto shrubs grow throughout South and Central America, the Caribbean, and in some parts of Mexico.

For the glaze:

1 cup honey

1 cup rice vinegar

¼ cup soy sauce

3 inches fresh ginger, sliced

1 teaspoon dark sesame oil

3 tablespoons five-spice powder

Prepare the brine: Place a 6- to 8-quart Dutch oven over medium-high heat, and when it is hot, add the oil. Add the ginger and garlic and cook for 2 to 3 minutes. Add the star anise, anise seeds, coriander, cinnamon stick, cloves, chilies, and annatto seeds. Cook, stirring regularly, until the spices are toasted and aromatic, 2 to 3 minutes.

Add the honey, bring to a boil and cook until caramelized, 4 to 5 minutes. Add the salt, soy sauce, and water, and bring to a boil.

Add the pork ribs and bring back to a boil. Then reduce the heat and simmer for 10 minutes. Remove the pan from the heat and allow the ribs to cool in the brine. Then refrigerate the ribs in the brine overnight, or up to 24 hours.

Prepare the glaze: Place the honey in a heavy saucepan over medium heat and bring to a boil. Allow to caramelize, 5 to 6 minutes. Carefully add the vinegar, soy sauce, ginger, sesame oil, and five-spice powder, and bring to a boil. Cook until reduced by one third, 5 to 6 minutes. Strain the glaze.

Build a mellow smoky fire in your grill. Slowly grill and smoke the rib racks for 30 to 45 minutes, brushing both sides with the glaze during the last 5 minutes of cooking.

To test for doneness: You should be able to pull a rib of the end of the rack rather easily.

Cut the racks into individual portions, and serve.

Serves 6

vegetarian entrees

Great vegetarian entrees are few and far between. People who make the choice to eat a primarily vegetable-based diet need to be concerned about balanced nutrition, especially sources of protein, so I always try to make vegetarian entrees as complete as possible. As often as I can, I combine grains, legumes, and vegetables, and I always aim for variety in both ingredients and flavor palettes. The measure of a great vegetable entree is how much it appeals to a steak eater. I think these do!

vegetable pie with spinach, raisins, and *ras el hanout*

The North African spice blend *ras el hanout* is said to be a powerful aphrodisiac. It contains rose petals and Spanish fly beetle along with a blend of many spices including nutmeg, ginger, and peppercorns. Although it can be ordered by mail and sometimes purchased at Middle Eastern groceries, it is not always easy to come by. An interesting and more readily available substitute is the Kashmiri spice blend *garam masala,* although, to my knowledge, there are no claims made for the same aphrodisiac qualities.

You can make this pie, as we do, with only a top crust of flavored cracked wheat, or you can bake it in a pastry shell. Serve Golden Shallot Relish (page 56), Spicy Eggplant Chutney (page 59), and a vegetable such as green beans or asparagus alongside.

For the filling:
1 tablespoon olive oil
1 tablespoon minced fresh ginger
4 garlic cloves, minced
2 small onions, diced
2 small carrots, diced
1 fennel bulb, diced
1 tablespoon ras el hanout
1 teaspoon kosher salt
½ teaspoon black pepper
½ cup dry white wine
½ cup raisins
2 bunches (about 1½ pounds) fresh spinach,
washed, stems removed, and cut in very thin strips
(chiffonade)

For the crust:

1 cup coarse bulgur

1 cup hot water

¼ cup orange juice

2 tablespoons lemon juice

1 bunch fresh thyme, stems removed

1½ teaspoons kosher salt

1 teaspoon black pepper

¾ cup walnut halves or pieces

1 tablespoon olive oil

Prepare the filling: Place a skillet over medium-high heat, and when it is hot, add the oil. Add the ginger and garlic and sauté until lightly caramelized, about 2 minutes. Add the onions, carrots, and fennel and sauté until all are lightly caramelized, 4 to 5 minutes. Add the *ras el hanout* and cook until very fragrant, about 1 minute. Add the salt, pepper, wine, and raisins. Bring to a boil and cook until the wine has evaporated, 3 to 5 minutes. Add the spinach and stir until just wilted, 1 to 2 minutes. Set aside to cool. (This can be made up to 1 day ahead. Cool to room temperature, cover tightly, and refrigerate until ready to use.)

Prepare the crust: Place the bulgur in a large mixing bowl, and add the hot water, orange juice, and lemon juice. Cover the bowl tightly with plastic wrap and allow it to stand until the bulgur is rehydrated, about 20 minutes. Then fluff the bulgur with a fork, and add the thyme, 1 teaspoon of the salt, and ½ teaspoon of the pepper. Mix to combine.

Preheat the oven to 375°F.

In a small bowl, toss the walnuts with the olive oil, remaining ½ teaspoon salt, and remaining ½ teaspoon pepper. Place the nuts in a single layer on a baking sheet and toast in the oven, turning once, until deep brown and very fragrant, 5 to 7 minutes. Add the walnuts to the bulgur and mix well. (Leave the oven on.)

Place the filling in six individual gratin dishes, a large casserole, or an ovenproof skillet. Top with the bulgur mixture and bake until the top is brown and slightly crisp, 10 to 12 minutes for individual gratin dishes, 18 to 20 minutes for a single large dish.

Serves 6

butternut squash, pearl onions, and bok choy with green curry

I first had this surprisingly easy and filling vegetarian curry when I was staying on a riverboat hostel in Ayutthaya, a preserved ancient city in Thailand. Served as a soup or an entree, it is best made ahead of time and kept refrigerated for 1 to 2 days to allow the flavors to develop (reheat and add the cilantro, scallions, and soy sauce just before serving). If you want to reduce the calorie content, you can substitute light coconut milk, available in most well-stocked grocery stores.

Serve the curry with steamed rice and a favorite chutney or the Tamarind Fruits (page 53).

1 tablespoon light sesame oil
1 cup (1 pint) pearl onions
1 carrot, diced
1 red bell pepper, diced
1 tablespoon minced fresh ginger
4 garlic cloves, minced
1 tablespoon Southeast Asian Green Curry Paste (page 29)
2 tablespoons Sweet Spice Mix (page 81)
1 14-ounce can unsweetened coconut milk
2 teaspoons kosher salt
1 teaspoon black pepper
1 head bok choy, cut into wide diagonal slices
1 butternut squash, cut into large dice
1 pound fingerling or other small potatoes, halved
2 cups Vegetable Stock (page 37) or water
¼ to 1 cup sliced fresh cilantro leaves
2 or 3 scallions, white and green parts, sliced
1 tablespoon soy sauce

Bok choy: Also known as Chinese mustard cabbage, bok choy has white celery-like stalks topped with large dark green leaves. Excellent in stir-fries and soups, cooked bok choy has a mild, sweet flavor. Bok choy is fat-free, low in calories and sodium, and an excellent source of vitamins C and A.

Place a 3- or 4-quart saucepan over medium heat, and when it is hot, add the oil. Add the pearl onions, reduce the heat to medium-low, and cook until caramelized, 4 to 5 minutes. Raise the heat to high and add the carrot and bell pepper. Cook, stirring often, until light brown and aromatic, 3 to 4 minutes. Add the ginger and garlic and cook until lightly browned and fragrant, 2 to 3 minutes. Add the green curry paste and Sweet Spice Mix and cook for 1 to 2 minutes. Add the coconut milk, salt, and pepper, and bring to a boil. Reduce the heat to low and simmer until reduced by half and very thick, about 5 minutes.

Add the bok choy, squash, potatoes, and stock, and bring back to a boil. Reduce the heat to low and simmer until the potatoes are tender and the squash is just beginning to fall apart, 15 to 20 minutes.

Remove the pan from the heat, and stir in the cilantro, scallions, and soy sauce. Serve immediately.

Serves 6

Organic
choy

roasted peanut soup
with pickled cucumbers

When I was growing up in the South, peanut soup was often served at the holidays. In fact, we ate peanuts boiled, roasted, raw, candied, and crushed! This Asian version is barely related to what I had growing up, but it is truly in the Salamander style and now I serve it at holidays. It is one of the most popular soups at the restaurant, where we often garnish it with vegetable or meat satay skewers, cilantro leaves, and julienned scallions. It can be prepared a day ahead.

For the cucumbers:

1 cup rice vinegar

1 cup mirin

1 tablespoon holy basil chili paste

1 teaspoon kosher salt

1 teaspoon black pepper

2 English (hothouse) cucumbers, halved lengthwise and thinly sliced on the diagonal

For the peanut soup:

1 tablespoon dark sesame oil

1 Spanish onion, diced

2 tablespoons minced fresh ginger

8 garlic cloves, minced

1 stalk lemongrass, outer husk discarded, inner heart sliced

¼ cup tomato paste

1 heaping cup natural unsweetened peanut butter

2 tablespoons holy basil chili paste

2 teaspoons ground coriander

6 cups Vegetable Stock (page 37)

1 14-ounce can unsweetened coconut milk

2 cups unsalted peanuts, toasted until dark golden brown

¼ cup soy sauce

½ cup rice vinegar

3 tablespoons mirin

1 teaspoon kosher salt

½ teaspoon black pepper

Prepare the cucumbers: Place the rice vinegar, mirin, chili paste, salt, and pepper in a bowl. Add the cucumbers, cover, and refrigerate overnight.

Prepare the soup: Place a 5-quart, heavy-bottomed soup pot over medium-high heat, and when it is hot, add the oil. Add the onion, ginger, garlic, and lemongrass, and cook until lightly caramelized, 3 to 4 minutes. Reduce the heat to low, and add the tomato paste, peanut butter, chili paste, and coriander. Cook, stirring constantly, until dark and fragrant (be careful not to let it scorch), 2 to 3 minutes.

Add the stock and coconut milk and bring to a boil. Reduce the heat to low and add the roasted peanuts, soy sauce, vinegar, and mirin. Simmer for 5 minutes. Transfer the soup to a blender and puree. Add the salt and pepper.

Reheat the soup, if necessary, and warm six soup plates. Divide the soup among the plates and garnish with the pickled cucumbers.

Serves 6

Holy basil chili paste: A mixture of holy basil (also Thai basil) and red chili paste, this spicy condiment is essential to many Thai dishes. It's available at Asian markets and specialty foods stores.

skillet of fragrant rice with tofu and asian greens

Somewhat like an Asian baked rice dish or paella, this quick one-pan meal is healthful, tasty, and satisfying. I often eat this late at night if I have had a long day. You can easily add or substitute ingredients you have on hand: mushrooms, squash, or spinach, for example.

1 tablespoon light sesame oil

1 tablespoon minced fresh ginger

1 tablespoon minced garlic

1 stalk lemongrass, outer husk discarded, inner heart minced

1 red onion, diced

½ cup diced napa cabbage

½ cup diced bok choy

1 carrot, diced

3 or 4 scallions, white and green parts, cut into 1-inch lengths

1½ cups jasmine rice

2 star anise pods

2 cardamom pods

½ teaspoon curry powder

2 cups Vegetable Stock (page 37) or water

1 14-ounce can unsweetened coconut milk

2 fresh or frozen kaffir lime leaves (see page 32)

2 teaspoons kosher salt

1 teaspoon black pepper

½ pound firm tofu, diced

¼ to 1 cup sliced fresh cilantro leaves

Garnish:

Scallion Oil (page 45)

Rice: I keep at least three types of rice at home: *basmati* (from India, a long-grain white rice with a delightful nutty flavor); *jasmine* (from Thailand, an intensely aromatic long-grain white rice); and *short grain,* or sticky rice; I like sticky rice for its flavor and its simple, basic, heart-warming sustenance. For steamed rice I use jasmine. The basmati is for pilaf and savory skillet or baked dishes because it holds its own when combined with strong spices or other ingredients.

Preheat the oven to 400°F.

Place a large ovenproof skillet over medium-high heat, and when it is hot, add the oil. Add the ginger, garlic, and lemongrass, and sauté until lightly caramelized, 1 to 2 minutes. Add the red onion, cabbage, bok choy, carrot, and scallions and cook until lightly browned and aromatic, 3 to 5 minutes. Add the rice, star anise, cardamon, and curry powder, and stir well. Then add the stock, coconut milk, lime leaves, salt, and pepper, and stir to combine. Bring to a boil. Stir in the tofu and cilantro, cover the skillet, and transfer it to the oven. Bake until the rice is tender, about 20 minutes.

Uncover and serve straight from the skillet, drizzled with Scallion Oil.

Serves 6

Rice in a Japanese rice measure

timbale of grains with wild mushrooms and a creamy feta sauce

This is one of my favorite meatless dishes—I love the hearty flavors and the textures of the grains. The sauce is easy to make and is creamy, dreamy, and delicious.

At the restaurant, one of the measures of a successful vegetarian dish is how broad its appeal is. This timbale is sure to please the meat-and-potatoes folks around your table. Serve it with sautéed green beans or steamed asparagus.

For the timbale:
½ cup pearl barley
½ cup wild rice
½ cup basmati rice
½ cup bulgur
1 teaspoon kosher salt
1 tablespoon unsalted butter
1 small onion, diced
2 small carrots, diced
1 small fennel bulb, diced
1 cup sliced fresh shiitake or portobello mushrooms
2 teaspoons minced garlic
½ bunch fresh thyme, stems removed
1 teaspoon kosher salt
1 teaspoon black pepper

For the sauce:
½ cup Vegetable Stock (page 37)
½ cup dry white wine
½ cup heavy cream
½ pound feta cheese
½ teaspoon black pepper
¼ bunch fresh thyme, stems removed

Prepare the timbale: Place the barley in a small saucepan, add cold water to cover, and season with ¼ teaspoon of the salt. Do the same thing with the wild rice (adding 1¼ cups water), basmati rice, and bulgur—each in its own saucepan. Bring the water in all four pans to a boil over medium heat, and boil until the grain is tender: 12 to 15 minutes for the barley, 20 to 25 minutes for the wild rice, 12 to 15 minutes for the basmati rice, and 4 to 5 minutes for the bulgur.

Drain the cooked grains thoroughly, and spread them out (now it's okay to mix them) on plates or on a baking sheet to cool.

Place a skillet over medium-high heat, and when it is hot, add the butter. Add the onion, carrots, fennel, mushrooms, and garlic and sauté until lightly caramelized, 5 to 6 minutes. Add the thyme, salt, pepper, and cooked grains. Stir to combine and cook until heated through, 4 to 6 minutes. Set aside.

Prepare the sauce: Place the stock and wine in a stainless-steel pot, and bring to a boil over high heat. Cook until reduced to ¼ cup, 5 to 6 minutes. Add the cream and bring back to a boil. Reduce the heat and simmer for 5 minutes. Add the feta and whisk until just melted. Season with the pepper and thyme.

Place a stainless-steel timbale ring (or large paper cup with the bottom cut off) in the center of each plate. Divide the grains mixture among the molds, packing it down firmly. Remove the rings and ladle the sauce around, but not on top of, the timbales.

Serves 6

Wild rice: Not really a rice, wild rice is actually the grain of a marsh grass. Prized for its chewy texture and nutty flavor, it takes longer to cook and is quite a bit more expensive than regular rice. Wild rice is delicious on its own or mixed into rice dishes or stuffings. It is sometimes marketed under the name "Indian rice."

persian turnovers with carrots, raisins, pine nuts, and goat cheese

We are always looking for great vehicles to create vegetarian entrees, and this one couldn't be more perfect. Essentially a spanakopita (spinach pie) with a North African twist, these turnovers are a bit of a departure from the flavors of the other recipes in this book.

I first ate *brik,* a savory deep-fried turnover usually filled with spicy meat or fish, in a Tunisian restaurant in southwestern France, and I marveled at the thin pastry layers. When I got back home, I began to experiment with a version of my own, but first I had to figure out where to find *brik* pastry. Thank goodness for the Internet: I found it in New Jersey. The *brik* wrappers are thin and very crispy after baking, but you can just as well use phyllo, spring roll wrappers, or lumpia wrappers. I serve these as a main course, but they are also great when made smaller to serve as an hors d'oeuvre, appetizer, or side dish.

Serve the turnovers with Ginger Garlic Spinach (page 232), Crisp Beans and Fresh Tomatoes with a Curry Vinaigrette (page 219), and Watermelon Pickles (page 68). If you like, you can prepare the sauce a day or two ahead.

For the turnovers:
1 tablespoon light sesame oil
4 onions, diced
4 carrots, diced
10 garlic cloves, minced
½ cup raisins
½ cup dried apricots, diced
½ teaspoon cumin seeds
¼ teaspoon ground cinnamon
⅛ teaspoon cayenne pepper
2 tablespoons lemon juice
2 tablespoons honey
2 teaspoons kosher salt
1 teaspoon black pepper
½ cup pine nuts, toasted
½ pound goat cheese

vegetarian entrees

Persian Turnovers with Carrots, Raisins, Pine Nuts, and Goat Cheese, and Ginger Garlic Spinach

1 package brik *or spring roll wrappers (12 wrappers)*
1 tablespoon unsalted butter, melted

For the sauce:
1 tablespoon light sesame oil
1 small onion, diced
1 tablespoon garam masala *(see page 251)*
¼ cup dry white wine
4 red bell peppers, roasted and peeled (see page 57)
1 cup Vegetable Stock (see page 37)
2 teaspoons lemon juice
½ teaspoon kosher salt
¼ teaspoon black pepper

Prepare the turnovers: Place a skillet over medium-high heat, and when it is hot, add the oil. Add the onions, carrots, and garlic and cook until deeply caramelized, 10 to 12 minutes. Transfer the vegetables to a large mixing bowl, and add the raisins, apricots, cumin seeds, cinnamon, and cayenne. Toss, and add the lemon juice, honey, salt, pepper, and pine nuts. Toss again to combine. Allow to cool for about 20 minutes. (If you are preparing this ahead of time, cover tightly and refrigerate for up to 2 days.)

Divide the goat cheese into twelve equal pieces.

Place one *brik* wrapper on a clean, flat surface and brush the top edge with melted butter. Place one twelfth of the filling in the center of the wrapper, and top with a piece of cheese. Fold the wrapper up envelope-style: fold in the sides, then fold up the bottom, followed by the top, to enclose the filling completely. Repeat with the remaining eleven wrappers, filling, and cheese. Cover and refrigerate for up to 4 hours.

Preheat the oven to 400°F.

Place the turnovers, seam side down, in a single layer on a parchment- or foil-lined baking sheet, and bake until golden and crisp, 8 to 10 minutes.

While the turnovers are baking, prepare the sauce: Place a small saucepan over medium-high heat, and when it is hot, add the oil. Add the onion and cook until lightly caramelized, 2 to 3 minutes. Add the *garam masala* and cook until fragrant, 1 minute. Add the wine, roasted peppers, and stock, and bring to a boil. Reduce the heat to low and simmer for 5 minutes.

Transfer the mixture to a blender or food processor, and add the lemon juice, salt, and pepper. Puree until smooth.

Place two turnovers on each plate, and spoon the sauce over them. Serve immediately.

Serves 6

salads

Fresh and crunchy, elegantly composed or warm and wilted, salads really turn people on. They are the choice of dieters and of those who love hot bacon vinaigrettes and crumbled blue cheese. I find that a composed salad is an excellent way to show off prized ingredients like crabmeat, asparagus, or beautiful prawns. Presentation is very important to salad craft. That wedge of iceberg lettuce can look great when arranged on a colorful platter with a thick drizzle of Green Goddess Dressing. Of course a summer salad, with tiny radishes and fancy-cut cucumbers tossed with all sorts of tomatoes and lettuces, is a beautiful thing.

The trick to making a good dressing is to use provocative and balanced flavors. Ingredients like mustard, curry, lots of herbs, quality oils, and interesting vinegars blend to become great vinaigrettes and dressings that harmonize and accentuate the ingredients of your salad. Always remember to season your dressing or vinaigrette well.

shrimp and avocado salad with tropical vinaigrette

Shrimp and avocado—a to-die-for combo that I cannot resist. Here it's made outrageously delicious with the addition of pineapple, ginger, mango, and lime. This dish really demonstrates how ingredients that are grown in the same climate together make sense when paired.

The vinaigrette itself is a great alternative to mayonnaise for a seafood or chicken salad, or for dressing a cold noodle dish with pork, chicken, or vegetables.

For the vinaigrette:
1 teaspoon coriander seeds, toasted
2 star anise pods
½ teaspoon Szechuan peppercorns
¼ cup mango juice
½ cup pineapple juice
¼ cup distilled vinegar
½ inch fresh ginger, sliced
1 teaspoon chili garlic paste (see page 82), or more to taste
½ cup soy oil
1 tablespoon dark sesame oil
1 tablespoon lime juice
2 teaspoons kosher salt
½ teaspoon black pepper

For the salad:
1½ pounds shrimp, peeled, deveined, and poached
2 perfectly ripe avocados, cut into small dice
1 pint cherry tomatoes, halved
⅓ cup sliced fresh Thai basil leaves

Garnish:
Cilantro Oil (page 46)

Cutting versus chopping soft herbs: With soft herbs, such as cilantro, basil, or mint, it is important to use a sharp knife and slice the leaves into slivers, or chiffonade. Using a dull knife or repeatedly chopping the herbs will bruise them, rendering them black and wilted.

Prepare the vinaigrette: Place the coriander, star anise, and Szechuan peppercorns in a saucepan over medium heat. Toast, stirring often, until the spices are darker and very fragrant, 1 to 2 minutes. Add the mango and pineapple juices, vinegar, and ginger and bring to a boil. Remove from the heat and allow to steep for 15 minutes. Then strain the mixture into a bowl and discard the solids.

Add the chili garlic paste, soy and sesame oils, lime juice, salt, and pepper to the strained mixture, and whisk until well combined. You should have about 2 cups. If you are making it ahead of time, transfer the dressing to a container, cover, and refrigerate for up to 2 weeks.

To make the salad, arrange the shrimp, avocado, and tomatoes on a platter. Drizzle with the vinaigrette, and garnish with the basil. Top with Cilantro Oil, and serve.

Serves 6

Light and herbaceous, this impressive salad appears to be far more complicated than it is. In a restaurant you might call it a timbale: layers of components that alone are fabulous and together are amazing. Each layer shows off the others.

The sweet, clean, ocean flavor of crabmeat makes it one of my favorite ingredients. Here it is nicely accented by the savory herbs, avocado, vegetables, and vinaigrette. The herbs are used as salad greens, but don't fret: These particular herbs have soft, mellow flavors that work well in large quantities.

The vinaigrette can be made ahead of time and used for any tossed green salad.

For the herbs:
2 bunches chives, cut into 1-inch lengths (about ½ cup)
1½ to 2 cups fresh cilantro leaves
½ cup fresh mint leaves
½ cup fresh Thai basil leaves

For the mustard vinaigrette:
½ cup plus 2 tablespoons extra-virgin olive oil
¼ cup fresh lemon juice (2 large lemons)
1 tablespoon grainy mustard
½ teaspoon kosher salt
½ teaspoon cracked black pepper

For the salad:
4 ripe avocados
1 tablespoon extra-virgin olive oil
1 tablespoon lemon juice
2 teaspoons kosher salt
1 teaspoon cracked black pepper

1½ pounds fresh crabmeat, picked over for shells
1 small carrot, cut into very small dice
1 small red bell pepper, cut into very small dice
3 shallots, cut into very small dice
Crackers or vegetable chips (optional)

Garnish:
Cilantro Oil (page 46) or Scallion Oil (page 45)

Prepare the herbs: Place the chives, cilantro, mint, and basil in a large bowl and toss to mix. Slice enough of the herb mixture to make ¼ cup, and reserve. Cover the remaining leaves with a moist paper towel, and set aside.

Make the vinaigrette: Place the olive oil, lemon juice, mustard, salt, and pepper in a bowl and whisk well. Set it aside.

Prepare the salad: Peel, pit, and coarsely smash the avocados and place in a bowl. Add the olive oil, lemon juice, half of the sliced herb mixture, 1 teaspoon of the salt, and ½ teaspoon of the pepper. Set aside.

Place the crabmeat, diced carrot, bell pepper, and shallots, and the remaining sliced herbs in a mixing bowl. Add ½ cup of the reserved vinaigrette and gently fold to combine. Season with the remaining 1 teaspoon salt and ½ teaspoon pepper, and refrigerate.

Use six timbale rings, or cut the top 1½ inches off six large paper cups, to mold the salad: Place a ring in the center of each plate, and divide the avocado mixture among them, packing it down gently with the back of a spoon.

Divide the crab salad among the rings, forming the second layer, and gently pack it down with the back of a spoon.

Toss the reserved unsliced herbs with the remaining vinaigrette, and crown each timbale with a portion of the herb salad.

Pull the rings up, and garnish the plates with crisp crackers or veggie chips, if desired. Drizzle with either Cilantro Oil or Scallion Oil, and serve.

Serves 6

chicken, orange, and cress salad with black bean vinaigrette

Fermented black beans are common in Chinese and Korean cooking and give a rich, earthy taste to any dish. They are very salty, so be sure to soak them in several changes of water before using them. This slightly sweet and spicy citrus-flavored vinaigrette is great on these bitter and crunchy greens, but I also like it on steamed vegetables, especially broccoli and asparagus, and on steamed fish, such as salmon fillet or snapper.

For the vinaigrette:
1 tablespoon light sesame oil
2 tablespoons fermented black beans, soaked, rinsed, and chopped
1 tablespoon minced fresh ginger
2 garlic cloves, minced
½ cup orange juice
¼ cup rice vinegar
1 tablespoon soy sauce
1 tablespoon mirin
⅓ cup soy oil
1 tablespoon dark sesame oil
1 tablespoon chili garlic paste (see page 82)
2 teaspoons kosher salt
½ teaspoon black pepper

For the salad:
3 bunches (2 to 2¼ pounds) watercress, stems removed
1½ pounds cooked chicken breast, diced
2 oranges, sectioned

Garnish:
Cilantro Oil (page 46)

Prepare the vinaigrette: Place a large skillet over medium-high heat, and when it is hot, add the oil. Add the beans, ginger, and garlic and cook until lightly browned, 2 to 3 minutes. Add the orange juice and bring to a boil. Transfer the mixture to a bowl and add the vinegar, soy sauce, mirin, soy and dark sesame oils, chili garlic paste, salt, and pepper. Whisk until well combined. You should have about 1½ cups. If you are not using it right away, transfer the dressing to a container, cover, and refrigerate for up to 2 weeks.

To make the salad, divide the watercress among six plates. Arrange the chicken and oranges on top of the cress, and generously drizzle the vinaigrette over each salad. Garnish with a drizzle of Cilantro Oil, and serve.

Serves 6

Fermented black beans: Also called salted black beans, these are aromatic, rich, pungent, and soft after being fermented with salt and spices. They are not interchangeable with the black beans usually called for in Mexican cooking. You can find them in specialty markets.

romaine and green bean salad with rice wine vinaigrette

Perfect for soft or crisp greens, spinach, or raw or steamed vegetables, this vinaigrette is a great example of how harmoniously rice vinegar and mirin work together. The small amount of dark sesame oil is just enough—you don't want to overwhelm the mellow flavors of the vinaigrette.

For the vinaigrette:

1 tablespoon minced fresh ginger
2 garlic cloves, minced
½ cup rice vinegar
¼ cup mirin
⅓ cup soy oil
1 tablespoon dark sesame oil
1 teaspoon coriander seeds, toasted and ground
½ teaspoon Szechuan peppercorns, toasted and ground
1 teaspoon kosher salt
½ teaspoon black pepper

For the salad:

1 head romaine lettuce, torn apart
½ pound green beans
1 small red onion, thinly sliced
¼ cup sliced almonds, toasted

Place all the vinaigrette ingredients in a container, cover, and shake until combined. You should have about 1 cup. If you are not using it right away, refrigerate the dressing for up to 1 month.

To make the salad, place the romaine, green beans, red onion, and almonds in a large salad bowl. Drizzle with 3 to 4 tablespoons of the dressing, and toss well. Serve immediately.

Serves 6

salads

melon and herb salad with lime vinaigrette

In Asian cuisines, ingredients are often put together in a way that seems uncharacteristic yet intriguing to an American palate: The point is to create combinations that are sweet and spicy, soft and crunchy, all at once. Take a chance—you will be hooked. The ingredients in this dish—melons, bell peppers, limes, and peanuts—all grow side by side.

This lime vinaigrette is a mainstay in the kitchen at Salamander, and is delicious in any napa cabbage–based salad or with crisp greens such as watercress, pea shoots, or tatsoi. It is also wonderful with cold chicken, crab, or shrimp salads—especially with the addition of Thai basil and mint. If you love the flavors and fragrances of lime, mint, basil, and cilantro as much as I do, you'll keep this vinaigrette on hand at all times!

This salad is great with Malaysian Sweet Spice–Rubbed Chicken (page 160). You can also serve it over a bed of spinach or watercress dressed with the same vinaigrette.

For the vinaigrette:
½ cup cold water
¼ cup sugar
4 star anise pods
½ inch fresh ginger, sliced
¼ cup rice vinegar
½ cup lime juice (3 or 4 limes)
⅓ cup soy oil
1 tablespoon dark sesame oil
2 teaspoons kosher salt
½ teaspoon black pepper

For the salad:
1 melon (cantaloupe, small Galia, or Charentais), diced
6 tablespoons unsalted peanuts, toasted
2 red bell peppers, roasted (see page 57) and cut into small dice
⅓ cup fresh mint leaves
¼ to 1 cup fresh cilantro leaves

Prepare the vinaigrette: Place the cold water, sugar, star anise, and ginger in a saucepan and bring to a boil over high heat. Reduce the heat to low and simmer for 2 to 3 minutes. Remove the pan from the heat and allow to steep for 15 minutes. Then strain the mixture into a bowl and discard the solids. Add the vinegar, lime juice, soy and sesame oils, salt, and pepper, and whisk until well combined. You should have about 1½ cups. If you are not using it right away, transfer the dressing to a container, cover, and refrigerate for up to 2 weeks.

To make the salad, place the melon, peanuts, bell peppers, mint, and cilantro in a large bowl and drizzle with ¼ cup of the vinaigrette. Serve immediately.

Serves 6

asian slaw with sweet and sour dressing

This boiled dressing provides the perfect balance of flavors for this crunchy and colorful Asian vegetable slaw. In colder weather, try turning it into a warm dish by quickly stir-frying the cabbage and other ingredients, adding the dressing while it's hot, and serving it straight from the pan. I've also used the slaw to dress fried tofu tossed with roasted peppers and roasted peanuts. The addition of cooked shrimp, lobster, pork, or chicken is especially delicious.

For the dressing:
3 arbol chilies
1 3-inch cinnamon stick
1 tablespoon coriander seeds
3 star anise pods
1 teaspoon Szechuan peppercorns
¼ cup sugar
½ cup cider vinegar
½ cup distilled vinegar
¾ cup pineapple juice
¾ cup mango juice
1 teaspoon chili garlic paste (see page 82)

For the salad:
1 head napa cabbage, cut into wide strips
1 English (hothouse) cucumber, sliced on the diagonal
6 radishes, sliced
2 carrots, julienned
1 small fennel bulb, julienned
1 small red onion, julienned
½ cup coarsely chopped unsalted peanuts, toasted
⅓ cup sliced fresh cilantro leaves
⅓ cup sliced fresh mint leaves
⅓ cup sliced fresh basil leaves
1 teaspoon salt
½ teaspoon black pepper

Prepare the dressing: Place the chilies, cinnamon stick, coriander, star anise, and peppercorns in a skillet over medium heat and cook until lightly toasted, about 2 minutes. Wrap the toasted spices in a cheesecloth bag, and place the bag in a medium-size saucepan. Add the sugar, both vinegars, both juices, and the chili garlic paste, and bring to a boil over high heat. Remove the pan from the heat and allow to steep for 1 hour. Discard the spice bag. If you will not be using it right away, transfer the dressing to a container, cover, and refrigerate for up to 1 month. You should have about 2 cups.

To make the salad, combine vegetables, peanuts, and herbs in a bowl and toss to mix. Add the salt, pepper, and ½ cup of the dressing, and toss again. Serve immediately.

Serves 6

crisp beans and fresh tomatoes with a curry vinaigrette

This perfect summer salad is made all the prettier if you have a variety of colors and shapes of beans and tomatoes to use. I look for heirloom tomatoes, such as Green Zebra and Cherokee Rose, as well as cherry tomatoes in all colors and shapes. Try to find both green and yellow beans. The vinaigrette is delicious on other salads, especially with cucumber or seafood, and on hot steamed vegetables such as broccoli or asparagus.

For the salad:
4 cups water
½ pound fresh beans (haricots verts, green beans, yellow wax beans)
1 pound ripe tomatoes, cut into wedges or large dice, or in half if small

For the dressing:
1½ teaspoons light sesame oil
1 tablespoon minced fresh ginger
1 teaspoon minced garlic
2 shallots, finely diced
1 teaspoon curry powder
2 tablespoons lemon juice
½ cup plain yogurt
1 tablespoon extra-virgin olive oil
3 to 4 tablespoons sliced fresh cilantro leaves
1 teaspoon kosher salt
1 teaspoon black pepper

Prepare an ice bath.

In a large saucepan, bring the water to a boil over high heat. Add the beans and cook until they are al dente and the color has intensified, 1 to 2 minutes. Drain the beans and place in the ice bath to stop the cooking process. Drain well. Combine the cooled beans and the tomatoes in a large mixing bowl.

Place a small skillet over medium-high heat, and when it is hot, add the oil. Add the ginger and garlic and cook until lightly caramelized, 1 to 2 minutes. Add the shallots and cook until lightly caramelized, 2 to 3 minutes. Transfer the mixture to a small bowl, and add the curry powder, lemon juice, yogurt, and olive oil. Whisk to mix well, and then add the cilantro, salt, and pepper.

Toss the dressing with the beans and tomatoes, and serve.

Serves 6

Crisp Beans and Fresh Tomatoes with a Curry Vinaigrette

salads

asian pear salad
with green beans and
glazed scallops

The ingredients in this salad lend themselves to a beautiful presentation. For ease of preparation, make the glaze and the vinaigrette, and toast the almonds the day before serving. Be sure to let your sauté pan get very hot before you add the scallops in order to get a really good sear.

For the vinaigrette:

1 shallot, minced

1 tablespoon minced fresh ginger

3 tablespoons rice vinegar

1 tablespoon mirin

2 tablespoons pear nectar

2 tablespoons light sesame oil

¼ cup canola oil

½ teaspoon kosher salt

¼ teaspoon black pepper

For the glaze:

¼ cup sugar

¼ cup water

1 inch fresh ginger, sliced

1 tablespoon pickling spice

¼ cup pear nectar

½ teaspoon kosher salt

¼ teaspoon black pepper

For the salad:

4 small heads frisée (curly endive), halved and roots removed

½ teaspoon kosher salt

¼ teaspoon black pepper

1 tablespoon vegetable oil

½ pound haricots verts or other fresh green beans, blanched

1 red bell pepper, finely julienned

½ pound mizuna

¼ pound tiny spinach leaves

1 head radicchio, coarsely chopped

4 Asian pears, or another variety, julienned

½ cup sliced almonds, toasted

Asian pears

For the scallops:

1 pound scallops, muscle removed

½ teaspoon kosher salt

¼ teaspoon black pepper

1 tablespoon vegetable oil

Place all the vinaigrette ingredients in a blender and process to combine. Set aside.

Prepare the glaze: Place the sugar, water, ginger, and pickling spice in a small saucepan over medium-high heat, and bring to a boil. Cook until reduced to a thick syrup, 2 to 3 minutes. Strain into a bowl, add the pear nectar, salt, and pepper, and set aside. Discard the solids.

Prepare the salad: Sprinkle the frisée with the salt and pepper. Place a large sauté pan over medium-high heat, and when it is hot, add the oil. Add the frisée and cook until just seared and beginning to wilt, 1 to 2 minutes. Transfer the frisée to a large bowl, and add the haricots verts, bell pepper, mizuna, spinach, radicchio, pears, and almonds. Add the reserved vinaigrette, and toss well. Divide the salad among eight large salad plates.

Sprinkle the scallops with the salt and pepper. Place a skillet over medium-high heat, and when it is hot, add the oil. Add the scallops and sear until golden brown, about 1 minute per side. Remove the pan from the heat and add the reserved glaze. Toss to combine, and divide the scallops among the salad plates. Serve immediately.

Serves 8

Asian pears: Asian pears have a crisp texture and refreshing character that falls between the flavor and crunch of an apple and the sweet fragrance of a pear.

Pickling spice: Pickling spice is a generic term used to describe any number of spice combinations used to pickle foods. Store-bought blends vary according to the manufacturer and may include any or all of the following: allspice berries, bay leaves, cardamom seeds, cinnamon stick, whole cloves, coriander seeds, ginger, brown and yellow mustard seeds, and peppercorns.

a variety of sweet peas
with green goddess dressing

I am a total, complete freak for Green Goddess Dressing. In fact, I consider myself a one-man crusade to return this creamy herbal dressing to the heart and kitchen of every food lover! We've often tried to determine what savory food Green Goddess would *not* go with—and other than a peanut butter sandwich, we've been hard pressed to come up with anything. Try it with everything from broiled salmon or chicken, to a turkey or ham sandwich, to a plate of sliced fresh tomatoes.

This is a nice salad to combine with a little leftover chicken breast or cooked bacon or salmon.

For the dressing:
1 garlic clove
2 or 3 anchovy fillets
1 tablespoon capers
½ cup packed spinach leaves
2 scallions, white and green parts, sliced
¼ cup fresh parsley leaves
⅛ cup fresh tarragon leaves
¼ cup sour cream
½ cup mayonnaise
1 teaspoon white wine vinegar
½ teaspoon kosher salt
¼ teaspoon black pepper

For the salad:
4 cups water
1 pound fresh peas and pod peas, mixed (regular garden peas, snow peas, sugar snap peas)
3 small heads baby lettuces, or 1 large head Bibb or red-leaf lettuce

Prepare the dressing: Place the garlic, anchovies, capers, spinach, scallions, parsley, and tarragon in a blender or food processor and process until smooth. Add the sour cream and blend until smooth. Transfer the mixture to a bowl, and add the mayonnaise, vinegar, salt, and pepper. Mix to combine. You should have 1 to 1¼ cups. Refrigerate until ready to use. The dressing may be made up to 1 week in advance.

Prepare an ice bath.

Place the water in a large saucepan and bring to a boil over high heat. Add all the peas and pods and cook for just 1 minute. Drain, and place in the ice bath to cool quickly. Then drain well.

Divide the lettuce among six plates, and top with the cooled peas. Drizzle (or ladle, as I do!) the dressing over the salad, and serve.

Serves 6

Picking pea pod leaves

shiitake salad with spring veggies and scallion vinaigrette

This lovely salad pairs woodsy shiitake mushrooms with delicate early asparagus, peas, beans, and baby carrots. I love this kind of salad for its variety of flavors, textures, and colors—a bit of flair goes a long way at the table. This would be an excellent appetizer or vegetarian luncheon entree. The vinaigrette would also be good on a simple lettuce and tomato salad.

For the vinaigrette:

1 shallot, minced

2 scallions, white and green parts, minced

2 teaspoons Dijon mustard

1 tablespoon white wine vinegar

1 tablespoon lemon juice

2 tablespoons soy oil

1 tablespoon extra-virgin olive oil

½ teaspoon kosher salt

¼ teaspoon black pepper

For the salad:

1 pound fresh shiitake mushrooms, sliced if desired

2 teaspoons light sesame oil

¼ pound small new potatoes

1 pound asparagus

4 cups water

¼ pound peas

½ pound baby carrots

¼ pound haricots verts

1 pint cherry tomatoes

½ pound baby salad greens (mesclun)
1 teaspoon kosher salt
½ teaspoon black pepper

Preheat the oven to 400°F.

Place all of the vinaigrette ingredients in a mixing bowl and whisk to combine. Set aside.

Toss the shiitake mushrooms with the oil, and spread them in a single layer on a baking sheet. Roast in the oven until browned and tender, 5 to 6 minutes. Set aside.

Place the potatoes in a medium saucepan and cover with cold water. Bring to a boil over high heat and cook until fork-tender, 8 to 10 minutes. Drain, and arrange in a single layer on a tray or plate to cool. Set aside.

Prepare an ice bath.

Fill a sauce pot with water and bring to a boil. Add the asparagus, and cook until bright green and barely tender, 3 to 4 minutes. Drain, and then place in the ice bath to cool.

Place the water in a saucepan and bring to a boil over high heat. Add the peas and cook for 1 minute. Remove the peas with a slotted spoon, and place in the ice bath to stop the cooking process. Bring the water back to a boil over high heat, and add the carrots. Cook until just al dente, 1 to 2 minutes. Remove the carrots with a slotted spoon, and place in the ice bath. Repeat with the haricots verts.

Drain the asparagus, peas, carrots, and haricots verts well, and place in a large mixing bowl. Add the reserved mushrooms and potatoes along with the tomatoes, lettuce, salt, and pepper. Add the vinaigrette, toss well, and divide among six salad plates.

Serves 6

vegetable side dishes

I love to see a table laden with platters of entrees, baskets of hot breads, and bowls of side dishes. This image is very Southern to me and reminds me of my high school days in Savannah, when we used to sneak off campus to go to Mrs. Wilkes's Boarding House for lunch. There you ate at large tables for ten or twelve people and shared family-style dishes like chicken and dumplings, Low Country boil, and deviled crab, all served with up to ten side dishes—mashed turnips, glazed sweet potatoes, mustard greens, black-eyed peas with ham hocks . . . Yummy!

Vegetable dishes will aways be part of an Asian table—that is one aspect of the inherent healthfulness of most Asian cuisines.

Although this was originally designed to pair with grilled fish, I like it as an accompaniment to almost anything spicy or rich, such as the Indian-Spiced Leg of Lamb with Creamy Yogurt Sauce (page 176) or the Cod Fillet with Curry Tomato Sauce (page 144). It provides a subtly flavored backdrop that is quite versatile. In the unlikely event that there are leftovers, you can make chickpea croquettes: Form the smash into patties and sauté them in olive oil or butter until browned, about 2 minutes on each side.

You can make this a day or two ahead and simply reheat it when you are ready to serve it.

1 cup dried chickpeas (garbanzo beans)
8 cups Vegetable Stock (page 37) or water
1 small onion, coarsely chopped
1 carrot, coarsely chopped
1 celery stalk, coarsely chopped
1 teaspoon kosher salt

1 tablespoon olive oil
1 tablespoon minced fresh ginger
4 garlic cloves, minced
2 small or 1 large onion, diced
½ teaspoon coriander seeds
½ teaspoon cumin seeds
½ teaspoon yellow mustard seeds
½ teaspoon fennel seeds
½ teaspoon curry powder
1 teaspoon kosher salt
½ teaspoon black pepper
½ cup plain yogurt

vegetable side dishes

Place the chickpeas in a bowl and cover with cold water by 3 to 4 inches. Soak for at least 6 hours, or preferably overnight.

Drain the chickpeas and place them in a 4-quart saucepan. Add the stock, onion, carrot, celery, and salt, and bring to a boil over high heat. Reduce the heat to low and simmer until the chickpeas are tender, about 1¼ hours.

Drain the chickpeas, reserving ½ cup of the cooking liquid. Discard the vegetables. Place the chickpeas and the reserved liquid in a mixing bowl.

Place a skillet over medium-high heat, and when it is hot, add the oil. Add the ginger and garlic and cook until lightly browned, 2 to 3 minutes. Add the onion and sauté until caramelized, 4 to 5 minutes. Add the coriander, cumin, mustard, and fennel seeds and the curry powder. Cook until very aromatic, about 1 minute. Add this mixture to the chickpeas, and stir to combine. Add the salt, pepper, and yogurt, and mash with a potato masher or fork. The mixture should remain a little chunky. Reheat if necessary, and serve.

Serves 6

Lightly stir-fried greens are attractive, nutritious, and delicious. I can eat this whole dish myself—I love the nutty garlic and toasted sesame flavors. The key to success with this simple recipe is to use a large, hot skillet, which will allow the garlic, sesame seeds, and ginger to brown, and then the spinach to cook just until it wilts and intensifies in color.

Try this same recipe with watercress, pea pod leaves, or mustard greens. Just be sure to spin the greens completely dry before they go into the hot pan.

2 pounds fresh flat-leaf spinach, stems removed
1 tablespoon dark sesame oil
2 tablespoons minced fresh ginger
4 garlic cloves, minced
1 tablespoon black and white sesame seeds, mixed
2 teaspoons kosher salt
1 teaspoon black pepper

Wash the spinach and dry it thoroughly. (If the spinach is wet when you cook it, it will steam instead of sautéing.)

Place a large skillet over medium-high heat, and when it is hot, add half the oil. Add half the ginger, half the garlic, and half the sesame seeds, and cook until caramelized, 1 to 2 minutes. Add half the spinach and toss with tongs to cook evenly and to combine with the other ingredients. Cook it quickly until it is lightly wilted and a deep and intense green, 1 to 2 minutes. Season with half of the salt and pepper, and remove to a serving dish. Wipe the skillet clean and repeat with the remaining half of the ingredients. Serve immediately.

Serves 6

vegetable side dishes

saffron potato cakes

Have you ever noticed the nearly universal love people have for potato pancakes? Whether it's latkes, hash browns, or pommes Anna, everyone loves the crisp edges, the buttery center, and the savoriness of this style of potato preparation. This version includes saffron, which creates not only a delicious pancake but a beautiful one as well. Use a nice flat, thick-bottomed pan. A friend told me she cooked and froze these cakes to enjoy on another occasion, with good results.

*2 to 2½ pounds of waxy potatoes such as Yukon gold, russet, or yellow Finn (avoid
     starchy potatoes like Idaho)*
1 tablespoon plus 1 teaspoon kosher salt
¼ cup dry white wine
12 to 16 saffron threads
8 cups water
3 tablespoons all-purpose flour
1 teaspoon black pepper
1 tablespoon olive oil

Peel and julienne the potatoes. (For an easy and even julienne, use a Japanese mandoline or the julienne disc of a food processor.)

Place the 1 tablespoon salt, wine, and saffron in a 3- to 4-quart saucepan. Bring to a boil over high heat and add the water. Add the potatoes and bring back to a boil. Cook until tender, 3 to 4 minutes. Drain the potatoes in a colander (do not rinse them), and then spread them out in a single layer on a baking sheet or plate to cool.

When the potatoes are cool, place them in a mixing bowl and add the flour, 1 teaspoon salt, and pepper. Mix to combine.

Place a large skillet over medium-high heat, and when it is hot, add the oil. Place all of the potato mixture in the pan and pat it down firmly with a spatula so you have one large, even pancake. Reduce the heat to medium and cook until golden brown on the bottom, 4 to 5 minutes. Invert a large plate over the skillet, and holding the two together, flip the pancake onto the plate. Then slide the pancake back into the skillet and cook on the second side until golden brown, 4 to 5 minutes. Cut into wedges and serve.

(Alternatively, you can divide the mixture into six portions and make individual cakes, following the same cooking directions.)

Serves 6

yogurt whipped potatoes

These whipped potatoes are light, a bit tangy, and completely irresistible. I make them as much for myself as for our guests. A food mill or ricer will give the fluffiest results. You can also use a stand mixer with the whisk attachment; just be careful not to overmix or the potatoes will turn gluey. Use a waxy, buttery potato such as a Yukon gold or yellow Finn.

3 pounds potatoes, peeled and cut into large dice
8 cups cold water
2 teaspoons kosher salt
½ cup heavy cream
4 tablespoons (½ stick) unsalted butter, at room temperature
1 cup plain yogurt
1 teaspoon black pepper

Place the potatoes, water, and 1 teaspoon of the salt in a large saucepan. Bring to a boil over high heat and cook until tender, 15 to 20 minutes. Drain well.

Place the cream in a small saucepan and bring it just to the boiling point. Set it aside.

Rice the potatoes and place them in a large mixing bowl; or mash them by hand. Stir in the butter, yogurt, scalded cream, pepper, and remaining 1 teaspoon salt.

Reheat gently if necessary, and serve immediately.

Serves 6

sesame parsnips

Sweet, creamy, and a touch smoky, these parsnips can be served in place of mashed potatoes alongside roast chicken or pork.

I have often said that I want to launch a root vegetable fan club. Parsnips are readily available, inexpensive, and delicious whether roasted, mashed, or used in a soup. Parsnips dug in the spring are extra-sweet from having been wintered over. Since I have had good luck with root vegetables like carrots and beets, I am going to try growing parsnips and turnips in my garden next year.

2 pounds parsnips, cut into 1-inch pieces
2 cups milk
3 teaspoons dark sesame oil
2 teaspoons kosher salt
1 teaspoon black pepper

Place the parsnips, milk, 2 teaspoons of the sesame oil, and 1 teaspoon of the salt in a saucepan. If necessary, add water so the parsnips are covered. Bring to a boil over medium-high heat. Reduce the heat to low and simmer until tender, 6 to 8 minutes. Drain parsnips, reserving ½ cup of the cooking liquid.

Place the parsnips and reserved liquid in a mixing bowl and mash by hand, with an electric mixer, or with a ricer. Season with the remaining 1 teaspoon sesame oil, 1 teaspoon salt, and pepper. Serve immediately.

Serves 6

Americans seem to have a taste for sweet sweet-potato dishes. Certainly the most common, and to me the worst, example is the marshmallow-topped sweet potatoes we eat at Thanksgiving (although I have to admit I always take a spoonful). These potatoes have a spicy-sweet glaze of guava or pineapple juice, honey, curry, and ginger. The natural sweetness of the sweet potatoes is set off by the tropical flavors and the curry powder.

Try these with Black Tea–Brined Chicken (page 153), Malaysian Sweet Spice–Rubbed Chicken (page 160), or Pork Tenderloin with Guava Glaze (page 189).

For the glaze:

1 cup guava juice, or 2 cups pineapple or mango juice
½ cup honey
1 tablespoon curry powder
2 tablespoons rice vinegar or cider vinegar
1 teaspoon minced fresh ginger
½ teaspoon kosher salt

For the sweet potatoes:

6 sweet potatoes (about 3 pounds total)
1 tablespoon vegetable or canola oil
1 teaspoon kosher salt
½ teaspoon black pepper

Preheat the oven to 375°F.

Prepare the glaze: Place all the glaze ingredients in a stainless steel–lined saucepan, and stir to combine. Bring to a boil over high heat. Reduce the heat to low and simmer until the glaze is reduced to ⅔ cup and is sticky to the touch, 15 to 20 minutes. Set aside.

Prepare the potatoes: Place the sweet potatoes in the oven and roast until just barely tender when pierced with a sharp paring knife or skewer, 15 to 18 minutes. Set aside to cool.

Peel the sweet potatoes and slice them into ⅟₁₆-inch-thick rounds. Place a 10- or 12-inch sauté pan over medium-high heat, and when it is hot, add the oil. Add the sweet potatoes in a single layer, sprinkle with the salt and pepper, and cook until lightly browned, 2 to 3 minutes. Turn the potatoes, reduce the heat to medium, and brown the second side, another 2 to 3 minutes. (You may need to brown the sweet potatoes in two batches; if so, simply return all the potatoes to the pan when browned.) Add the glaze and continue to cook, tossing, until all the potatoes are well coated. Serve immediately.

Serves 6

Sweet potatoes and yams: The confusion surrounding the difference between the sweet potato and the yam is legendary. A large part of that confusion can be faulted to the United States, where canned sweet potatoes are often marketed and labeled as yams. The truth is that the two come from different plant species. There are over 150 different varieties of yam grown around the world, but almost none of those varieties is grown or sold in the United States. There are many different varieties of sweet potato as well, though only two are widely available commercially: the pale sweet potato and the dark-skinned, orange-fleshed variety that most Americans erroneously call a yam. The bottom line? If you really and truly need a yam, not a sweet potato, visit a superior grocer and be sure to check with the produce manager.

FRIED NOODLES

INGREDIENTS: Wheat Flour, Pasteurized Egg, Soybean Oil, Water, Cornstarch, Salt, Sodium Benzoate, FD&C Yellow #5, FD&C Yellow #6, Potassium Carbonate.

Packed By:
HO TOY NOODLE COMPANY
78-79 Essex St. Boston, MA 02111
Tel: 617-426-0247

Sell By:
Net Wt:

rice and noodles

Rice and noodles are the mainstays of the cuisines that have influenced my cooking. These foodstuffs, in their myriad variations, have sustained people for centuries, whether at everyday meals or at high-style banquets and celebrations.

Rice cultivation is so widespread across Asia that it truly is the staff of life. Whether long-grain or short-grain, jasmine or basmati, purple, polished, or red, rice is revered and is used in many intriguing ways. From steamed and stir-fried, to noodles and wrappers of rice flour, to congee and sushi, rice is a daily part of eating.

Noodles can be made of wheat or rice flour, buckwheat, mung bean, and sweet potato. They can be steamed, stir-fried, served in soup, made into crispy cakes, stuffed, boiled . . . The variety is endless and delicious!

peanut noodles with sesame spinach

Do you remember eating Dan Dan noodles for the first time? I do. I was nine years old and in New York City's Chinatown with my Uncle Howard. I still enjoy ordering that spicy peanut noodle dish. Sammy's Noodle Restaurants in New York City serve a very good version.

This dish is simple, quick, and filling. A good peanut sauce should be smooth and moist and should coat the noodles evenly. The spinach adds a nice complement of color, texture, and nutritional balance.

For the spinach:

1 tablespoon sesame oil

1 tablespoon minced garlic

1 tablespoon chopped fresh ginger

2 tablespoons black and/or white sesame seeds

1 teaspoon ground coriander

1 teaspoon crushed red chili flakes

1 pound spinach, stems removed

1 teaspoon kosher salt

½ teaspoon black pepper

For the peanut noodles:

½ cup unsweetened peanut butter

½ cup hot water

2 tablespoons soy sauce

2 tablespoons light sesame oil

2 tablespoons rice vinegar

1½ teaspoons chopped fresh ginger

1 teaspoon ground coriander

¼ cup chopped unsalted peanuts, toasted

■■■

1 pound fresh yellow Chinese noodles
1 carrot, julienned
1 red onion, julienned
1 bunch (about 8) scallions, white and green parts, minced
½ teaspoon kosher salt
¼ teaspoon black pepper

Garnish:
Scallion Oil (page 45)

Prepare the spinach: Place a large sauté pan over medium heat, and when it is hot, add the oil. Add the garlic, ginger, sesame seeds, coriander, and chili flakes and cook until browned, about 2 minutes. Add the spinach, salt, and pepper and cook until the spinach is lightly wilted. Transfer to a large plate, cover, and refrigerate.

Prepare the noodles: Place the peanut butter, hot water, soy sauce, sesame oil, vinegar, ginger, and coriander in a blender and mix until smooth. Add the peanuts and set aside.

Bring a large pot of water to a boil over high heat. Add the noodles and cook until al dente, 2 to 3 minutes. Drain, and spread the noodles on a baking sheet or plate to cool.

When the noodles are cool, transfer them to a large mixing bowl. Add the carrot, red onion, and scallions and toss to combine. Add the peanut sauce, and stir to coat the noodles evenly. Season with the salt and pepper.

Divide the noodles among six plates, and top each serving with a portion of the cold spinach. Drizzle with Scallion Oil, and serve.

Serves 6

pan-seared somen noodle cake

Similar in size to the more familiar angel-hair pasta, somen are delicate, thinly cut Japanese noodles made of wheat flour. Versatile and delicious, these cakes are great for lunch when topped with stir-fried vegetables. Drop Somen into a soup broth. Or use them for cold noodle salads. Try them at your favorite Japanese restaurant—they are fun and delicious.

The soft, subtle, sweet flavors of these cakes make them a good accompaniment to the Crispy Sole Fillets with Wild Mushroom Stew (page 148) or the Marinated Skate with Lightly Pickled Vegetables (page 136). Note that the noodle cake sets overnight in the refrigerator before it is cooked.

1 tablespoon plus 1 teaspoon kosher salt
1½ pounds somen noodles
1 carrot, julienned
4 scallions, white and green parts, julienned
1 red bell pepper, julienned
½ cup snow peas, julienned
1 tablespoon dark sesame oil
1 teaspoon black pepper
1½ teaspoons light sesame oil

Line a 9-inch square baking pan with plastic wrap, leaving 5 to 6 inches extra hanging over all four sides.

Bring a large pot of water to a boil over high heat. Add 1 tablespoon of the salt and the somen noodles. Return to a boil and cook until al dente, 1 to 2 minutes. Drain the noodles in a colander (do not rinse), and transfer them to a large mixing bowl. Add the carrot, scallions, bell pepper, and snow peas. Toss to combine. Add the dark sesame oil, the remaining 1 teaspoon salt, and pepper, and toss until evenly coated.

Pour the noodles into the prepared pan and pack them down tightly. Wrap the overhang over the top of the noodles, sealing the packet. Place the pan in the refrigerator overnight to set.

Remove packet from the pan and remove the plastic wrap. Slice the noodle cake into six equal pieces with a thin, sharp knife.

Place a skillet over medium-high heat, and when it is hot, add the light sesame oil. Add the cakes and sear until deep golden, crisp, and heated through, 3 to 4 minutes per side. Serve immediately.

Serves 6

Japanese udon noodles are the perfect choice for these individual cakes. Thick, chewy, and delicious, these little cakes crisp up beautifully and are great with chicken, pork, or grilled fish. You can make a great vegetarian meal by topping these with a quick stir-fry of mixed vegetables. In restaurants you will more often find udon served in soups.

2 teaspoons kosher salt
1½ pounds udon noodles, frozen or dried
1 bunch (about 8) scallions, white and green parts, sliced
1 teaspoon black pepper
1 tablespoon light sesame oil

Bring a large pot of water to a boil over high heat, and add 1 teaspoon of the salt. Add the udon noodles and return to a boil. Cook until the noodles are al dente, 1 to 2 minutes if frozen, 5 to 6 minutes if dried. Drain the noodles (do not rinse them), and spread them out on a baking sheet to cool.

Place the cooled noodles in a mixing bowl and add the scallions. Add the remaining 1 teaspoon salt and the pepper, and toss to combine. Divide into six portions and shape into cakes.

Place a large skillet over medium-high heat, and when it is hot, add the oil. Add the noodle cakes and sear until crisp and brown, 3 to 4 minutes. Flip them over and cook until the second side is crisp and brown, 2 to 3 minutes. Serve immediately.

Serves 6

indonesian coconut rice with spinach and peanuts

This hearty casserole-like dish is made exotic with coconut, Sweet Spice Mix, and lemongrass.

Rice could be my staple cereal grain. I enjoy everything about it: its texture, its flavor, the way it takes to so many other flavors and cooking techniques, and its ability to sustain so many diverse cultures. Rice has affordably taken care of over half the world in the best and worst of times. Serve this hearty side dish with roasted chicken or baked fish.

1 tablespoon light sesame oil
1 tablespoon minced fresh ginger
6 garlic cloves, minced
1 tablespoon minced lemongrass
1 tablespoon minced galangal (see page 30), or 1 additional tablespoon fresh ginger
1 red bell pepper, finely diced
1 small red onion, finely diced
2 teaspoons shrimp paste (see page 187)
2 teaspoons tomato paste
1 tablespoon unsweetened peanut butter
1 teaspoon holy basil chili paste (see page 199)
1 tablespoon Sweet Spice Mix (page 81)
4 cups cooked jasmine rice, cooled
¼ cup mango juice
2 tablespoons fish sauce
2 ounces Tamarind Juice (page 54)
1½ tablespoons lime juice
1 14-ounce can unsweetened coconut milk
¾ pound spinach, leaves cut into thin strips
¼ cup sliced fresh cilantro leaves
¼ cup sliced fresh mint leaves
Kosher salt
Black pepper

Garnish:

½ cup unsalted peanuts, toasted and coarsely chopped
Cilantro sprigs
Mint sprigs

Place a wok or a large skillet over medium-high heat, and when it is hot, add the oil. Add the ginger, garlic, lemongrass, and galangal, and cook until lightly caramelized, 1 to 2 minutes. Add the bell pepper and red onion, and cook 1 minute longer. Add the shrimp paste, tomato paste, peanut butter, holy basil chili paste, and Sweet Spice Mix. Cook, stirring constantly, for 1 to 2 minutes. Add the rice and cook, stirring constantly, for 2 to 3 minutes. Add the mango juice, fish sauce, tamarind juice, lime juice, and coconut milk, and stir to combine. Bring quickly to a boil, and then remove from the heat.

Add the spinach, cilantro, and mint. Season with salt and pepper, and garnish with the chopped peanuts and herb sprigs. Serve immediately.

Serves 6

curried rice sticks with chicken, shrimp, and sprouts

The first time I had this dish was with my mentor and pal Jasper White. When I worked at Jasper's, which was very close to Chinatown, we often went for Chinese food after work and almost always ordered Singapore rice sticks, a one-pan meal that really packs a punch. Inspired by all the great flavors and not wanting to be without it too long, I came home and created my own version of this classic dish. You can make a meal of these noodles, or serve them as an accompaniment to grilled or baked fish or poultry.

If you want it hotter, add a little chili garlic sauce.

3 teaspoons light sesame oil
1 cup shredded cooked chicken in large pieces (approximately 1 breast or 2 thighs)
½ pound shrimp (16–20 count), peeled and deveined
1 small red onion, julienned
1 small red bell pepper, julienned
1 small carrot, julienned
2 scallions, white and green parts, cut into 1-inch pieces
1 tablespoon minced fresh ginger
4 cloves garlic, minced
1 tablespoon minced lemongrass
1 tablespoon Yellow Curry Paste (page 31)
1 teaspoon Sweet Spice Mix (page 81)
1 pound rice vermicelli, soaked in cold water for 10 minutes and drained well
1 cup Chicken Stock (page 34)
½ cup pineapple juice
1 tablespoon lime juice
2 tablespoons fish sauce
¾ cup sliced fresh cilantro leaves
⅓ cup sliced fresh mint leaves
½ cup fresh pea shoots (optional)
1 cup fresh mung bean sprouts
1 teaspoon kosher salt
½ teaspoon black pepper

Garnish:

Cilantro sprigs
Mint sprigs
Lime wedges

Place a wok or skillet over medium-high heat, and when it is hot, add 1 teaspoon of the oil. Add the chicken and cook until crisp on all sides, 2 to 3 minutes. Transfer the chicken to a large plate, and add the shrimp to the wok. Sear the shrimp until brown, 1 minute per side. Place the shrimp on the plate with the chicken, and set aside.

Curried Rice Sticks with Chicken, Shrimp, and Sprouts

Reheat the wok, add 1 teaspoon of the oil, and when it is hot, add the onion, bell pepper, and carrot. Cook until lightly caramelized but still crunchy, 1 to 2 minutes. Remove from the wok and set aside with the shrimp and chicken.

Reheat the wok, add the remaining 1 teaspoon oil, and when it is hot, add the scallions, ginger, garlic, and lemongrass. Cook until lightly caramelized, 1 minute. Add the curry paste and Sweet Spice Mix, and cook for 1 minute.

Add the noodles and cook for 1 to 2 minutes. Add the reserved chicken, shrimp, and vegetables along with the chicken stock, pineapple and lime juices, and fish sauce. Bring to a boil and cook until the liquids have completely evaporated, leaving the noodles wet and shiny, 2 to 3 minutes. Remove the wok from the heat and add the cilantro, mint, pea shoots (if using), sprouts, salt, and pepper. Toss well.

Garnish with the herb sprigs and lime wedges, and serve.

Serves 6

rice and noodles

chilled soba noodles with a tamari wasabi vinaigrette

Good soba noodles are made with buckwheat flour and are hard to beat. I suppose I like chilled soba the best because it can really show off the quality of the noodles, the particular flavor (soba comes in so many variations including green tea, yam, and wakame), and the other ingredients or accompaniments. I serve this with Miso Vegetable Pickles (page 66) on the side.

You can add crabmeat, chilled shrimp, or shredded chicken breast to this dish.

For the noodles:
3 quarts water
1 pound soba noodles
½ teaspoon light sesame oil

For the vinaigrette:
2 teaspoons wasabi powder (see page 78)
1 teaspoon water
¼ cup rice vinegar
2 tablespoons mirin
2 tablespoons tamari
2 tablespoons soy oil
1 tablespoon dark sesame oil
1 teaspoon minced fresh ginger
1 teaspoon kosher salt
½ teaspoon cracked black pepper

For the vegetables:
1 red bell pepper, cut into fine julienne
3 inches daikon, cut into fine julienne
3 scallions, white and green parts, cut into fine julienne
1 English (hothouse) cucumber, cut into fine julienne
½ teaspoon kosher salt
½ teaspoon cracked black pepper

Garnish:
12 sprigs cilantro or mint
Scallion Oil (page 45)

Place the water in a saucepan and bring to a boil over high heat. Add the soba noodles and cook until al dente, 5 to 6 minutes. Drain the noodles in a colander (do not rinse them), and then toss with the sesame oil to evenly coat. Spread them out to cool on a baking sheet or platter.

Prepare the vinaigrette: Place the wasabi powder and water in a small bowl and mix together with a fork. Whisking constantly, add the vinegar, mirin, tamari, soy and sesame oils, ginger, salt, and pepper.

Toss the noodles with ⅓ cup of the vinaigrette and divide them among six plates.

Place the bell pepper, daikon, scallions, and cucumber in a small bowl. Add the salt, pepper, and remaining vinaigrette, and toss to combine. Place a portion of the vegetables on top of each serving of noodles. Garnish with the cilantro sprigs, drizzle with Scallion Oil, and serve.

Serves 6

exotically spiced
basmati rice pilaf

Good basmati is a true wonder. Unlike short-grain rice, which is creamy, starchy, and sticky, basmati rice is nutty and cooks into individual grains, making it a perfect canvas for the sublime flavors of this pilaf. Serve this the same way you would serve steamed rice—which for me is with just about anything. Be sure to measure the water and rice carefully; it really does make a difference.

Garam masala: An Indian spice mixture with a more complex flavor and aroma than curry powder, *garam masala* is most often made by the cook rather than purchased premixed. As a result, the mixture varies greatly from home to home and from region to region. The combination may include any or all of the following: cumin, fennel, coriander, cardamom, cinnamon, saffron, pepper, chilies, and caraway seed. *Garam masala* is also used as a condiment, added to a dish at the very end of cooking. It's available at specialty markets.

1 tablespoon light sesame oil
1 tablespoon minced fresh ginger
4 cloves garlic, minced
2 shallots, minced
1 tablespoon garam masala
2 cups basmati rice
2 cups water
1½ teaspoons kosher salt
¼ teaspoon cracked black pepper

Heat a 1½-quart saucepan over medium heat, and when it is hot, add the oil. Add the ginger, garlic, and shallots and cook until lightly caramelized, 2 minutes. Add the *garam masala* and cook, stirring constantly, until toasted and aromatic, 1 minute. Add the rice and stir until each grain is well coated with spices and oil, 1 minute. Then add the water and bring to a boil. Reduce the heat to low, cover, and simmer until the rice is fluffy and tender, 18 to 20 minutes. Remove the pan from the heat and let it stand for 3 minutes. Add the salt and pepper, and serve immediately.

Serves 6

The flavor combinations and the look of this dish are classic Cantonese (now Guangzhou). One note of interest is that there is no soy sauce in this recipe—a nice change from a lot of fried-rice recipes, especially for anyone sensitive to sodium, wheat and gluten.

The finest fried rice is made with rice that has been cooked earlier and completely cooled, so if you want good results, don't rush it. Remember to use a large skillet. This dish is great with grilled or roasted beef or pork.

1 tablespoon light sesame oil
1 tablespoon minced fresh ginger
4 cloves garlic, minced
1 small red bell pepper, finely diced
1 small red onion, finely diced
1 cup peas, blanched
1 cup diced ham, (½ pound)
½ pound shrimp (16–20 count), peeled and deveined
3 eggs, beaten and scrambled in large curds
4 cups cooked jasmine rice
2 scallions, white and green parts, thinly sliced
1 teaspoon Sweet Spice Mix (page 81)
1 teaspoon kosher salt
½ teaspoon cracked black pepper

Place a wok or skillet over medium-high heat, and when it is hot, add the oil. Add the ginger and garlic and cook until lightly caramelized, about 1 minute. Add the bell pepper and red onion, and cook for 2 minutes. Add the peas, ham, and shrimp and cook, stirring constantly, for 2 to 3 minutes. Add the eggs and rice and keep things moving; don't let the rice stick to the sides of the pan. Add the scallions, Sweet Spice Mix, salt, and pepper, continuing to stir until heated throughout, 3 to 4 minutes. Serve immediately.

Serves 6

sweets and treats

When I crave something sweet, what I look for is the treats of childhood: candy, cookies, ice cream. In this chapter, you will learn some interesting and helpful candy-making and chocolate-handling skills. In order to do them well, you will need a heavy stainless steel—lined small saucepan and a good candy thermometer. And remember to read the instructions very carefully and to proceed with caution, especially when working around children: The caramels, toffees, and cooked sugar stages reach extremely high temperatures.

sweet ginger syrup and candied ginger

I am very fond of candied ginger and use a lot of it, especially in desserts such as the Gingery Lemon Meringue Tart (page 286) and the Ginger Spice Cookies (page 259). The syrup is used to flavor sauces and baked goods, such as the Chocolate Lemon Ginger Madeleines (page 257).

4 cups cold water
2½ cups sugar
½ cup light corn syrup
½ pound (10 inches) fresh ginger, cut into ¼-inch-thick slices (2 cups)

Line a cookie sheet with parchment paper.

Prepare the Sweet Ginger Syrup: Place the water, 2 cups of the sugar, and the corn syrup in a heavy saucepan and bring to a boil over medium heat. Stir to dissolve the sugar. Add the ginger and reduce the heat to low. Simmer until the liquid is reduced by half, the ginger is tender, and the syrup is thick enough to coat the back of a spoon, about 20 minutes.

Strain the syrup into a glass or ceramic container and set the ginger aside. Allow the syrup to cool to room temperature. Cover and refrigerate for up to 2 weeks.

Make the Candied Ginger: Place the drained ginger on the prepared cookie sheet and let it dry at room temperature until firm, usually overnight. Toss with the remaining ½ cup sugar to coat. Store in a covered plastic container at room temperature and at low humidity for up to 1 month.

2½ to 3 cups ginger syrup; 1 cup candied ginger

chocolate lemon
ginger madeleines

Madeleines are delicious cakelike cookies that are baked in a special pan that has shell-shaped molds. My version uses lemon zest to add a citrus complement to the chocolate—but if you wish, you can substitute orange zest, a more common pairing. You can also add a pinch of cinnamon or cloves to the batter.

Madeleine pans are not expensive and are readily available. You really should have one because once you taste these cookies, you won't be able to resist them. You can also use mini muffin pans; of course, you won't get the classic shape.

4 tablespoons (½ stick) unsalted butter, at room temperature
¼ cup sugar
½ tablespoon Sweet Ginger Syrup (page 256)
1 large egg
2 large egg yolks
Grated zest of 1 lemon
¼ cup all-purpose flour
¼ cup unsweetened cocoa powder
½ teaspoon baking powder
1 teaspoon ground ginger
¼ teaspoon kosher salt

Preheat the oven to 350°F. Butter a madeleine pan.

Place the butter and sugar in the bowl of a stand mixer fitted with the paddle (or use a hand-held mixer), and beat on medium-high speed until light and fluffy, 3 to 4 minutes. Scrape down the sides of the bowl with a rubber spatula. Lower the speed to medium, and add the ginger syrup. Add the egg and egg yolks, one at a time, beating until each is fully incorporated. Then add the lemon zest and mix to combine. Scrape down the sides of the bowl again.

Sift the flour, cocoa powder, baking powder, ginger, and salt together in a bowl, and add to the butter mixture. Mix until just combined; do not overmix.

Spoon the batter carefully into the prepared pan, being careful to wipe up any that spills outside the molds. Transfer the pan to the oven and bake until the cookies spring

Chocolate Lemon Ginger Madeleines

back when touched or until a skewer draws out cleanly, 14 to 15 minutes (6 to 8 minutes for the small madeleines). Set aside to cool for 10 minutes. Then unmold the madeleines and let them cool on a cake rack.

When they are completely cooled, store the madeleines in a well-sealed airtight container for up to 3 days.

24 standard or 48 small madeleines
(the mini-madeleines are really cute)

ginger spice cookies

I could be happy the rest of my days with just ice cream and cookies—especially these sweet, crumbly, cakelike, gingerbread-like ginger cookies, which are not to be confused with gingersnaps. Best when made fairly small, they are great with almost any kind of ice cream. These are particularly nice over the winter holidays—the flavors of ginger and molasses seem destined for warm fires and blustery days.

8 tablespoons (1 stick) unsalted butter, at room temperature
1½ cups sugar
1 large egg
½ cup molasses
4 cups all-purpose flour
1 tablespoon baking soda
1 tablespoon ground ginger
½ cup whole milk
2 tablespoons chopped Candied Ginger (page 256 or store-bought)

Preheat the oven to 350°F. Line a cookie sheet with parchment paper.

Place the butter and sugar in the bowl of a stand mixer fitted with the paddle (or use a hand-held mixer), and beat on medium-high speed until light and fluffy, 3 to 4 minutes. Scrape down the sides of the bowl with a rubber spatula. Lower the speed to medium and add the egg, beating until fully incorporated. Scrape down the sides again, and add the molasses. Mix until combined.

Sift the flour, baking soda, and ground ginger together in a bowl, and add to the butter mixture. Just before the flour is fully incorporated, add the milk and candied ginger. Mix until just combined; do not overmix.

Place teaspoonfuls of the batter 2 inches apart on the prepared cookie sheet, and transfer to the oven. Bake until the edges are lightly browned, 10 to 12 minutes. Let the cookies cool on the cookie sheet. Repeat with the remaining batter.

When they are completely cooled, store the cookies in a well-sealed airtight container for up to 3 days.

About 50 cookies

259

chewy oatmeal cookies
with apricots and cashews

These are one of my favorite kinds of cookies. When I was a kid I loved old-fashioned oatmeal-raisin cookies; in fact, they were one of the first sweets I learned to bake. This variation replaces the raisins with dried apricots and adds rich, buttery cashews. You can use other combinations of dried fruits and nuts (cherries and almonds, dried blueberries and pecans . . .), as long as you stick to the same proportions.

What is sour cream doing in a cookie? It gives the cookies their moist, soft, chewy texture.

This dough freezes well: Form it into logs, wrap them in parchment and then aluminum foil, and freeze. Simply slice through the frozen dough with a serrated knife and cook as directed below.

Dicing dried fruit: If you wipe the knife very lightly with soy oil or butter cooking spray, dried fruits will not stick to the knife when you dice them.

1 cup (2 sticks) unsalted butter, at room temperature
1 cup sugar
1 large egg
¼ cup sour cream
2 cups all-purpose flour
½ tablespoon baking powder
1 teaspoon kosher salt
2 cups rolled oats
1 cup diced dried apricots
½ cup chopped unsalted cashews, toasted

Place the butter and sugar in the bowl of a stand mixer fitted with the paddle (or use a hand-held mixer), and beat on medium-high speed until light and fluffy, 3 to 4 minutes. Scrape down the sides of the bowl with a rubber spatula. Lower the speed to medium and add the egg, beating until fully incorporated. Scrape down the sides again and add the sour cream. Continue mixing until just combined.

Sift the flour, baking powder, and salt together in another bowl and add to the butter mixture. Just before the flour is fully incorporated, add the oats, apricots, and cashews. Mix until just combined; do not overmix.

Place the dough on a sheet of parchment or wax paper and form it into three 1½- to 2-inch-thick logs. Wrap them up tightly in plastic wrap and refrigerate until firm, at least 1 hour (you can hold them for up to 1 week).

Preheat the oven to 350°F.

Slice each dough log into twelve rounds and arrange them on two cookie sheets. Bake until golden, 10 to 12 minutes. Allow the cookies to cool on the sheets.

Store the cooled cookies, tightly covered, at room temperature for up to 3 days.

About 36 cookies

Chewy Oatmeal Cookies with Apricots and Cashews

These delicious cookies are a delightful twist on the classic chocolate chip. We call for un-salted pistachios, but I've found that salted roasted pistachios are more commonly available in the supermarket, so if that is what you have, just eliminate the salt from the dough.

Other good combinations include almond and raisin, walnut and golden raisin, and apricot and pecan. It's amazing how much my appreciation for a classic like Toll House cookies has been renewed by varying the recipe.

1 cup (2 sticks) unsalted butter, at room temperature
¼ cup sugar
½ cup packed light brown sugar
2 large eggs
1 tablespoon vanilla extract
2½ cups all-purpose flour
1 teaspoon baking soda
1 teaspoon kosher salt
2 cups semisweet chocolate chips
½ cup dried cherries
1 cup unsalted pistachios, toasted and fully cooled

Place the butter, sugar, and brown sugar in the bowl of a stand mixer fitted with the paddle (or use a hand-held mixer), and beat on medium-high speed until light and fluffy, 3 to 4 minutes. Scrape down the sides of the bowl with a rubber spatula. Lower the speed to medium and add the eggs, one at a time, beating until each is fully incorporated. Scrape down the sides again and add the vanilla extract. Mix until just combined.

Sift the flour, baking soda, and salt together in another bowl, and add to the butter mixture. Just before the flour is fully incorporated, add the chocolate chips, dried cherries, and pistachios. Mix until just combined; do not overmix. The dough should appear fine and sandy.

Place the dough on a sheet of parchment or wax paper, and form it into a 1½- to 2-inch-thick log. Wrap it in plastic wrap and refrigerate until firm, at least 1 hour (you can store the dough for up to 1 week).

Preheat the oven to 350°F. Line a cookie sheet with parchment paper.

Slice the dough into twelve rounds and place six on the prepared cookie sheet. Bake until golden, 12 to 14 minutes. Let the cookies cool on the sheet. Repeat with the remaining six rounds.

Store the cooled cookies in an airtight container at room temperature for up to 3 days.

12 large cookies

pine nut shortbread

Along with custard and caramel, shortbread is one of the most addictive sweets I know. The trick to good shortbread is in creaming the butter and sugar just right. In this recipe, do not whip too much air into the butter.

1 cup (2 sticks) unsalted butter, at room temperature
¾ cup sugar
1½ tablespoons vanilla extract
2 cups all-purpose flour
½ teaspoon kosher salt
¼ cup pine nuts, toasted and cooled

Vanilla extract: Always buy pure vanilla extract and good-quality vanilla beans. There truly is a difference. Store the extract, tightly closed, in a dark place.

Preheat the oven to 350°F.

Place the butter and sugar in the bowl of a stand mixer fitted with the paddle (or use a hand-held mixer), and beat on medium-high speed until light but not too fluffy, 2 to 3 minutes. Scrape down the sides of the bowl with a rubber spatula. Add the vanilla extract, and mix until just combined.

Sift the flour and salt together in another bowl, and add to the butter mixture. Just before the flour is fully incorporated, add the pine nuts. Mix until just combined; do not overmix. The dough should appear fine and sandy.

Place a sheet of parchment paper on your countertop, and place the dough on the paper. Top with an additional sheet, and using a rolling pin, roll the dough out to ¼-inch thickness. Place the flattened dough on a cookie sheet and refrigerate for 30 minutes. (At this point the dough can be wrapped tightly in plastic wrap and frozen for up to 2 months.)

Remove the top layer of parchment and cut the dough into twelve squares, triangles, hearts, or whatever shape you like, using a sharp knife or a cookie cutter. Using a spatula to move the delicate dough, transfer half the cookies to a plate, and spread the remaining ones across the cookie sheet. Discard the bottom sheet of parchment. Transfer the cookie sheet to the oven and bake until the edges of the cookies are golden, 12 to 14 minutes. Allow the cookies to cool completely before removing them from the sheet. Repeat with the remaining dough.

Store the cooled cookies in an airtight container at a cool temperature for up to 1 week.

12 large cookies

sweets and treats

sugar-and-spice walnuts

My mother was crazy for football. On Sundays she would serve a big brunch, and then afterward she would be tuned into the professional games all day. Not a true couch potato, she was always rushing around greeting guests or neighbors who regularly dropped in. She would make little snacks throughout the day: deviled eggs, quiche, and these sweet-and-savory walnuts. Although I am more of a basketball fan, sometimes I make these on Sunday afternoons too. They never last long.

1 large egg white
2 cups walnut halves, pecan halves, or a combination
6 tablespoons sugar
1 teaspoon salt
1 teaspoon ground ginger
1 teaspoon ground cinnamon
¼ teaspoon ground cloves

Preheat the oven to 350°F. Line a cookie sheet with parchment paper.

Place the egg white in a stainless-steel bowl and whisk until light, doubled in volume, and forming soft peaks, 3 to 5 minutes. Add the walnuts and toss to coat. Add the sugar, salt, and spices, and toss to coat.

Spread the nuts evenly across the prepared cookie sheet, separating them so they don't create clumps, and transfer to the oven. Bake for 10 minutes. Stir the nuts and continue baking until they have taken on a lovely toasted color and are appealingly fragrant, 5 minutes. Set aside to cool slightly before eating (if you are able).

Store the nuts in a covered plastic container at room temperature for up to 1 week.

2 cups

chocolate-covered stout caramel candies

I am a sucker for anything and everything caramel! These chewy, stick-to-your-teeth, creamy caramel sweets are the kind you really want to last forever, even as they melt away. The stout adds a wonderful roasted malt flavor that acts as a kind of bitter foil to the sweetness. Ohhhh, these are *so* good.

¾ cup stout (such as Guinness, Murphy's, or
  Samuel Smith Oatmeal Stout)
½ cup light corn syrup
½ cup packed light brown sugar
½ cup sugar
6 tablespoons (¾ stick) unsalted butter
1 cup heavy cream
1 pound bittersweet chocolate, chopped

Generously butter an 8- or 9-inch loaf pan.

Place the stout, corn syrup, and both sugars in a heavy stainless-steel saucepan and bring to a boil over medium heat. Boil, stirring to dissolve the sugars, for 5 minutes. The stout will foam a lot at the start but will settle down after a few minutes.

Add the butter and cream and bring to a boil again. Stir, and continue cooking until the mixture reaches the soft ball stage (240°F on your candy thermometer), 12 to 14 minutes. (You can test the syrup by dropping a small amount into a bowl of ice water. When it's cold, the syrup should form a soft, pliable mass that you can shape between your fingers.)

Pour the mixture into the prepared pan and let it cool completely at room temperature overnight.

Remove the caramel from the pan and place it on a cutting board lined with parchment paper. Cut it into thirty-six 1-inch pieces.

Bring a small pot of water to a boil and then remove it from the heat. Place the chocolate in a dry stainless-steel bowl, and place the bowl over the hot water so that it rests on the pan without touching the hot water. Stir the chocolate continuously while it melts, until there are just a few little unmelted bits. Remove the bowl from the heat and continue stirring to finish melting. (Allowing the chocolate to finish melting off the heat allows it to cool slightly.)

Line a cookie sheet with parchment paper. Using two forks, dip the caramels into the melted chocolate and lift them out, allowing the excess chocolate to run back into the bowl. Place the caramels on the prepared sheet and allow the chocolate to set for 10 to 15 minutes.

Place a piece of parchment paper in the bottom of a plastic container, and arrange one layer of caramels on it. Top with another piece of parchment and another layer of caramels. Repeat until all the caramels have been stored. Cover and store in the refrigerator or at room temperature, away from humidity, for up to 1 week.

36 pieces

Chocolate: The word "chocolate" comes from the Aztec word *xocolatl,* which means "bitter water." While we think of chocolate as sweet, cocoa beans in their purest form are quite bitter. When cocoa beans are roasted and ground to a paste, the result is called chocolate liquor. The taste of chocolate is determined by the amount of chocolate liquor it contains. The higher the percentage of chocolate liquor, the more bitter the flavor. Unsweetened baking chocolate is generally pure chocolate liquor. Bittersweet or semisweet chocolate is 35 percent chocolate liquor. Milk chocolate has a low percentage of chocolate liquor, usually only 10 percent, and it also contains milk (usually 12 percent). White chocolate contains cocoa butter but no chocolate liquor, and therefore is not technically chocolate.

This is a fabulous candy. Once you master the toffee (which is easier if you have a candy thermometer), you are on your way to making this treat—and many variations—on a regular basis. Try milk chocolate and almonds or pecans, or white chocolate and pistachios.

Remember to be careful when making candies—the caramelized sugar is extremely hot!

Serve these as a treat, with coffee after dinner or crumbled over ice cream.

½ cup (1 stick) unsalted butter
¼ cup sugar
¼ cup packed light brown sugar
2½ tablespoons light corn syrup
2½ tablespoons heavy cream
Pinch of kosher salt
1½ cups sliced almonds, toasted and cooled
½ pound bittersweet chocolate

Line a cookie sheet with parchment paper. Butter an offset spatula.

Place the butter, white and brown sugars, corn syrup, and cream in a small heavy saucepan and cook over medium heat until the butter melts and the sugar dissolves, 3 to 5 minutes. Reduce the heat to low and simmer, stirring once or twice until the mixture takes on a lovely caramel hue. Continue cooking the toffee until it reaches 280°F on a candy thermometer, 10 to 12 minutes. (This is the soft crack stage: You can test the toffee without a thermometer by dropping a spoonful onto a lightly buttered plate or cookie sheet and letting it cool quickly. The cooled toffee should break with a snap but not be brittle or hard on the teeth.)

Add the salt and ½ cup of the almonds, and stir to combine. Carefully pour the toffee onto the prepared cookie sheet, spreading it out as thin as possible with the prepared offset spatula. Cool to room temperature.

While the toffee is cooling, melt the chocolate: Bring a small pot of water to a boil and then remove it from the heat. Break the chocolate into pieces and place the pieces in a dry stainless-steel bowl. Place the bowl on the pan but do not allow it to actually touch the hot water. Stir the chocolate continuously while it melts, until there are just

sweets and treats

a few little unmelted bits. Then remove the bowl from the pan and continue stirring until the chocolate has melted completely.

Break the toffee into serving-size pieces. Place the remaining 1 cup toasted almonds on a plate or in a shallow dish.

Using tongs or two forks, dip the toffee pieces in the melted chocolate and lift them out, allowing the excess chocolate to run back into the bowl. Then roll them in the almonds, and set aside to cool on parchment paper for 20 minutes.

Place a piece of parchment paper in the bottom of a plastic container and add one layer of toffee pieces. Top with another piece of parchment and another layer of toffee. Repeat until all the toffee has been stored. Cover and store in the refrigerator or at room temperature, away from humidity, for up to 2 weeks.

24 to 30 small candies

Although this is a candy that children will love to eat, it may not be a good one to make with them: The sugar must be taken to a high temperature (above 300°F) and then cooked slowly. The result: a crisp caramel candy that shatters when broken and is crunchy when eaten. Great for a snack just about any time—or ground and stirred into a cake frosting or sprinkled over frosted cupcakes.

1 cup sugar

½ cup water

¼ cup light corn syrup

1 cup macadamia nuts, toasted, cooled, and coarsely chopped

½ teaspoon kosher salt

1 tablespoon unsalted butter

½ teaspoon vanilla extract

½ teaspoon baking soda

Lightly butter a cookie sheet and an offset spatula.

Place the sugar, water, and corn syrup in a small, heavy stainless steel–lined saucepan and bring to a boil over medium heat. Stir until the sugar has dissolved. Reduce the heat and simmer until the syrup turns a light caramel color (like a camel-hair coat) and reaches 320°F on a candy thermometer, 14 to 16 minutes.

Stir in the macadamia nuts. Then add the salt, butter, vanilla, and baking soda, one at a time, stirring gently after each addition.

Carefully pour the brittle onto the prepared cookie sheet, spreading it out as thin as possible with the prepared spatula. Set aside to cool to room temperature, about 20 minutes.

Break the brittle into twenty-four to thirty small pieces.

Place a piece of parchment paper in the bottom of a plastic container and add one layer of the brittle. Top with another piece of parchment and another layer of brittle. Repeat until all the brittle has been stored. Cover and store at room temperature, away from humidity, for up to 2 weeks.

24 to 30 small pieces

sweets and treats

caramelized lemongrass lemonade

I first had the idea for this lemonade when I taught a kids' cooking class several years ago. We've since made it for almost every special event, especially those on hot summer days. For adults, I am convinced that vodka is the best addition, but gin and dark rum have been rather pleasing as well. Serve this by the pitcher over ice, garnished with mint and sliced lemons, oranges, and limes.

4 cups sugar
1 cup cool water
2 stalks lemongrass, outer husk discarded, inner heart cut into 3-inch lengths
2 cups lemon juice, fresh or frozen
6 cups boiling water

Garnish:
Fresh mint leaves
2 lemons, thinly sliced, or about
*   12 stalks lemongrass, outer*
*   husk discarded*
1 orange, thinly sliced
2 limes, thinly sliced

Place a heavy-bottomed stainless steel–lined saucepan over medium heat. Add the sugar and cool water, and cook, stirring, until the sugar is dissolved. Brush the sides of the pot with a little extra water to be sure no sugar crystals remain. Cook until the sugar syrup is a light golden brown, 5 to 8 minutes. Then add the lemongrass and reduce the heat. Do not stir, or the caramel may crystallize.

Caramelized Lemongrass Lemonade

Cook until the caramel is a deep golden brown, 10 to 12 minutes, and then carefully remove the pan from the heat. If you are using a candy thermometer, the caramel should be approximately 330°F.

Cool the caramel in the pan for 2 to 3 minutes, and then carefully add the lemon juice. Pour the boiling water over the caramel-lemon mixture, and stir until the caramel is completely dissolved. Transfer the mixture to a plastic or ceramic pitcher, cover, and refrigerate for up to 5 days.

Serve over ice and garnish with the mint and the lemon, orange, and lime slices.

About 3 quarts

desserts

Rice pudding. Layer cake. Lemon meringue pie. All familiar and homey desserts to which I have added a simple flavor twist: The rice pudding gets exotic spices, the chocolate layer cake is combined with banana and tea flavors, and the lemon meringue pie is accented with fresh ginger.

At Salamander, the challenge with desserts is that traditional Asian sweets tend not to satisfy the Western sweet tooth. So I try to come up with desserts that are well matched to the savory side of Salamander's cuisine, like the coconut spring rolls. But the majority of the recipes here bridge East and West by expanding the flavors of our old favorites with a hint of the exotic.

ginger ice cream

I love ice cream! When I was a child, ice-cream-making was a whole-family endeavor: We had an old hand-cranked machine and we all had to get in on the act. Today there are lots of high-quality machines on the market that require no ice, no salt, and fewer participants. I don't know—is that good or bad? Either way, this is a nice base to vary from as your imagination and seasonal ingredients inspire you.

1 cup whole milk
4 cups heavy cream
1⅓ cups sugar
1 vanilla bean, split lengthwise
5 inches fresh ginger, thinly sliced
10 large egg yolks

Place the milk, cream, ⅔ cup of the sugar, vanilla bean, and ginger in a stainless steel–lined saucepan and bring just to a boil over medium-high heat. Remove from the heat.

Place the egg yolks and the remaining ⅔ cup sugar in a large mixing bowl and whisk together. Ladle 1 cup of the hot milk mixture into the egg mixture and whisk together to temper the egg mixture. Add the tempered egg mixture to the milk mixture and carefully bring to a boil over medium heat, stirring continually. Cook until the custard is thick enough to coat a spoon, 5 to 8 minutes.

Strain the custard into a ceramic, glass, or metal bowl and discard the solids. Cover and refrigerate. Freeze in an ice cream maker according to the manufacturer's instructions.

Vanilla beans: Vanilla beans should be kept tightly wrapped in plastic. After using a bean, submerge the pod in white sugar; within a few days the sugar will be perfumed by the vanilla. Or store it in a bottle of Kahlúa or rum and then use the liqueur to bake with, or pour it into your coffee.

Variations

Berry: Fold 1 or more cups of crushed blackberries or strawberries into the custard when it is almost frozen.

Toasted Coconut: Fold 1 cup toasted coconut into the ice cream as it comes out of the freezer.

Spice: Add two 3-inch cinnamon sticks, 2 star anise pods, and 2 whole cloves to the milk mixture when bringing it to a boil. Strain, and discard the spices along with the other solids.

Slightly more than 1 quart

white chocolate ice cream

White chocolate has an exotic, luxurious appeal. It's a tricky ingredient to use, however, because it contains so much cocoa butter. In order to compensate for the high fat content, I put more milk in the custard and then, because that rich composition is unstable, add the last cup of cream to the finished custard so that it quickly cools to the gentle temperature that white chocolate prefers.

You can't substitute dark or milk chocolate for the white, but you can swirl in ½ to 1 cup of chopped chocolate chips as the ice cream comes out of the machine.

2 cups whole milk
3 cups heavy cream
1⅓ cups sugar
1 vanilla bean, split lengthwise
10 large egg yolks
5 ounces white chocolate, finely chopped

Place the milk, 2 cups of the cream, ⅔ cup of the sugar, and the vanilla bean in a stainless steel–lined saucepan and bring just to a boil over medium-high heat. Remove from the heat.

Place the egg yolks and the remaining ⅔ cup sugar in a large mixing bowl and whisk together. Ladle 1 cup of the hot milk mixture into the egg mixture and whisk together to temper the egg mixture. Add the tempered egg mixture to the milk mixture and carefully bring to a boil over medium heat, stirring continually. Cook until the custard is thick enough to coat a spoon, 5 to 6 minutes.

Strain the custard and discard the solids. Add the white chocolate and whisk until the chocolate has melted and the mixture is smooth. Whisk in the remaining 1 cup cream. Cover and refrigerate. Freeze in an ice cream maker according to the manufacturer's instructions.

1½ quarts

peanut butter and chocolate ice cream parfait

Do you remember the Nutty Buddy ice cream bars? I love the combination of peanuts and dark chocolate: I have to admit that the Nutty Buddy combo was the inspiration for this dish.

You can add toasted peanuts and chocolate chips between the layers if you want more texture and intensity. Serve this with a chocolate or caramel sauce, if desired, and Ginger Spice Cookies (page 259).

2 cups whole milk
4 cups heavy cream
1 cup sugar
10 large egg yolks
½ cup natural unsweetened, unsalted peanut butter
½ pound unsweetened chocolate, chopped into small pieces

Place the milk, cream, and ½ cup of the sugar in a stainless steel–lined saucepan and bring just to a boil over medium-high heat. Remove from the heat.

Place the egg yolks and the remaining ½ cup sugar in a large mixing bowl and whisk together. Ladle 1 cup of the hot milk mixture into the egg mixture and whisk together to temper the egg mixture. Add the tempered egg mixture to the milk mixture and carefully bring to a boil over medium heat, stirring continually. Cook until the custard is thick enough to coat a spoon, about 6 minutes.

Strain the custard and discard the solids. Divide the custard evenly between two containers. Add the peanut butter to one container and whisk until the mixture is smooth. Add the chocolate to the other and whisk until the chocolate has melted and the mixture is smooth. Cover both and refrigerate. Freeze each in an ice cream maker according to the manufacturer's instructions.

Line an 8- or 9-inch loaf or baking pan with plastic wrap, leaving a generous overhang on all four sides.

Spoon alternating layers of each ice cream into the prepared pan and smooth them out. Freeze overnight.

To serve, unmold and slice the ice cream.

Serves 12

simple and rich rice pudding

Puddings delight the kid in us all, no matter what age we are. When I had food shops in Boston and Cambridge, we always sold the homiest desserts: crumb cakes, individual pies, butter-scotch pudding, chocolate pudding, and, of course, rice pudding. This is a very simple and ba-sic recipe, although many variations come to mind: Try adding golden raisins, dried cranberries, almonds, pistachios . . . I also like to brûlée (brown) the top for a little extra touch.

1 cup Japanese sushi rice or short-grain rice
1½ cups sugar
8 cups whole milk
4 cardamom pods
1 cup heavy cream
2 large eggs
4 large egg yolks
1 teaspoon kosher salt

Place the rice, sugar, milk, and cardamom pods in a heavy stainless-steel saucepan and bring to a boil over medium heat. Reduce the heat to low and simmer, stirring oc-casionally, until the rice is tender, 20 to 25 minutes.

Place the cream, eggs, egg yolks, and salt in a large mixing bowl and whisk to-gether. Ladle 1 cup of the hot cooked rice into the egg mixture and whisk together to temper the egg mixture. Add the tempered egg mixture to the rice mixture and care-fully bring just barely to a boil over medium heat, stirring continually.

Immediately transfer the pudding to a ceramic or glass container, and lay plastic wrap directly on the top of the pudding (to prevent a skin from forming while the pudding cools). Refrigerate for at least 2 hours and up to 2 days. Remove the car-damom pods before serving.

Serves 12

old-fashioned honey pound cake

My grandmother, Carrie Boyd, and her sister, Arah, baked the most wonderful pound cakes. My grandmother never measured, she never fretted . . . she just knew. She would serve slices of buttery moist cake, toasted, with glasses of ice-cold fresh raw milk. I have always appreciated the influence my grandmother had on me: She was a very serious woman who expressed her love through her cooking, her kitchen, and the table she set.

Serve this honey-scented pound cake with fresh berries and either whipped cream or ice cream.

1¼ cups (2½ sticks) unsalted butter, at room temperature
1 cup sugar
1 cup honey
4 extra-large eggs, at room temperature
3 cups all-purpose flour
2 teaspoons baking powder
½ teaspoon kosher salt
1 cup whole milk
2 teaspoons vanilla extract

Preheat the oven to 350°F. Butter and flour a 10-inch Bundt pan.

Place the butter and sugar in the bowl of a stand mixer fitted with the paddle (or use a hand-held mixer), and beat at high speed until very light and fluffy, 4 to 5 minutes. Scrape down the sides of the bowl with a rubber spatula. Gradually add the honey, still beating. Scrape down the bowl again. Reduce the speed to medium and add the eggs, one at a time, allowing each to be fully incorporated before adding the next.

In a separate bowl, sift together the flour, baking powder, and salt.

In another bowl, combine the milk and vanilla.

Alternate adding the dry and wet ingredients to the egg mixture in two or three batches, finishing with dry. Spoon the batter into the prepared Bundt pan. Transfer it to the oven and bake until a tester comes out clean, 50 to 60 minutes.

Set the pan on a wire rack to cool for 10 to 15 minutes before unmolding the cake. Let the cake finish cooling on the wire rack.

Serves 12

easy chocolate cake with bananas and raspberry-tea syrup

This moist and easy chocolate cake has a beautiful texture.

If I am feeling very adventurous and have a little extra time, I like to sauté the bananas with butter and brown sugar, and sometimes rum. I spread this mixture across the split cake before frosting. Mmmm.

Well wrapped, it keeps nicely for up to 3 days.

8 tablespoons (1 stick) unsalted butter, at room temperature
1 cup sugar
2 large eggs
¾ cup cake flour
¼ teaspoon baking powder
1 teaspoon baking soda
½ teaspoon kosher salt
3 tablespoons unsweetened cocoa powder
¾ cup whole milk
½ tablespoon vanilla extract

For the raspberry tea syrup:
1 tablespoon raspberry tea leaves, or 3 teabags
2 cups hot water
1½ cups sugar
½ cup light corn syrup
½ cup frozen raspberries

1 cup heavy cream, whipped
3 or 4 ripe bananas, thinly sliced
Confectioners' sugar, for dusting

Cake flour: A soft wheat flour with a high starch content and very fine texture, cake flour yields delicate and tender cakes and pastries.

Preheat the oven to 350°F. Butter an 8- or 9-inch springform pan.

Make the cake: Place the butter and sugar in the bowl of a stand mixer fitted with the paddle (or use a hand-held mixer) and beat on medium-high speed until light and fluffy, 3 to 4 minutes. Scrape down the sides of the bowl with a rubber spatula. Lower the speed to medium and add the eggs, beating until fully incorporated. Scrape down the sides again.

Sift the flour, baking powder, baking soda, salt, and cocoa powder together in another bowl.

Place the milk and vanilla extract in a small bowl and stir to combine.

Easy Chocolate Cake with Bananas and Raspberry-Tea Syrup

Add the flour mixture and the milk mixture alternately to the egg mixture. Do not overmix. Pour the batter into the prepared springform pan and transfer it to the oven. Bake until the cake springs back when touched and a tester comes out clean, 30 to 40 minutes. Set the cake aside in the pan to cool to room temperature. Then unmold and cool completely on a wire rack.

To make the raspberry-tea syrup: Place the tea in the hot water and set aside to steep for 3 to 4 minutes. Strain into a saucepan and discard the solids. Add the sugar, corn syrup, and raspberries to the tea and bring to a boil over high heat. Cook until reduced to 2 cups. Cover, and refrigerate until completely cooled.

Slice the cake in half horizontally, and spread the bottom half with the whipped cream. Arrange the bananas over the whipped cream, and replace the top half of the cake.

Pour a pool of raspberry-tea syrup on each plate, and place a slice of cake next to it. Dust the cake with confectioner's sugar.

Serves 10

These are fun to make and to eat (with your fingers). If your kids love coconut, this is a perfect recipe to work on together—everyone can get their hands into it and have fun shaping the spring rolls.

I always push our bakers to come up with dishes that complement the rest of the menu; this crispy coconut dessert was one of our most inspired ideas. The rolls can be frozen; simply thaw them before baking.

For frozen blackberries, I recommend Cascadian Farms. Try other berries too.

¼ *cup light corn syrup*
1¼ *cups finely grated unsweetened coconut, toasted and cooled*
4 *tablespoons (½ stick) unsalted butter, melted*
⅓ *cup sugar*
2 *large egg whites*
2 *teaspoons all-purpose flour*
½ *teaspoon vanilla extract*
¼ *teaspoon kosher salt*
12 *spring roll or lumpia wrappers*

For the dipping sauce:
1 *cup Sweet Ginger Syrup (page 256)*
1 *cup fresh or frozen blackberries*

Garnish:
Fresh mint leaves

Preheat the oven to 350°F. Line a cookie sheet with parchment paper.

Place the corn syrup, coconut, 2 tablespoons of the melted butter, the sugar, egg whites, flour, vanilla, and salt in a stainless-steel bowl. Using a wooden spoon, combine until well mixed and slightly sticky to the touch.

Place one spring roll wrapper on a cutting board or on a clean kitchen towel, and position it so that one point is toward you, forming a diamond shape. Cut off the bottom 1½ inches of the diamond. Place about ⅓ cup of the filling in the center of the wrapper. Fold and tuck the sides in, envelope-style, to close off the ends, and then fold the wrapper once around the filling. Continue rolling and tightening until you get to the pointed end. Seal the edges with some of the remaining melted butter. Repeat with the remaining filling and spring roll wrappers. Cover and refrigerate until ready to bake, or for up to 24 hours. (See photo, page 73.)

Place the spring rolls, seam side down, on the prepared cookie sheet and transfer to the oven. Bake until they are a deep golden color and crispy-crunchy, 20 to 25 minutes.

Meanwhile, prepare the sauce: Place the ginger syrup and blackberries in a food processor or blender, and blend until smooth. Transfer the sauce to a small dish.

Place two spring rolls on each plate, and pass the sauce as a dipping sauce.

Garnish with mint leaves, if desired.

Serves 6

Everyone should have a wonderful recipe for a pineapple upside-down cake! Now that you do, make sure you use a cast-iron skillet as your cake pan; it conducts the heat well, properly caramelizes the pineapple, and bakes the cake evenly. If you can find them, use the sweeter golden pineapples—they're more flavorful than the white ones.

You can substitute apples, pears, mangoes, or cherries for the pineapple.

This is great with Ginger or White Chocolate Ice Cream (pages 274, 276).

For the streusel:

½ cup all-purpose flour

⅓ cup packed light brown sugar

8 tablespoons (1 stick) cold unsalted butter, cut into cubes

For the pineapple:

8 tablespoons (1 stick) cold unsalted butter, cut into cubes

1½ cups sugar

1 ripe pineapple, golden if possible, cored and cut into ¼-inch-thick slices

For the cake:

3 large eggs, separated

½ cup sugar

½ teaspoon kosher salt

2¼ cups whole milk

2 teaspoons vanilla extract

2¼ cups all-purpose flour

½ teaspoon baking powder

½ teaspoon ground cinnamon

Preheat the oven to 350°F.

Prepare the streusel: Place the flour, brown sugar, and cold cubed butter in a food processor and process until it forms pea-size crumbs. Set aside.

Prepare the pineapple: Place a 12-inch cast-iron skillet over medium heat, and when it is hot, add the butter and sugar and stir to dissolve the sugar. Watching carefully, cook until the sugar is lightly caramelized, 4 to 5 minutes. Remove the skillet from the heat and add the pineapple slices, arranging them decoratively in a single layer, and top with the streusel.

Make the cake: Place the egg yolks and sugar in a stand mixer fitted with the whisk attachment (or use a hand-held mixer) and whip at high speed until light and doubled in volume, 3 to 4 minutes. The mixture should form ribbons when it falls from the beater.

In a separate bowl, combine the egg whites and salt. Whisk until they form stiff peaks. Fold the whites into the yolks, trying not to lose the volume. Then fold in the milk and vanilla.

Sift the flour, baking powder, and cinnamon together in a bowl, and gently fold into the egg mixture. Pour the batter over the pineapples. Transfer the skillet to the oven and bake until fully cooked, about 45 minutes (a cake tester should come out clean). Set the skillet aside to cool for 10 minutes. Then invert the cake onto a serving platter so that the caramelized pineapples are on top. Serve warm or at room temperature.

Serves 10

gingery lemon meringue tart

My mother regularly made Key lime and lemon meringue pies when I was a child. Later, when I worked at a French restaurant in Atlanta, I had to prepare and send out an endless stream of baked Alaskas. After that, I just had to take a break from meringues! Now that I am back in the groove, I have added ginger syrup to the meringue, and candied ginger to the rich lemony custard. This recipe will show you how to make an Italian meringue: a finer, more stable meringue than simply whipping egg whites and sugar (although of course you can do that if you want).

This recipe makes two tart shells—freeze one to make the next tart that much quicker to prepare!

For the tart dough:
2¼ cups all-purpose flour
1½ teaspoons kosher salt
¾ cup (1½ sticks) cold unsalted butter, cut into cubes
½ cup ice-cold water
1 teaspoon fresh lemon juice

For the filling:
8 tablespoons (1 stick) unsalted butter, melted
1 cup sugar
1 cup eggs (4 or 5 large eggs)
½ cup fresh lemon juice (2 to 3 lemons)
¼ cup chopped Candied Ginger (page 256)

For the meringue:
½ cup sugar
2 tablespoons Sweet Ginger Syrup (page 256)
2 tablespoons fresh lemon juice
3 large egg whites

Garnish:
Candied Lemon Slices (recipe on page 289)

Prepare the tart dough: Place the flour and salt in a stainless-steel bowl and toss together. Add the butter, and using your fingertips only, rub the butter into the flour until it forms large coarse flakes about the size and shape of thick corn flakes.

Add the cold water and the lemon juice, and toss together with a fork. Do not overwork the dough or it may become tough. The dough should come together easily when pressed between your hands.

Divide the dough in half and form each half into a ball. Flatten them into disks, wrap in plastic wrap, and refrigerate for at least 30 minutes and up to 3 or 4 days (or freeze for up to 1 month).

Remove one of the portions of dough from the refrigerator. If it has been refrigerated for several hours or days, allow the dough to soften for 10 to 20 minutes. The dough should be chilled, but if it is too cold you will have to work it too hard and may not be able to roll it; if the dough is too warm, there is a chance that the butter may melt.

Place the dough on a very lightly floured work surface. Rub a little flour into a rolling pin, and rolling from the center of the dough to the edges, roll it out to form a rough circle approximately 12 inches in diameter (use your tart pan as a guide—you need about an inch extra on all sides).

Fold the dough in half and then in quarters, or roll it around your pin, to make it easier to move it to the tart pan. Line the tart pan with the dough; do not stretch the dough. Press the dough firmly into the sides of the pan. Refrigerate the dough-lined pan for at least 30 minutes and, covered, up to 24 hours.

Preheat the oven to 350°F.

Line the tart shell with parchment paper or aluminum foil, and fill it with rice or beans or pie weights. Bake the tart shell for 30 minutes. Remove the parchment and rice, and bake for another 5 to 6 minutes. Set the shell aside to cool. Leave the oven on.

While the tart shell is cooling, prepare the filling: Place the melted butter and the sugar in the bowl of a stand mixer fitted with the whisk attachment (or use a hand-held mixer), and whisk until the sugar is dissolved, 1 to 2 minutes. Add the eggs and whisk until smooth, 1 to 2 minutes. Add the lemon juice and candied ginger, and whisk until completely combined. Pour the filling into the cooled tart shell.

Place the tart on a cookie sheet, transfer it to the oven, and bake until the filling is firmly set and does not jiggle when shaken, 18 to 20 minutes. Transfer the tart to a wire rack and allow to cool completely.

Reset the oven to broil (or use a cook's torch).

Gingery Lemon Meringue Tart

Prepare the meringue: Place the sugar, ginger syrup, and lemon juice in a small, heavy stainless steel–lined saucepan and bring to a boil over medium-high heat. Cook for 8 to 10 minutes, until the syrup reaches 240°F on a candy thermometer. (This is the soft ball stage. You can test the syrup by dropping a small amount into a bowl of ice water. When it's cold, the syrup should form a soft, pliable mass that you can shape between your fingers.)

Place the egg whites in the bowl of a stand mixer fitted with the whisk (or use a hand-held mixer), and whisk on high speed until they form soft peaks. Reduce the speed to medium and carefully drizzle in the hot syrup. Whisk until they form firm peaks and all the syrup has been incorporated.

Spread the lemon ginger meringue over the cooled lemon tart, or pipe it decoratively, and brown it under the broiler or with a torch. Garnish with the candied lemon slices.

Serves 8 to 10

candied lemon slices

1½ cups water
1 cup sugar, plus additional for dusting
1 lemon, very thinly sliced

Line a cookie sheet with parchment paper.

Place the water and sugar in a stainless-steel saucepan and bring to a boil over high heat. Cook for 2 to 4 minutes, and then add the lemon slices. Reduce the heat to low and gently simmer until the lemon is tender, 10 to 12 minutes.

Transfer the lemon slices to the prepared sheet and spread them out to dry in a single layer for 4 to 6 hours. Store them, layered between sheets of parchment paper, in a closed container for 2 to 5 days. They will stay somewhat soft and pliable. Dust with additional sugar before using.

About 10 slices

Strangely enough, my dad does not like chocolate but has a tremendous sweet tooth—he usually orders two desserts just for himself whenever we go out to dinner. This is one of his favorite desserts and a great example of how you can incorporate an Asian ingredient into a familiar recipe. I have to admit to ordering coconut cream pie any time I'm at a diner.

This is the same tart shell as on page 286—the recipe makes two shells. If you froze the extra one there, you can skip all that preparation here.

I usually brown the top of this tart just prior to serving it with a dollop of fresh whipped cream and a sprinkling of coconut.

For the tart dough:

2¼ cups all-purpose flour
1½ teaspoons kosher salt
¾ cup (1½ sticks) cold unsalted butter, cut into cubes
½ cup ice-cold water
1 teaspoon fresh lemon juice

For the filling:

3 large eggs, at room temperature
¾ cup sugar
1 cup whole milk
½ cup unsweetened coconut milk
1 teaspoon vanilla extract
¾ cup shredded unsweetened coconut, toasted and cooled
1 cup heavy cream, whipped (optional)

Prepare the tart shell: Place the flour and salt in a stainless-steel bowl and toss together. Add the butter, and using your fingertips only, rub the butter into the flour until it forms large coarse flakes about the size and shape of thick corn flakes.

Add the cold water and the lemon juice, and toss together with a fork. Do not overwork the dough or it may become tough. The dough should come together easily when pressed between your hands.

290 | desserts

Divide the dough in half and form each half into a ball. Flatten them into disks, wrap in plastic wrap, and refrigerate for at least 30 minutes and up to 3 or 4 days (or freeze for up to 1 month).

Remove one of the portions of dough from the refrigerator. If it has been refrigerated for several hours or days, allow the dough to soften for 10 to 20 minutes. The dough should be chilled, but if it is too cold you will have to work it too hard and may not be able to roll it; if the dough is too warm, there is chance that the butter may melt.

Place the dough on a very lightly floured work surface. Rub a little flour into a rolling pin, and rolling from the center of the dough to the edges, roll it out to form a rough circle approximately 12 inches in diameter (use your tart pan as a guide—you will need about an inch extra on all sides).

Fold the dough in half and then quarters, or roll it around your pin, to make it easier to move it to the tart pan. Line the tart pan with the dough; do not stretch the dough. Press the dough firmly into the sides of the pan. Refrigerate the dough-lined pan for at least 30 minutes and, covered, up to 24 hours.

Preheat the oven to 350°F.

Line the tart shell with parchment paper or aluminum foil, and fill it with rice or beans or pie weights. Bake the tart shell for 20 minutes. Remove the parchment and rice, and bake for another 5 to 6 minutes. Set the shell aside to cool. Reduce the oven heat to 300°F.

While the tart shell is cooling, prepare the filling:

Place the eggs and sugar in the bowl of a stand mixer fitted with the whisk (or use a hand-held mixer), and whisk on high speed until the sugar is dissolved, 1 to 2 minutes. Add the milk, coconut milk, and vanilla, and whisk until well combined, about 1 minute. Add ¼ cup of the coconut. Pour into the cooled tart shell.

Place the tart on a cookie sheet, transfer it to the oven, and bake until the custard is firmly set and jiggles slightly when shaken, 50 to 60 minutes. Transfer the tart pan to a rack and allow to cool completely

If desired, spread the whipped cream over the cooled tart (or pipe it decoratively). Sprinkle with the remaining ½ cup coconut.

This pie will keep for up to 3 days (if it lasts that long!), tightly wrapped, in the refrigerator.

Serves 8 to 10

These sweet banana-filled wontons are an easy treat to make. I created them for the dessert menu at the opening of Salamander in 1994, and they became one of our most frequently requested items. They still make an appearance on the menu at the new Copley Square restaurant.

It is a good idea to make the filling and the anglaise ahead of time, but don't fill and seal the wontons more than 2 or 3 hours before cooking. You can add nuts or chocolate chips to the filling for a twist that will please the kids. These are delicious with Ginger Ice Cream (page 274) or Macadamia Nut Brittle (page 270).

For the anglaise:
6 large egg yolks
¾ cup sugar
1 cup whole milk
1 cup heavy cream
2 to 3 tablespoons dark rum

For the filling:
2 tablespoons unsalted butter
2 or 3 ripe bananas, sliced into ¼-inch-thick rounds (about 2 cups)
¼ cup packed dark brown sugar
2 tablespoons dark rum

For the wontons:
1 large egg
1 tablespoon water
36 (1 package) square wonton wrappers
1 cup soy oil

Prepare the anglaise: Place the egg yolks and sugar in a bowl and whisk to combine. Place the milk and cream in a stainless steel–lined saucepan and gently bring to a boil over medium heat. Add 1 cup of the hot milk mixture to the eggs, and whisk until smooth. Return the egg mixture to the pan and whisk until thickened enough to coat a spoon, 4 to 6 minutes. Add the rum and mix to combine. Strain, and discard the solids. Cover and refrigerate for at least 2 hours and up to 3 days.

Prepare the filling: Place a skillet over medium heat, and when it is hot, add the butter. Add the bananas, brown sugar, and rum, and cook until the bananas are tender and the mixture is reduced by nearly half and is no longer liquidy, 8 to 10 minutes. Remove from pan. Cover and refrigerate until completely chilled, at least 1 and up to 24 hours.

To make the wontons: Place the egg and water in a small bowl and whisk to combine. Line two cookie sheets with parchment paper.

Lay eighteen wonton wrappers on a work surface and brush each edge with the egg wash. (You may want to do this in batches.) Place 1 tablespoon of the filling onto the

Bananas

center of each wrapper, and then place a second wrapper over the top. Press down on all four sides to seal completely. Transfer to the prepared cookie sheets, cover with plastic wrap, and refrigerate until ready to cook.

Preheat the oven to 250°F.

To cook the wontons, place a large skillet over medium heat and add the oil. When the oil is shimmering (325°F), add six wontons and cook until deeply golden, 2 to 3 minutes per side. Drain the wontons on paper towels and then transfer them to the oven to keep warm. Repeat with the remaining wontons. (You can also bake the wontons on a buttered pan at 400°F for 3 to 5 minutes, but they will not be as crisp—and therefore not as good.)

Serve three wontons per person in a soup plate or on a large dinner plate, topped with a large spoonful of the rum anglaise.

Serves 6

classic crème brûlée

There is no resisting crème brûlée! Depriving yourself of such a delightful treat can lead to deep depression. Go out and buy some cute little ramekins and a cook's torch or a salamander. Then just give yourself over to the crunchy sweet caramelized top and the lush sweet vanilla custard underneath. I always do.

Crème brûlée: Crème brûlée, literally "burnt cream" in French, is a smooth and creamy chilled custard topped with a brittle crust that is created by sprinkling the top with sugar and caramelizing it just prior to serving. The best tool to use for caramelizing the top is called a salamander; it's a flat metal iron that allows the top to brown quickly without heating the custard itself. A cook's blowtorch works well also.

1½ cups whole milk
1 cup heavy cream
1 2-inch-long strip of orange zest
   (about ¼ orange)
1 vanilla bean, split lengthwise
12 tablespoons sugar
6 large egg yolks

Preheat the oven to 300°F.

Place the milk, cream, orange zest, vanilla bean, and 6 tablespoons of the sugar in a stainless steel–lined saucepan and bring just to a boil over medium-high heat. Remove from the heat.

Place the egg yolks and 2 tablespoons of the sugar in a stainless-steel bowl and whisk together. Add 1 cup of the hot milk mixture and whisk well. Add the remaining hot milk and whisk well. Strain into a glass, ceramic, or stainless-steel container, and discard the solids. Ladle the mixture into six shallow 6-ounce (¾-cup) ramekins.

Place the ramekins in a shallow roasting pan, and fill the pan with hot water to reach at least halfway up the sides of the ramekins. Bake until each custard jiggles like Santa's belly, 45 to 60 minutes. Let cool, still in the roasting pan, at room temperature for 10 minutes. Then remove from the pan, cover, and refrigerate for at least 2 hours and up to 2 days.

Before serving, allow the custard to stand at room temperature for 1 hour.

Sprinkle the remaining 4 tablespoons sugar over the custards, and caramelize with a salamander or a cook's torch. (If using a torch, set the flame at about ½ to ¾ inch and wave it 1 inch above the sugar until the sugar is melted and caramelized, 1 to

2 minutes. If using a salamander, heat the iron on a medium-high burner, and when it is hot, touch the flat side lightly to the sugar and burn the topping to a dark caramel, about 1 minute. Be very careful: the salamander will make a lot of smoke, so work right under your exhaust fan.)

Serve immediately.

Serves 6

Variations

Summer berry: Stir 1 cup berries into the custard after straining.

Cassia (the Asian cousin of cinnamon): Add two 3-inch pieces when bringing the milk mixture to a boil.

Jasmine tea: Add 1 tablespoon loose tea or two tea bags to the boiled milk mixture. Just prior to straining, steep for 2 to 3 minutes.

Index

A

accompaniments:

basmati rice pilaf, exotically spiced, 251

beans, crisp, and fresh tomatoes with curry vinaigrette, 219–20, *220*

chickpea smash, East Indian, 230–31

coconut rice with spinach and peanuts, Indonesian, 245–246

fried rice, Yang Chow, 252, *253*

lentil and vegetable fritters, 94–95

melon and herb salad with lime vinaigrette, 215–16

noodle cake, crispy, 181–82

parsnips, sesame, 235

peas, sweet, variety of, with green goddess dressing, 224–25

potato cakes, saffron, 233

potatoes, yogurt whipped, *186*, 234

rice sticks, curried, with chicken, shrimp, and sprouts, 247–48, *248*

romaine and green bean salad with rice wine vinaigrette, 214

scallion and oyster popovers, 97–98

scallion noodle cakes, *109*, 244

scallion popovers, 85

shrimp fritters, Vietnamese-style, 82–83

slaw, Asian, with sweet and sour dressing, 217–18

somen noodle cake, pan-seared, 242–43

spinach, ginger garlic, *205*, 232

sweet potatoes, glazed, 236–37

see also condiments

allspice, 158

almond and dark chocolate toffee, 268–69

amchoor (mango powder), 27

anglaise, dark rum, banana wontons with, 292–94

annatto seeds, 191

appetizers, *see* starters

apricots, chewy oatmeal cookies with cashews and, 260–61, *261*

arbol chilies, 44

Asian pear(s), *222*, 223

salad with green beans and glazed scallops, 221–23

asparagus:

chilled jumbo shrimp with cucumber mango relish and, 119–20

shiitake salad with spring veggies and scallion vinaigrette, 226–27

vegetable nori rolls, 76–78, *77*

avocado(s):

crabmeat in mustard vinaigrette with fresh herb salad, 210–11

and shrimp salad with tropical vinaigrette, 208–9

vegetable nori rolls, 76–78, *77*

B

baking, 23

banana(s):

easy chocolate cake with raspberry-tea syrup and, 280–81, *281*

wontons with dark rum anglaise, 292–94

barbecued pork ribs, honey and five-spice, 191–92

barbecue sauce, tamarind, 104–5

barley, in timbale of grains with wild mushrooms and creamy feta sauce, 202–3

basil:

holy, chili paste, 199

Thai, 131

Thai, in fresh herb salad with crabmeat in mustard vinaigrette, 210–11

basmati rice, 200

pilaf, exotically spiced, 251

basting sauce, 117–18

bean curd, *see* tofu

beans, *see* black bean(s), fermented; chickpea; green bean(s); lentil

beef:

flank steak, grilled soy-soaked, over crispy noodles, 180–82

rib-eye steak, Szechuan peppercorn–rubbed, with ginger demi-glace, 185–86, *186*

short ribs braised with sweet and sour onions, 183–84

sirloin steak, grilled, with spicy stir-fried shrimp and watercress, 187–88

berry(ies):

blackberry ginger dipping sauce, coconut spring rolls with, 282–83

berry(ies) (*cont.*):

  ice cream, 275

  raspberry-tea syrup, easy chocolate cake with bananas and, 280–81, *281*

  summer, crème brûlée, 296

beverages:

  caramelized lemongrass lemonade, *271*, 271–72

  sake, 133

bird chilies, Thai, 32

black bean(s), fermented, 213

  vinaigrette, chicken, orange, and cress salad with, 212–13

blackberry ginger dipping sauce, coconut spring rolls with, 282–83

black tea–brined chicken, 153–154, *154*

blanching vegetables, ice baths for, 45

bok choy (Chinese mustard cabbage), 196

  butternut squash, and pearl onions with green curry, 196–97

  skillet of fragrant rice with tofu and Asian greens, 200–201

braised:

  beef short ribs with sweet and sour onions, 183–84

  ginger and mustard rabbit with wild mushrooms, 178–179

braising, 23

bread crumbs, panko, 140

brik wrappers, 204

brines, 191–92

  black tea, 153–54

  cider lemongrass, 158–59

  ginger citrus, 106–7

  tamarind, 173–74

brining, 107

brittle, macadamia nut, 270

broiling, 23

broths, 33

  dashi, seared tuna in, with chewy fat noodles, 138–39

  dashi, versatile, 38–39

  saffron, tuna steaks in, with spicy pepper puree, 140–41

  see also stocks

bulgur:

  crust, 195

  timbale of grains with wild mushrooms and creamy feta sauce, 202–3

buns, pork and tofu steamed, 80–81

butter, flavored, 187–88

butternut squash, pearl onions, and bok choy with green curry, 196–97

C

cabbage:

  Chinese mustard, *see* bok choy

  napa, chi *(kim chi)*, 63–64, *64*

  napa, in Asian slaw with sweet and sour dressing, 217–18

cake flour, 280

cakes (savory):

  noodle, crispy, 181–82

  saffron potato, 233

  scallion noodle, *109*, 244

  somen noodle, pan-seared, 242–43

cakes (sweet):

  chocolate, with bananas and raspberry-tea syrup, easy, 280–81, *281*

  honey pound, old-fashioned, 279

  pineapple skillet, upside-down, 284–85

candied:

  ginger, sweet ginger syrup and, 256

  lemon slices, 289

candies:

  chocolate-covered stout caramel, 266–67

  dark chocolate and almond toffee, 268–69

  macadamia nut brittle, 270

caramel:

  garlic sauce, grilled quail with cilantro and, 171–72

  stout candies, chocolate-covered, 266–67

caramelized lemongrass lemonade, *271*, 271–72

carrot(s):

  Asian slaw with sweet and sour dressing, 217–18

  lentil and vegetable fritters, 94–95

  miso vegetable pickles, 66

  Persian turnovers with raisins, pine nuts, goat cheese and, 204–6, *205*

  roll-cutting, 67

  shiitake salad with spring veggies and scallion vinaigrette, 226–27

  tomato and roasted vegetable soup with seared red snapper fillet, 130–31

  vegetable nori rolls, 76–78, *77*

  vegetable pie with spinach, raisins, and *ras el hanout*, 194–95

  vegetable udon, 138–39

cashew(s):

  chewy oatmeal cookies with apricots and, 260–61, *261*

  -crusted chicken breasts with coconut curry sauce, 155–57

-crusted salmon fillet, 146–47

sauce, curry-basted grilled jumbo scallops with, 117–118

cassia crème brûlée, 296

cauliflower, in miso vegetable pickles, 66

ceviche (Asian marinated salmon), *124*, 124–25

char-grilled shrimp satay with tamarind barbecue sauce, 104–5

cheese:

feta sauce, creamy, timbale of grains with wild mushrooms and, 202–3

goat, Persian turnovers with carrots, raisins, pine nuts and, 204–6, *205*

toasts with red lentil dip, 92–93

cherry-pistachio chocolate chip cookies, 262–63

chewy oatmeal cookies with apricots and cashews, 260–261, *261*

chi, napa cabbage *(kim chi)*, 63–64, *64*

chicken, 151–69

black tea–brined, 153–54, *154*

breasts, cashew-crusted, with coconut curry sauce, 155–157

breasts, pan-roasted, with Japanese eggplant and mushrooms, 162–63

coconut five-spice, 152

curried rice sticks with shrimp, sprouts and, 247–248, *248*

Malaysian sweet spice–rubbed, 160–61

orange, and cress salad with black bean vinaigrette, 212–13

and peanut lettuce cups, 84

stir-fried, with sesame and spiced walnuts, 164–66

stock, 34–35

twice-cooked Philippines-style, with papaya relish, 167–69

wings, cider lemongrass–brined, 158–59

chickpea:

croquettes, 230

smash, East Indian, 230–31

chickpea flour, 95

chiffonade technique, for soft herbs, 208

chili(es):

arbol, 44

bird, Thai, 32

flakes, Korean, 64

garlic paste, 82

holy basil paste, 199

powder, Korean vs. American, 28

spice blend, Korean, 28

and spice oil, fragrant, 44

sweet and hot pepper relish, *50*, 55

chilled:

jumbo shrimp with asparagus and cucumber mango relish, 119–20

soba noodles with tamari wasabi vinaigrette, 249–50

Chinese flavors, dishes with:

chicken, black tea–brined, 153–54, *154*

chicken, coconut five-spice, 152

fried rice, Yang Chow, 252, *253*

hoisin and spice dipping sauce, 48

peanut noodles with sesame spinach, 240–41

pork and tofu steamed buns, 80–81

rib-eye steak, Szechuan peppercorn–rubbed, with ginger demi-glace, 185–86, *186*

rice sticks, curried, with chicken, shrimp, and sprouts, 247–48, *248*

sweet spice mix, 81

wontons: filling and variations, 86–89

Chinese ingredients:

bok choy (Chinese mustard cabbage), 196

fermented black beans, 213

hoisin, 48

hot mustard powder, 170

star anise, 30, *30*

Szechuan peppercorns, 153

wonton wrappers, 72

yellow noodles, fresh, 180

Chinese steamers, 80

chives, in fresh herb salad with crabmeat in mustard vinaigrette, 210–11

chocolate, 267

cake with bananas and raspberry-tea syrup, easy, 280–81, *281*

chip cookies, pistachio-cherry, 262–63

-covered stout caramel candies, 266–67

dark, and almond toffee, 268–269

ice cream and peanut butter parfait, 277

lemon ginger madeleines, 257–58, *258*

white, ice cream, 276

chutneys:
eggplant, spicy, 59–60
mango, sweet curried, 58, *190*
tamarind fruits, 53–54, *54*
see also relishes
cider lemongrass–brined chicken
wings, 158–59
cilantro:
fresh herb salad with crabmeat in mustard vinai-
grette, 210–11
grilled quail with caramel
garlic sauce and, 171–72
herb and melon salad with
lime vinaigrette, 215–16
oil, 46
cinnamon sticks, toasting, 53
citrus:
dipping sauce, 50
ginger brined shrimp, 106–7
zest, flavoring oil with, 45
see also specific citrus fruits
clams, *100*
Indonesian-style red seafood
curry, 115–16, *116*
pan-roasted mussels and, with
fragrant lime leaves, 113–
114, *114*
coconut:
curry sauce, cashew-crusted
chicken breasts with, 155–
157
custard tart, 290–91
five-spice chicken, 152
rice with spinach and peanuts,
Indonesian, 245–46
spring rolls with ginger blackberry dipping sauce, 282–
283
toasted, ice cream, 275
toasting, 156
coconut milk, 108
cod fillet with curry tomato
sauce, 144–45

coffee grinders, grinding spices
in, 19
condiments, 43–69
butter, flavored, 187–88
chili and spice oil, fragrant, 44
cilantro oil, 46
citrus dipping sauce, 50
cucumber pickles, sweet, 65
curry oil, 47
daikon, spicy, 62, *186*
eggplant chutney, spicy, 59–60
hoisin and spice dipping
sauce, 48
lime dip, cool, *50,* 51
mango chutney, sweet curried,
58, *190*
miso vegetable pickles, 66
napa cabbage *chi (kim chi),*
63–64, *64*
papaya relish, 168–69
peanut dipping sauce, spicy,
49
scallion oil, 45
sesame sauce, spicy, 52
shallot relish, golden, *50,* 56–
57
sweet and hot pepper relish,
50, 55
tamarind fruits, 53–54, *54*
tropical fruit pickles, 61
watermelon pickles, 68–69
see also spice rubs and pastes;
vinaigrettes
consommés, 34
cookies:
chocolate lemon ginger
madeleines, 257–58, *258*
ginger spice, 259
oatmeal, with apricots and
cashews, chewy, 260–61,
261
pine nut shortbread, 264
pistachio-cherry chocolate
chip, 262–63

cooking methods, 23
cookware, 22
cool lime dip, *50,* 51
coriander (seed), *20,* 59
-spiced diver scallops with
pear glaze, 102–3
corn and sweet potato curry,
spicy grilled lobster with,
108–10, *109*
crabmeat:
in mustard vinaigrette with
fresh herb salad, 210–11
nori rolls, 78
cracking seeds and peppercorns,
115
crème brûlée:
cassia, 296
classic, 295–96
jasmine tea, 296
summer berry, 296
cress, *see* watercress
crisp beans and fresh tomatoes
with curry vinaigrette,
219–20, *220*
crispy:
noodles, grilled soy-soaked
flank steak over, 180–82
sole fillets with wild mushroom stew, 148–49
croquettes, chickpea, 230
crusts:
bulgur, 195
cashew, 155–56
cucumber(s):
Asian slaw with sweet and
sour dressing, 217–18
mango relish, chilled jumbo
shrimp with asparagus and,
119–20
pickled, roasted peanut soup
with, 198–99
pickles, sweet, 65
vegetable nori rolls, 76–78,
77

curry(ied):

-basted grilled jumbo scallops with cashew sauce, 117–18

clams and mussels, pan-roasted, with fragrant lime leaves, 113–14, *114*

coconut, sauce, cashew-crusted chicken breasts with, 155–57

corn and sweet potato, spicy grilled lobster with, 108–110, *109*

green, butternut squash, pearl onions, and bok choy with, 196–97

lobster, in rich and poor man's lobster, 142–43

mango chutney, sweet, 58, *190*

oil, 47

red seafood, Indonesian-style, 115–16, *116*

rice sticks with chicken, shrimp, and sprouts, 247–248, *248*

salmon fillet, cashew-crusted, 146–47

tomato sauce, cod fillet with, 144–45

vinaigrette, crisp beans and fresh tomatoes with, 219–220, *220*

curry pastes:

green, Southeast Asian, 29

making quick curry dishes with, 30

as marinades, 32

red, 32

yellow, 31

curry powder, 58

curry pastes vs., 30

custard tart, coconut, 290–91

cutting techniques:

for dried fruit, 260

for ginger, 47

roll-cutting, 67

for soft herbs, 208

D

daikon, spicy, 62, *186*

dark chocolate and almond toffee, 268–69

dark rum anglaise, banana wontons with, 292–94

dashi:

seared tuna in, with chewy fat noodles, 138–39

versatile, 38–39

demi-glace, ginger, Szechuan peppercorn–rubbed rib-eye steak with, 185–86, *186*

desserts, 273–96

banana wontons with dark rum anglaise, 292–94

chocolate cake with bananas and raspberry-tea syrup, easy, 280–81, *281*

coconut custard tart, 290–91

coconut spring rolls with ginger blackberry dipping sauce, 282–83

crème brûlée, classic, 295–96

gingery lemon meringue tart, 286–89, *288*

honey pound cake, old-fashioned, 279

peanut butter and chocolate ice cream parfait, 277

pineapple skillet cake, upside-down, 284–85

rice pudding, simple and rich, 278

see also ice cream; sweets and treats

deviled game hens, 170

dip, red lentil, cheese toasts with, 92–93

dipping sauces, 48–52

citrus, 50

ginger blackberry, 282–83

hoisin and spice, 48

lime, cool, *50,* 51

peanut, spicy, 49

sesame, spicy, 52

dressings, *see* salad dressings; vinaigrettes

dried fruit, dicing, 260

dry measure equivalencies, 297

duck, slow-roasted tamarind, 173–74

E

East Indian dishes:

chickpea smash, 230–31

spice blend, 26

East Indian ingredients:

amchoor (mango powder), 27

coriander seed, 59

curry powder, 58

palm sugar (jaggery), 55

turmeric, 31

eggplant:

chutney, spicy, 59–60

Japanese, pan-roasted chicken breasts with mushrooms and, 162–63

miso vegetable pickles, 66

egg roll skins (spring roll wrappers), 72, *73*

entrees:

Asian pear salad with green beans and glazed scallops, 221–23

beef short ribs braised with sweet and sour onions, 183–184

butternut squash, pearl onions, and bok choy with green curry, 196–97

chicken, black tea–brined, 153–54, *154*

chicken, coconut five-spice, 152

entrees (*cont.*):

chicken, Malaysian sweet spice–rubbed, 160–61

chicken, orange, and cress salad with black bean vinaigrette, 212–13

chicken, stir-fried, with sesame and spiced walnuts, 164–66

chicken, twice-cooked Philippines-style, with papaya relish, 167–69

chicken breasts, cashew-crusted, with coconut curry sauce, 155–57

chicken breasts, pan-roasted, with Japanese eggplant and mushrooms, 162–63

chicken wings, cider lemongrass–brined, 158–59

clams and mussels, pan-roasted, with fragrant lime leaves, 113–14, *114*

cod fillet with curry tomato sauce, 144–45

crabmeat in mustard vinaigrette with fresh herb salad, 210–11

duck, slow-roasted tamarind, 173–74

flank steak, grilled soy-soaked, over crispy noodles, 180–82

game hens, deviled, 170

grains, timbale of, with wild mushrooms and creamy feta sauce, 202–3

halibut, teriyaki glazed, with sake pine-nut sauce, 132–33

hot and sour soup with ginger tamari–glazed seafood, 126–28

lamb, Indian-spiced leg of, with creamy yogurt sauce, 176–77

lobster, rich and poor man's, 142–43

lobster, spicy grilled, with corn and sweet potato curry, 108–10, *109*

lobster tempura, 111–12

peanut, roasted, soup with pickled cucumbers, 198–99

pork ribs, honey and five-spice barbecued, 191–92

pork tenderloin with guava glaze, 189–90, *190*

quail, grilled, with caramel garlic sauce and cilantro, 171–72

rabbit, ginger and mustard braised, with wild mushrooms, 178–79

rib-eye steak, Szechuan peppercorn–rubbed, with ginger demi-glace, 185–86, *186*

rice, fragrant, skillet of, with tofu and Asian greens, 200–201

rice sticks, curried, with chicken, shrimp, and sprouts, 247–48, *248*

salmon, Asian marinated, *124*, 124–25

salmon fillet, cashew-crusted, 146–47

salmon fillet, sweet tamari-glazed, 129

salmon steaks, grilled, with fresh oyster sauce, *134*, 134–35

scallops, coriander-spiced diver, with pear glaze, 102–3

scallops, curry-basted grilled jumbo, with cashew sauce, 117–18

seafood curry, Indonesian-style red, 115–16, *116*

shiitake salad with spring veggies and scallion vinaigrette, 226–27

shrimp, chilled jumbo, with asparagus and cucumber mango relish, 119–20

shrimp, ginger citrus brined, 106–7

shrimp and avocado salad with tropical vinaigrette, 208–9

shrimp satay, char-grilled, with tamarind barbecue sauce, 104–5

sirloin steak, grilled, with spicy stir-fried shrimp and watercress, 187–88

skate, marinated, with lightly pickled vegetables, 136–137

soba noodles, chilled, with tamari wasabi vinaigrette, 249–50

sole fillets, crispy, with wild mushroom stew, 148–49

striped bass, honey tamari–brined, 122–23

tomato and roasted vegetable soup with seared red snapper fillet, 130–31

tuna, seared, in dashi with chewy fat noodles, 138–139

tuna steaks in saffron broth with spicy pepper puree, 140–41

turnovers with carrots, raisins, pine nuts, and goat cheese, Persian, 204–6, *205*

vegetable pie with spinach, raisins, and *ras el hanout*, 194–95

equipment, 22–23

Chinese steamers, 80

for grilling, 23

knives, 22

pots and pans, 22

resource list for, 21

sushi mats, 76

essentials, 17–23

cooking methods, 23

equipment, 22–23

pantry items, 18–21

resource list for, 21

exotically spiced basmati rice
pilaf, 251

extracts, 19–21

vanilla, 264

F

fennel:

Asian slaw with sweet and
sour dressing, 217–18

miso vegetable pickles,
66

tomato and roasted vegetable
soup with seared red snapper fillet, 130–31

vegetable pie with spinach,
raisins, and *ras el hanout*,
194–95

feta sauce, creamy, timbale of
grains with wild mush-
rooms and, 202–3

Filipino cooking, *see* Philippines-style cooking

first courses, *see* starters

fish, 121–49

buying, 121

cod fillet with curry tomato
sauce, 144–45

fumet, 40

halibut, teriyaki glazed, with
sake pine-nut sauce, 132–
133

hot and sour soup with ginger
tamari–glazed seafood,
126–28

monkfish, in rich and poor
man's lobster, 142–43

red snapper fillet, seared,
tomato and roasted veg-
etable soup with, 130–31

skate, marinated, with lightly
pickled vegetables, 136–37

sole fillets, crispy, with wild
mushroom stew, 148–49

striped bass, honey tamari–
brined, 122–23

tips for cooking, 121

tuna, seared, in dashi with
chewy fat noodles, 138–39

tuna steaks in saffron broth
with spicy pepper puree,
140–41

see also salmon

fish sauce, 51, *63*

five-spice:

coconut chicken, 152

and honey barbecued pork
ribs, 191–92

marinade, 152

flank steak, grilled soy-soaked,
over crispy noodles, 180–82

flours:

cake, 280

chickpea, 95

fragrant chili and spice oil, 44

freezer pantry items, 21

fried rice, Yang Chow, 252, *253*

fritters:

lentil and vegetable, 94–95

shrimp, Vietnamese-style, 82–
83

fruit(s):

dried, dicing, 260

fresh, in pantry, 21

tamarind, 53–54, *54*

tropical, pickles, 61

see also specific fruits

frying, 23

fumet, fish, 40

G

galangal, 30

game hens, deviled, 170

garam masala, 194

garlic:

caramel sauce, grilled quail
with cilantro and, 171–72

chili paste, 82

flavoring oil with, 45

ginger spinach, *205*, 232

ginger, 27, *27*

blackberry dipping sauce,
coconut spring rolls with,
282–83

chocolate lemon madeleines,
257–58, *258*

chopping, 47

citrus brined shrimp, 106–7

demi-glace, Szechuan peppercorn–rubbed rib-eye steak
with, 185–86, *186*

galangal as substitute for, 30

garlic spinach, *205*, 232

ice cream, 274–75

lemon meringue tart, 286–89,
288

and mustard braised rabbit
with wild mushrooms, 178–
179

spice cookies, 259

syrup, sweet, and candied
ginger, 256

tamari–glazed seafood, hot
and sour soup with, 126–28

glazed:

grilled shrimp with peanut
coating, 96

sweet potatoes, 236–37

glazes:

ginger tamari, 126–28

guava, 189–90, *190*

guava, pineapple, or mango,
236

honey and five-spice, 192

glazes (*cont.*):

lemongrass, 155–56

pear, 102–3, 221–23

goat cheese, Persian turnovers with carrots, raisins, pine nuts and, 204–6, *205*

golden shallot relish, *50,* 56–57

grains:

timbale of, with wild mushrooms and creamy feta sauce, 202–3

see also rice

green bean(s):

Asian pear salad with glazed scallops and, 221–23

crisp, and fresh tomatoes with curry vinaigrette, 219–20, *220*

and romaine salad with rice wine vinaigrette, 214

shiitake salad with spring veggies and scallion vinaigrette, 226–27

green curry(ies):

butternut squash, pearl onions, and bok choy with, 196–97

pan-roasted clams and mussels with fragrant lime leaves, 113–14, *114*

paste, Southeast Asian, 29

green goddess dressing, variety of sweet peas with, 224–225

greens:

Asian, skillet of fragrant rice with tofu and, 200–201

see also specific greens

grilled:

char-, shrimp satay with tamarind barbecue sauce, 104–5

flank steak, soy-soaked, over crispy noodles, 180–82

lobster, spicy, with corn and sweet potato curry, 108–10, *109*

pork ribs, honey and five-spice barbecued, 191–92

pork tenderloin with guava glaze, 189–90, *190*

quail with caramel garlic sauce and cilantro, 171–72

rib-eye steak, Szechuan peppercorn–rubbed, with ginger demi-glace, 185–86, *186*

salmon steaks with fresh oyster sauce, *134,* 134–35

scallops, curry-basted jumbo, with cashew sauce, 117–18

shrimp, ginger citrus brined, 106–7

shrimp, glazed, with peanut coating, 96

sirloin steak with spicy stir-fried shrimp and watercress, 187–88

grilling, 23

equipment for, 23

grinders, for spices, 19

guava:

glaze, pork tenderloin with, 189–90, *190*

juice, in glazed sweet potatoes, 236–37

paste, 155

H

halibut, teriyaki glazed, with sake pine-nut sauce, 132–33

herb(s):

cutting vs. chopping, 208

-flavored oil, 45

fresh, salad, crabmeat in mustard vinaigrette with, 210–11

green goddess dressing, 224–25

and melon salad with lime vinaigrette, 215–16

see also specific herbs

hoisin, 48

and spice dipping sauce, 48

holy basil chili paste, 199

honey:

and five-spice barbecued pork ribs, 191–92

pound cake, old-fashioned, 279

tamari–brined striped bass, 122–23

hors d'oeuvres, *see* starters

hot and sour soup with ginger tamari–glazed seafood, 126–28

I

ice baths, 45

ice cream:

berry, 275

ginger, 274–75

parfait, peanut butter and chocolate, 277

spice, 275

toasted coconut, 275

white chocolate, 276

Indian flavors, dishes with:

cheese toasts with red lentil dip, 92–93

chickpea smash, East Indian, 230–31

lamb, Indian-spiced leg of, with creamy yogurt sauce, 176–77

lentil and vegetable fritters, 94–95

spice blend, East Indian, 26

tuna steaks in saffron broth with spicy pepper puree, 140–41

Indian ingredients:

amchoor (mango powder), 27

basmati rice, 200

chickpea flour, 95

coriander seed, *20*, 59

curry powder, 58

palm sugar (jaggery), 55

turmeric, 31

Indonesian-style red seafood curry, 115–16, *116*

ingredients:

allspice, 158

amchoor (mango powder), 27

annatto seeds, 191

arbol chilies, 44

Asian pears, *222, 223*

basmati rice, 200

bok choy (Chinese mustard cabbage), 196

brik wrappers, 204

cake flour, 280

chickpea flour, 95

chili garlic paste, 82

Chinese hot mustard powder, 170

chocolate, 267

coconut milk, 108

coriander seed, *20*, 59

curry powder, 58

fermented black beans, 213

fish sauce, 51

fruits and vegetables, fresh, 21

galangal, 30

ginger, 27, *27*

guava paste, 155

hoisin, 48

holy basil chili paste, 199

jasmine rice, 200

konbu (kombu or kelp), 38

Korean chili flakes, 64

lemongrass, 127, *127*

lime leaves, 32

lumpia wrappers, 72

mirin (rice wine), 49

miso, 67

mizuna, 102

nori, 28

palm sugar (jaggery), 55

panko, 140

refrigerator and freezer items, 21

resource list for, 21

rice paper wrappers, 72

saffron, 57

sake, 133

salt, kosher, 85

scallops, diver, 102

sesame oil, light vs. dark, 46

sesame seeds, 28

shrimp paste, 187

soy oil, 27

spices and extracts, 19–21

spring roll wrappers (egg roll skins), 72, *73*

staples, 18–19

star anise, *20*, 30, *30*

sweet potatoes and yams, 237

Szechuan peppercorns, 153

tamarind, 53

Thai basil, 131

Thai bird chilies, 32

tofu (bean curd), 90

turmeric, 31

vanilla beans, 274

vanilla extract, 264

wasabi powder, 78

watermelon, 69

wild rice, 203

wonton wrappers, 72

yellow Chinese noodles, fresh, 180

J

jaggery (palm sugar), 55

Japanese equipment:

mandolines, 22

sushi mats, 76

Japanese flavors, dishes with:

citrus dipping sauce, 50

crabmeat nori rolls, 78

daikon, spicy, 62, *186*

dashi, versatile, 38–39

lobster tempura, 111–12

miso soup, 99

miso vegetable pickles, 66

salmon nori rolls, 78

scallion noodle cakes, *109, 244*

scallion popovers, 85

soba noodles, chilled, with tamari wasabi vinaigrette, 249–50

somen noodle cake, pan-seared, 242–43

sushi rice, 79

tuna, seared, in dashi with chewy fat noodles, 138–39

vegetable nori rolls, 76–78, *77*

Japanese ingredients, 28

konbu (kombu or kelp), 38

mirin (rice wine), 49

miso, 67

mizuna, 102

nori, 28

sake, 133

tofu (bean curd), 90

wasabi powder, 78

jasmine rice, 200

jasmine tea crème brûlée, 296

K

kaffir lime leaves, 32

kelp (konbu or kombu), 38

kim chi (napa cabbage *chi*), 63, *64*

knives, 22

konbu (kombu or kelp), 38

dashi, versatile, 38–39

Korean ingredients:

chili flakes, 64

chili spice blend, 28

fermented black beans, 213

Korean napa cabbage *chi (kim chi)*, 63–64, *64*

kosher salt, 85

L

lamb, Indian-spiced leg of, with
    creamy yogurt sauce, 176–
    177
leeks:
    vegetable udon, 138–39
    washing, 138
lemon:
    chocolate ginger madeleines,
        257–58, *258*
    meringue tart, gingery, 286–
        289, *288*
    slices, candied, 289
lemonade, caramelized lemon-
    grass, *271,* 271–72
lemongrass, 127, *127*
    caramelized, lemonade, *271,*
        271–72
    cider–brined chicken wings,
        158–59
    glaze, 155–56
lentil:
    red, dip, cheese toasts with,
        92–93
    and vegetable fritters, 94–95
lettuce:
    cups, chicken and peanut, 84
    romaine and green bean salad
        with rice wine vinaigrette,
        214
lime:
    dip, cool, *50,* 51
    vinaigrette, melon and herb
        salad with, 215–16
lime leaves, 32
    fragrant, pan-roasted clams
        and mussels with, 113–14,
        114
    preparing, 152
liquid measure equivalencies,
    297
lobster:
    rich and poor man's, 142–43
    spicy grilled, with corn and

sweet potato curry, 108–10,
    109
tempura, 111–12
lumpia wrappers, 72

M

macadamia nut brittle, 270
madeleines, chocolate lemon
    ginger, 257–58, *258*
main dishes, *see* entrees; vege-
    tarian entrees
maki (vegetable nori rolls), 76–
    78, *77*
Malaysian sweet spice–rubbed
    chicken, 160–61
mandolines, Japanese, 22
mango:
    chutney, sweet curried, 58, *190*
    cucumber relish, chilled
        jumbo shrimp with aspara-
        gus and, 119–20
    juice, in glazed sweet potatoes,
        236–37
    juice, in tropical vinaigrette,
        208–9
    powder (amchoor), 27
    tropical fruit pickles, 61
marinades:
    for chicken, 32, 46, 152
    cilantro oil, 46
    coconut five-spice, 152
    curry pastes as, 32
    for meats, 32, 180–81
    for seafood, 32, 46, 125, 134–
        135, 136–37
    soy, 180–81
marinated:
    salmon, Asian, *124,* 124–25
    skate with lightly pickled
        vegetables, 136–37
meats, 175–92
    beef short ribs braised with
        sweet and sour onions, 183–
        184

flank steak, grilled soy-soaked,
    over crispy noodles, 180–82
lamb, Indian-spiced leg of,
    with creamy yogurt sauce,
    176–77
pork ribs, honey and five-spice
    barbecued, 191–92
pork tenderloin with guava
    glaze, 189–90, *190*
rabbit, ginger and mustard
    braised, with wild mush-
    rooms, 178–79
rib-eye steak, Szechuan pep-
    percorn–rubbed, with
    ginger demi-glace, 185–86,
    186
sirloin steak, grilled, with
    spicy stir-fried shrimp and
    watercress, 187–88
melon and herb salad with lime
    vinaigrette, 215–16
meringue tart, gingery lemon,
    286–89, *288*
metric equivalencies, 297
mint:
    fresh herb salad with crab-
        meat in mustard vinai-
        grette, 210–11
    herb and melon salad with
        lime vinaigrette, 215–16
mirin (rice wine), 49
    vinaigrette, romaine and
        green bean salad with,
        214
miso, 67
    soup, 99
    vegetable pickles, 66
mizuna, 102
monkfish:
    hot and sour soup with ginger
        tamari–glazed seafood,
        126–28
    rich and poor man's lobster,
        142–43

mushroom(s):
  pan-roasted chicken breasts
    with Japanese eggplant
    and, 162–63
  shiitake salad with spring
    veggies and scallion vinai-
    grette, 226–27
  wild, ginger and mustard
    braised rabbit with, 178–79
  wild, stew, crispy sole fillets
    with, 148–49
  wild, timbale of grains with,
    and creamy feta sauce,
    202–3
mussels:
  Indonesian-style red seafood
    curry, 115–16, *116*
  pan-roasted clams and, with
    fragrant lime leaves, 113–
    114, *114*
mustard:
  deviled game hens, 170
  and ginger braised rabbit with
    wild mushrooms, 178–79
  powder, Chinese hot, 170
  vinaigrette, crabmeat in, with
    fresh herb salad, 210–11
mustard cabbage, Chinese, *see*
  bok choy

N

napa cabbage:
  Asian slaw with sweet and
    sour dressing, 217–18
  chi (kim chi), 63–64, *64*
noodle(s), 259
  cakes, scallion, *109*, 244
  chewy fat, seared tuna in
    dashi with, 138–39
  crispy, grilled soy-soaked flank
    steak over, 180–82
  fresh yellow Chinese, 180
  peanut, with sesame spinach,
    240–41

rice sticks, curried, with
  chicken, shrimp, and
  sprouts, 247–48, *248*
rice vermicelli, in Vietnamese
  summer rolls, 74–75, *75*
soba, chilled, with tamari
  wasabi vinaigrette, 249–
  250
somen, cake, pan-seared, 242–
  243
nori, 28
nori rolls, 76–79, *79*
  crabmeat, 78
  salmon, 78
  sushi rice for, 79
  vegetable, 76–78, *77*
North African flavors, dishes
  with:
  Persian turnovers with car-
    rots, raisins, pine nuts, and
    goat cheese, 204–6, *205*
  vegetable pie with spinach,
    raisins, and *ras el hanout*,
    194–95
nuts:
  toasting, 96
  see also specific nuts

O

oatmeal cookies with apricots
  and cashews, chewy, 260–
  261, *261*
oils:
  sesame, light vs. dark, 46
  soy, 27
oils, flavored, 44–47
  chili and spice, fragrant, 44
  cilantro, 46
  curry, 47
  with fresh ingredients, 45
  herb, 45
  scallion, 45
old-fashioned honey pound cake,
  279

onion(s):
  lentil and vegetable fritters,
    94–95
  pearl, butternut squash, and
    bok choy with green curry,
    196–97
  pearl, in miso vegetable
    pickles, 66
  sweet and sour, beef short ribs
    braised with, 183–84
  tomato and roasted vegetable
    soup with seared red snap-
    per fillet, 130–31
  vegetable pie with spinach,
    raisins, and *ras el hanout*,
    194–95
orange, chicken, and cress salad
  with black bean vinai-
  grette, 212–13
oyster(s):
  fresh, sauce, grilled salmon
    steaks with, *134*, 134–35
  and scallion popovers, 97–98
  shucking, *97*

P

palm sugar (jaggery), 55
pancake, savory rice noodle and
  tofu, 90–91
panko, 140
pan-roasted:
  chicken breasts with Japanese
    eggplant and mushrooms,
    162–63
  clams and mussels with fra-
    grant lime leaves, 113–14,
    114
pans, 22
pan-seared somen noodle cake,
  242–43
pantry essentials, 18–21
  fresh fruits and vegetables, 21
  refrigerator and freezer items,
    21

pantry essentials (*cont.*):
  resource list for, 21
  spices and extracts, 19–21
  staples, 18–19
papaya(s), *169*
  relish, twice-cooked Philip-
    pines-style chicken with,
    167–69
  tamarind fruits, 53–54, *54*
  tropical fruit pickles, 61
parfait, peanut butter and chocolate ice cream, 277
parsley, in green goddess dressing, 224–25
parsnips:
  roll-cutting, 67
  sesame, 235
pastes, *see* spice rubs and pastes
peanut(s):
  butter and chocolate ice cream
    parfait, 277
  and chicken lettuce cups, 84
  coating, glazed grilled shrimp
    with, 96
  dipping sauce, spicy, 49
  Indonesian coconut rice with
    spinach and, 245–46
  noodles with sesame spinach,
    240–41
  roasted, soup with pickled
    cucumbers, 198–99
pear(s):
  Asian, *222, 223*
  Asian, salad with green beans
    and glazed scallops, 221–23
  glaze, coriander-spiced diver
    scallops with, 102–3
  tamarind fruits, 53–54, *54*
peas:
  shiitake salad with spring
    veggies and scallion vinai-
    grette, 226–27
  sweet, variety of, with green
    goddess dressing, 224–25

pepper(s):
  flavoring oil with, 45
  lentil and vegetable fritters,
    94–95
  miso vegetable pickles, 66
  puree, spicy, tuna steaks in
    saffron broth with, 140–41
  roasting, 57
  sweet and hot, relish, *50,* 55
  vegetable nori rolls, 76–78,
    77
  vegetable udon, 138–39
  see also chili(es)
peppercorn(s):
  cracking, 115
  Szechuan, 153
  Szechuan, –rubbed rib-eye
    steak with ginger demi-
    glace, 185–86, *186*
Persian turnovers with carrots,
  raisins, pine nuts, and goat
  cheese, 204–6, *205*
Philippines-style cooking:
  lumpia wrappers, 72
  twice-cooked chicken with
    papaya relish, 167–69
pickle(d)(s), 61–69
  cucumber, sweet, 65
  cucumbers, roasted peanut
    soup with, 198–99
  daikon, spicy, 62, *186*
  miso vegetable, 66
  napa cabbage *chi (kim chi),*
    63–64, *64*
  tropical fruit, 61
  vegetables, marinated skate
    with, 136–37
  watermelon, 68–69
pickling spice, 223
pie, vegetable, with spinach,
  raisins, and *ras el hanout,*
  194–95
pilaf, exotically spiced basmati
  rice, 251

pineapple:
  juice, in glazed sweet potatoes,
    236–37
  juice, in tropical vinaigrette,
    208–9
  tamarind fruits, 53–54, *54*
  tropical fruit pickles, 61
  upside-down skillet cake, 284–
    285
pine nut(s):
  Persian turnovers with car-
    rots, raisins, goat cheese
    and, 204–6, *205*
  sake sauce, teriyaki glazed
    halibut with, 132–33
  shortbread, 264
pistachio-cherry chocolate chip
  cookies, 262–63
poaching, 23
popovers:
  scallion, 85
  scallion and oyster, 97–98
pork:
  ribs, honey and five-spice
    barbecued, 191–92
  tenderloin with guava glaze,
    189–90, *190*
  and tofu steamed buns, 80–
    81
potato(es):
  cakes, saffron, 233
  new, in shiitake salad with
    spring veggies and scallion
    vinaigrette, 226–27
  yogurt whipped, *186,* 234
pots and pans, 22
poultry, 151–74
  duck, slow-roasted tamarind,
    173–74
  game hens, deviled, 170
  quail, grilled, with caramel
    garlic sauce and cilantro,
    171–72
  see also chicken

pound cake, honey, old-fashioned, 279

pudding, rice, simple and rich, 278

puree, spicy pepper, 140–41

Q

quail, grilled, with caramel garlic sauce and cilantro, 171–72

R

rabbit, ginger and mustard braised, with wild mushrooms, 178–79

radishes, in Asian slaw with sweet and sour dressing, 217–18

raisins:
    Persian turnovers with carrots, pine nuts, goat cheese and, 204–6, *205*
    tamarind fruits, 53–54, *54*
    vegetable pie with spinach, *ras el hanout* and, 194–195

ras el hanout, vegetable pie with spinach, raisins and, 194–195

raspberry-tea syrup, easy chocolate cake with bananas and, 280–81, *281*

ravioli, two-piece (wontons), 89

red curry(ies):
    -basted grilled jumbo scallops with cashew sauce, 117–18
    coconut, sauce, cashew-crusted chicken breasts with, 155–57
    paste, 32
    seafood, Indonesian-style, 115–16, *116*

red lentil dip, cheese toasts with, 92–93

red snapper fillet, seared, tomato and roasted vegetable soup with, 130–31

refrigerator pantry items, 21

relishes:
    cucumber mango, chilled jumbo shrimp with asparagus and, 119–20
    papaya, twice-cooked Philippines-style chicken with, 167–69
    shallot, golden, *50,* 56–57
    sweet and hot pepper, *50,* 55
    see also chutneys

resource list, for pantry essentials and equipment, 21

rib-eye steak, Szechuan peppercorn–rubbed, with ginger demi-glace, 185–86, *186*

ribs:
    beef short, braised with sweet and sour onions, 183–84
    pork, honey and five-spice barbecued, 191–92

rice, 239
    basmati, pilaf, exotically spiced, 251
    coconut, with spinach and peanuts, Indonesian, 245–46
    fragrant, skillet of, with tofu and Asian greens, 200–201
    fried, Yang Chow, 252, *253*
    pudding, simple and rich, 278
    sushi, 79
    timbale of grains with wild mushrooms and creamy feta sauce, 202–3
    types of, 200

rice paper wrappers, 72

rice vermicelli (rice sticks):
    curried, with chicken, shrimp, and sprouts, 247–48, *248*
    and tofu pancake, savory, 90–91

Vietnamese summer rolls, 74–75, *75*

rice wine (mirin), 49
    vinaigrette, romaine and green bean salad with, 214

rich and poor man's lobster, 142–143

roasted peanut soup with pickled cucumbers, 198–99

roll-cutting, 67

rolls:
    spring, 72–73
    summer, Vietnamese, 74–75, *75*
    see also nori rolls

romaine and green bean salad with rice wine vinaigrette, 214

rubs, *see* spice rubs and pastes

rum, dark, anglaise, banana wontons with, 292–94

S

saffron, 57
    broth, tuna steaks in, with spicy pepper puree, 140–41
    golden shallot relish, *50,* 56–57
    potato cakes, 233

sake, 133
    pine-nut sauce, teriyaki glazed halibut with, 132–33

salad dressings, 207
    green goddess, 224–25
    sweet and sour, 217–18
    see also vinaigrettes

salads, 207–27
    Asian pear, with green beans and glazed scallops, 221–23
    beans, crisp, and fresh tomatoes with curry vinaigrette, 219–20, *220*
    chicken, orange, and cress, with black bean vinaigrette, 212–13

salads (*cont.*):

herb, fresh, crabmeat in mustard vinaigrette with, 210–11

melon and herb, with lime vinaigrette, 215–16

mizuna greens for, 102

peas, sweet, variety of, with green goddess dressing, 224–25

romaine and green bean, with rice wine vinaigrette, 214

scallops, coriander-spiced diver, with pear glaze, 102–103

shiitake, with spring veggies and scallion vinaigrette, 226–27

shrimp and avocado, with tropical vinaigrette, 208–9

slaw, Asian, with sweet and sour dressing, 217–18

Salamander, 15–16

salmon:

Asian marinated, *124*, 124–25

fillet, cashew-crusted, 146–47

fillet, sweet tamari-glazed, 129

hot and sour soup with ginger tamari–glazed seafood, 126–28

nori rolls, 78

steaks, grilled, with fresh oyster sauce, *134*, 134–35

salts, *20*

kosher, 85

satay, char-grilled shrimp, with tamarind barbecue sauce, 104–5

sauces:

basting, 117–18

caramel garlic, 171–72

cashew, 118

citrus dipping, 50

coconut curry, 155–57

curry tomato, 144–45

dark rum anglaise, 292–93

feta, creamy, 202–3

ginger demi-glace, 185–86

hoisin and spice dipping, 48

Japanese eggplant and mushroom, 162–63

lime dip, cool, *50*, 51

oyster, fresh, 135

peanut, spicy, 49

sake pine-nut, 132–33

sesame, spicy, 52

sweet and sour onion, 183–84

tamarind barbecue, 104–5

yogurt, creamy, 176–77

see also vinaigrettes

sautéing, 23

savory rice noodle and tofu pancake, 90–91

scallion(s):

green goddess dressing, 224–225

lentil and vegetable fritters, 94–95

noodle cakes, *109*, 244

oil, 45

and oyster popovers, 97–98

popovers, 85

vegetable nori rolls, 76–78, *77*

vegetable udon, 138–39

vinaigrette, shiitake salad with spring veggies and, 226–27

scallops:

coriander-spiced diver, with pear glaze, 102–3

diver, 102

glazed, Asian pear salad with green beans and, 221–23

Indonesian-style red seafood curry, 115–16, *116*

jumbo, curry-basted grilled, with cashew sauce, 117–18

seafood, *see* fish; salmon; shellfish; shrimp

seared tuna in dashi with chewy fat noodles, 138–39

seaweed:

konbu (kombu or kelp), 38

nori, 28

seeds:

cracking, 115

toasting, 52

see also specific seeds

serving accompaniments, *see* condiments

sesame (seed)(s), 28

parsnips, 235

sauce, spicy, 52

spinach, peanut noodles with, 240–41

stir-fried chicken with spiced walnuts and, 164–66

sesame oil, light vs. dark, 46

shallot relish, golden, *50*, 56–57

shellfish, 101–20

buying and storing, 101

clams and mussels, pan-roasted, with fragrant lime leaves, 113–14, *114*

crabmeat in mustard vinaigrette with fresh herb salad, 210–11

crabmeat nori rolls, 78

lobster, rich and poor man's, 142–43

lobster, spicy grilled, with corn and sweet potato curry, 108–10, *109*

lobster tempura, 111–12

oyster sauce, fresh, grilled salmon steaks with, *134*, 134–35

red seafood curry, Indonesian-style, 115–16, *116*

scallops, coriander-spiced diver, with pear glaze, 102–3

scallops, curry-basted grilled jumbo, with cashew sauce, 117–18

scallops, glazed, Asian pear salad with green beans and, 221–23

stock, 41

see also shrimp

shiitake salad with spring veggies and scallion vinaigrette, 226–27

shortbread, pine nut, 264

short grain rice (sticky rice), 200

short ribs, beef, braised with sweet and sour onions, 183–184

shrimp:

and avocado salad with tropical vinaigrette, 208–9

chilled jumbo, with asparagus and cucumber mango relish, 119–20

curried rice sticks with chicken, sprouts and, 247–248, *248*

fritters, Vietnamese-style, 82–83

ginger citrus brined, 106–7

glazed grilled, with peanut coating, 96

hot and sour soup with ginger tamari–glazed seafood, 126–28

Indonesian-style red seafood curry, 115–16, *116*

paste, 187

satay, char-grilled, with tamarind barbecue sauce, 104–5

spicy stir-fried, grilled sirloin steak with watercress and, 187–88

side dishes, *see* accompaniments; vegetable side dishes

simple and rich rice pudding, 278

sirloin steak, grilled, with spicy stir-fried shrimp and watercress, 187–88

skate, marinated, with lightly pickled vegetables, 136–137

skillet cake, upside-down pineapple, 284–85

skillet of fragrant rice with tofu and Asian greens, 200–201

slaw, Asian, with sweet and sour dressing, 217–18

slow-roasted tamarind duck, 173–74

snacks:

spiced walnuts, 166

sugar and spice walnuts, 265

see also sweets and treats

soba noodles, chilled, with tamari wasabi vinaigrette, 249–50

sole fillets, crispy, with wild mushroom stew, 148–49

somen noodle cake, pan-seared, 242–43

soups:

hot and sour, with ginger tamari–glazed seafood, 126–28

miso, 99

roasted peanut, with pickled cucumbers, 198–99

tomato and roasted vegetable, with seared red snapper fillet, 130–31

Southeast Asian flavors, dishes with:

chicken, Malaysian sweet spice–rubbed, 160–61

green curry paste, 29

red seafood curry, Indonesian-style, 115–16, *116*

see also Thai flavors, dishes with; Vietnamese flavors, dishes with

Southeast Asian ingredients:

fish sauce, 51

lemongrass, 127, *127*

lime leaves, 32

see also Thai ingredients

soy:

oil, 27

-soaked flank steak, grilled, over crispy noodles, 180–82

spice(s), 19–21

allspice, 158

and chili oil, fragrant, 44

Chinese hot mustard powder, 170

cinnamon sticks, toasting, 53

coriander seed, *20*, 59

curry powder, 58

garam masala, 194

ginger cookies, 259

and hoisin dipping sauce, 48

ice cream, 275

Malaysian sweet, –rubbed chicken, 160–61

pickling, 223

ras el hanout, 194

saffron, 57

star anise, *20*, 30, *30*

storing, 19

sugar and, walnuts, 265

sweet, mix, 81

Szechuan peppercorns, 153

turmeric, 31

whole vs. ground, 19

spiced walnuts, 166

spice rubs and pastes, 25–32

curry pastes, as marinades, 32

curry pastes, making quick curry dishes with, 30

East Indian spice blend, 26

Korean chili spice blend, 28

spice rubs and pastes (*cont.*):
   Malaysian sweet spice rub,
     160–61
   red curry paste, 32
   Southeast Asian green curry
     paste, 29
   yellow curry paste, 31
spicy:
   daikon, 62, *186*
   eggplant chutney, 59–60
   grilled lobster with corn and
     sweet potato curry, 108–10,
     109
   peanut sauce, 49
   sesame sauce, 52
   stir-fried shrimp, grilled
     sirloin steak with water-
     cress and, 187–88
spinach:
   ginger garlic, *205*, 232
   green goddess dressing, 224–
     225
   Indonesian coconut rice with
     peanuts and, 245–46
   sesame, peanut noodles with,
     240–41
   vegetable pie with raisins, *ras
     el hanout* and, 194–95
spring rolls, 72–73
   coconut, with ginger black-
     berry dipping sauce, 282–
     283
spring roll wrappers (egg roll
   skins), 72, 73
spring veggies, shiitake salad
   with, and scallion vinaigrette, 226–27
sprouts, curried rice sticks with
   chicken, shrimp and, 247–
   248, *248*
squash, butternut, pearl onions,
   and bok choy with green
   curry, 196–97
staples, 18–19

star anise, *20*, 30, *30*
   toasting, 30
starters, 71–99
   cheese toasts with red lentil
     dip, 92–93
   chicken and peanut lettuce
     cups, 84
   clams and mussels, pan-
     roasted, with fragrant lime
     leaves, 113–14, *114*
   crabmeat nori rolls, 78
   lentil and vegetable fritters,
     94–95
   miso soup, 99
   peanut noodles with sesame
     spinach, 240–41
   pork and tofu steamed buns,
     80–81
   rice noodle and tofu pancake,
     savory, 90–91
   salmon nori rolls, 78
   scallion and oyster popovers,
     97–98
   scallion popovers, 85
   shiitake salad with spring
     veggies and scallion vinai-
     grette, 226–27
   shrimp, chilled jumbo, with
     asparagus and cucumber
     mango relish, 119–20
   shrimp, glazed grilled, with
     peanut coating, 96
   shrimp fritters, Vietnamese-
     style, 82–83
   spring rolls, 72–73
   summer rolls, Vietnamese,
     74–75, *75*
   turnovers with carrots, raisins,
     pine nuts, and goat cheese,
     Persian, 204–6, *205*
   vegetable nori rolls, 76–78,
     77
   wontons: filling and varia-
     tions, 86–89

steaks:
   flank, grilled soy-soaked, over
     crispy noodles, 180–82
   rib-eye, Szechuan pepper-
     corn–rubbed, with ginger
     demi-glace, 185–86, *186*
   sirloin, grilled, with spicy stir-
     fried shrimp and water-
     cress, 187–88
steamers, Chinese, 80
stews:
   ginger and mustard braised
     rabbit with wild mush-
     rooms, 178–79
   wild mushroom, crispy sole
     fillets with, 148–49
sticky rice (short grain rice), 200
stir-fry(ied):
   chicken with sesame and
     spiced walnuts, 164–66
   shrimp, spicy, grilled sirloin
     steak with watercress and,
     187–88
   vegetable, 181–82
stir-frying, 23
stocks, 33–41
   chicken, 34–35
   fish fumet, 40
   shellfish, 41
   tips for, 34
   veal, 36
   vegetable, 37
   see also broths
stout caramel candies, chocolate-
   covered, 266–67
striped bass, honey tamari–
   brined, 122–23
sugar, palm (jaggery), 55
summer rolls, Vietnamese, 74–
   75, *75*
sushi mats, 76, 77
sushi rice, 79
sweet:
   cucumber pickles, 65

curried mango chutney, 58, *190*

ginger syrup and candied ginger, 256

and hot pepper relish, *50*, 55

spice mix, 81

tamari-glazed salmon fillet, 129

sweet and sour:

dressing, Asian slaw with, 217–18

onions, beef short ribs braised with, 183–84

sweet potato(es), 237

and corn curry, spicy grilled lobster with, 108–10, *109*

glazed, 236–37

sweets and treats, 255–72

chocolate-covered stout caramel candies, 266–67

chocolate lemon ginger madeleines, 257–58, *258*

dark chocolate and almond toffee, 268–69

ginger spice cookies, 259

ginger syrup, sweet, and candied ginger, 256

lemonade, caramelized lemongrass, *271*, 271–72

lemon slices, candied, 289

macadamia nut brittle, 270

pine nut shortbread, 264

pistachio-cherry chocolate chip cookies, 262–63

sugar and spice walnuts, 265

see also desserts

syrups:

ginger, sweet, and candied ginger, 256

raspberry-tea, easy chocolate cake with bananas and, 280–81, *281*

Szechuan peppercorn(s), 153

–rubbed rib-eye steak with ginger demi-glace, 185–86, *186*

T

tamari:

citrus dipping sauce, 50

ginger–glazed seafood, hot and sour soup with, 126–128

-glazed salmon fillet, sweet, 129

honey–brined striped bass, 122–23

wasabi vinaigrette, chilled soba noodles with, 249–50

tamarind, 53

barbecue sauce, 104–5

duck, slow-roasted, 173–74

fruits, 53–54, *54*

juice, 54

tarragon, in green goddess dressing, 224–25

tart(s):

coconut custard, 290–91

gingery lemon meringue, 286–89, *288*

shells, 286–87

tea:

black, –brined chicken, 153–154, *154*

jasmine, crème brûlée, 296

raspberry, syrup, easy chocolate cake with bananas and, 280–81, *281*

tempura, lobster, 111–12

teriyaki glazed halibut with sake pine-nut sauce, 132–33

Thai basil, 131

fresh herb salad with crab-meat in mustard vinai-grette, 210–11

Thai flavors, dishes with:

butternut squash, pearl onions, and bok choy with green curry, 196–97

green curry paste, Southeast Asian, 29

salmon, Asian marinated, *124*, 124–25

shrimp, glazed grilled, with peanut coating, 96

striped bass, honey tamari–brined, 122–23

Thai ingredients:

coconut milk, 108

fish sauce, 51

galangal, 30

holy basil chili paste, 199

jasmine rice, 200

lemongrass, 127, *127*

lime leaves, 32

Thai basil, 131

Thai bird chilies, 32

timbale of grains with wild mushrooms and creamy feta sauce, 202–3

toasted coconut ice cream, 275

toasting:

cinnamon sticks, 53

coconut, 156

nuts, 96

seeds, 52

star anise, 30

toasts, cheese, with red lentil dip, 92–93

toffee, dark chocolate and almond, 268–69

tofu (bean curd), 90

and pork steamed buns, 80–81

and rice noodle pancake, savory, 90–91

skillet of fragrant rice with Asian greens and, 200–201

tomato(es):
cherry, in shiitake salad with
spring veggies and scallion
vinaigrette, 226–27
curry sauce, cod fillet with,
144–45
fresh, and crisp beans with
curry vinaigrette, 219–20,
220
and roasted vegetable soup
with seared red snapper
fillet, 130–31
tropical:
fruit pickles, 61
vinaigrette, shrimp and
avocado salad with, 208–9
tuna:
seared, in dashi with chewy
fat noodles, 138–39
steaks in saffron broth with
spicy pepper puree, 140–41
turmeric, 31
turnovers with carrots, raisins,
pine nuts, and goat cheese,
Persian, 204–6, *205*
twice-cooked Philippines-style
chicken with papaya relish,
167–69

U

udon noodle(s):
cakes, scallion, *109*, 244
seared tuna in dashi with
chewy fat noodles, 138–39
upside-down pineapple skillet
cake, 284–85

V

vanilla:
beans, 274
extract, 264
variety of sweet peas with green
goddess dressing, 224–25
veal stock, 36

vegetable(s):
blanching, ice baths for, 45
fresh, in pantry, 21
and lentil fritters, 94–95
lightly pickled, marinated
skate with, 136–37
nori rolls, 76–78, *77*
pickles, miso, 66
pie with spinach, raisins, and
ras el hanout, 194–95
roasted, and tomato soup with
seared red snapper fillet,
130–31
spring, shiitake salad with,
and scallion vinaigrette,
226–27
stir-fry, 181–82
stock, 37
udon, 138–39
see also specific vegetables
vegetable side dishes, 229–37
chickpea smash, East Indian,
230–31
parsnips, sesame, 235
potato cakes, saffron, 233
potatoes, yogurt whipped, *186*,
234
spinach, ginger garlic, *205*,
232
sweet potatoes, glazed, 236–
237
see also accompaniments
vegetarian entrees, 193–206
butternut squash, pearl
onions, and bok choy with
green curry, 196–97
grains, timbale of, with wild
mushrooms and creamy
feta sauce, 202–3
peanut, roasted, soup with
pickled cucumbers, 198–99
rice, fragrant, skillet of, with
tofu and Asian greens, 200–
201

shiitake salad with spring
veggies and scallion vinaigrette, 226–27
turnovers with carrots, raisins,
pine nuts, and goat cheese,
Persian, 204–6, *205*
vegetable pie with spinach,
raisins, and *ras el hanout*,
194–95
vermicelli, rice (rice sticks):
curried, with chicken, shrimp,
and sprouts, 247–48, *248*
and tofu pancake, savory, 90–91
Vietnamese summer rolls, 74–
75, *75*
Vietnamese flavors, dishes with:
hot and sour soup with ginger
tamari–glazed seafood,
126–28
quail, grilled, with caramel
garlic sauce and cilantro,
171–72
shrimp fritters, 82–83
summer rolls, 74–75, *75*
vinaigrettes, 207
black bean, 212–13
curry, 219–20, *220*
lime, 215–16
mustard, 210–11
pear, 102–3, 221–23
rice wine, 214
scallion, 226–27
tamari wasabi, 249–50
tropical, 208–9

W

walnuts:
spiced, stir-fried chicken with
sesame and, 164–66
sugar and spice, 265
wasabi:
powder, 78
tamari vinaigrette, chilled
soba noodles with, 249–50

watercress:

    chicken, and orange salad with black bean vinaigrette, 212–13

    grilled sirloin steak with spicy stir-fried shrimp and, 187–188

watermelon, 69

    pickles, 68–69

web sites, 21

white chocolate ice cream, 276

wild rice, 203

    timbale of grains with wild mushrooms and creamy feta sauce, 202–3

wine:

    rice (mirin), 49

    rice (mirin), vinaigrette, romaine and green bean salad with, 214

    sake, 133

wontons, 86–89

    banana, with dark rum anglaise, 292–94

    classic soup fold, 88

    filling for, 86

    four-corner fold, 87

    simple triangle fold, 87

    two-piece ravioli, 89

wonton wrappers, 72

Y

yams, 237

Yang Chow fried rice, 252, *253*

yellow Chinese noodles, fresh, 180

    crispy, grilled soy-soaked flank steak over, 180–82

    peanut noodles with sesame spinach, 240–41

yellow curry(ies):

    lobster, in rich and poor man's lobster, 142–43

paste, 31

rice sticks with chicken, shrimp, and sprouts, 247–248, *248*

salmon fillet, cashew-crusted, 146–47

sweet potato, spicy grilled lobster with corn and, 108–110, *109*

yogurt:

    sauce, creamy, Indian-spiced leg of lamb with, 176–77

    whipped potatoes, *186*, 234

Z

zucchini, in lentil and vegetable fritters, 94–95

Metric Equivalencies

Liquid and Dry Measure Equivalencies

CUSTOMARY	METRIC
¼ teaspoon	1.25 milliliters
½ teaspoon	2.5 milliliters
1 teaspoon	5 milliliters
1 tablespoon	15 milliliters
1 fluid ounce	30 milliliters
¼ cup	60 milliliters
⅓ cup	80 milliliters
½ cup	120 milliliters
1 cup	240 milliliters
1 pint *(2 cups)*	480 milliliters
1 quart *(4 cups, 32 ounces)*	960 milliliters *(.96 liter)*
1 gallon *(4 quarts)*	3.84 liters
1 ounce *(by weight)*	28 grams
¼ pound *(4 ounces)*	114 grams
1 pound *(16 ounces)*	454 grams
2.2 pounds	1 kilogram *(1,000 grams)*